Counter-Narratives and Organization

This book brings new insight to the emergent, negotiated practice of organizational narrative, with clear implications for the conditions that create and sustain the vitality of the organization as a storytelling system.
—Benjamin D. Golant, Newcastle University Business School, UK

Counter-Narratives and Organization brings the concept of "counter-narrative" into an organizational context, illuminating these complex elements of communication as intrinsic yet largely unexplored aspect of organizational storytelling. Departing from dialogical, emergent and processual perspectives on "organization," the individual chapters focus on the character of counter-narratives, along with their performative aspects, by addressing questions such as

- How do some narratives gain dominance over others?
- How do narratives intersect, relate and reinforce each other? and
- How are organizational members and external stakeholders engaged in the telling and retelling of the organization?

The empirical case studies provide much-needed insights on the function of counter-narratives for individuals, professionals and organizations in navigating, challenging, negotiating and replacing established dominant narratives about "who we are," "what we believe," "what we do" as a collective. The book has an interdisciplinary scope, drawing together ideas from storytelling in organization studies, the communicative constitution of organization (CCO) from organizational communication and traditional narratology from humanities. *Counter-Narratives and Organization* reflects an ambition to spark readers' imagination, recognition, and discussion of organization and counter-narratives, offering a route to bring this important concept to the center of our understandings of organization.

Sanne Frandsen is a postdoc in the Department of Business Administration at Lund University, Sweden.

Timothy Kuhn is a professor in the Department of Communication at the University of Colorado at Boulder, USA.

Marianne Wolff Lundholt is an associate professor at the Department of Design and Communication at the University of Southern Denmark, Denmark.

Routledge Studies in Management, Organizations and Society

For a full list of titles in this series, please visit www.routledge.com ·

This series presents innovative work grounded in new realities, addressing issues crucial to an understanding of the contemporary world. This is the world of organised societies, where boundaries between formal and informal, public and private, local and global organizations have been displaced or have vanished, along with other nineteenth century dichotomies and oppositions. Management, apart from becoming a specialized profession for a growing number of people, is an everyday activity for most members of modern societies.

Similarly, at the level of enquiry, culture and technology, and literature and economics, can no longer be conceived as isolated intellectual fields; conventional canons and established mainstreams are contested. **Management, Organizations and Society** addresses these contemporary dynamics of transformation in a manner that transcends disciplinary boundaries, with books that will appeal to researchers, student and practitioners alike.

39 **Counter-Narratives and Organization**
Edited by Sanne Frandsen, Timothy Kuhn and Marianne Wolff Lundholt

Other titles in this series:

Casting the Other
Maintaining gender inequalities in the workplace
Edited by Barbara Czarniawska and Heather Höpfl

Gender, Identity and the Culture of Organizations
Edited by Iiris Aaltio and Albert J. Mills

Text/Work
Representing organization and organizing representation
Edited by Stephen Linstead

The Social Construction of Management
Texts and identities
Nancy Harding

Management Theory
A critical and reflexive reading
Nanette Monin

Counter-Narratives and Organization

Edited by
Sanne Frandsen, Timothy Kuhn
and Marianne Wolff Lundholt

NEW YORK AND LONDON

First published 2017
by Routledge
711 Third Avenue, New York, NY 10017

and by Routledge
2 Park Square, Milton Park, Abingdon, Oxon OX14 4RN

Routledge is an imprint of the Taylor & Francis Group, an informa business

© 2017 Taylor & Francis

The right of the editors to be identified as the authors of the editorial material, and of the authors for their individual chapters, has been asserted in accordance with sections 77 and 78 of the Copyright, Designs and Patents Act 1988.

All rights reserved. No part of this book may be reprinted or reproduced or utilised in any form or by any electronic, mechanical, or other means, now known or hereafter invented, including photocopying and recording, or in any information storage or retrieval system, without permission in writing from the publishers.

Trademark notice: Product or corporate names may be trademarks or registered trademarks, and are used only for identification and explanation without intent to infringe.

Library of Congress Cataloging-in-Publication Data
Names: Frandsen, Sanne, editor. | Kuhn, Timothy, editor. | Lundholt, Marianne Wolff, editor.
Title: Counter-narratives and organization / edited by Sanne Frandsen, Timothy Kuhn and Marianne Wolff Lundholt.
Description: New York : Routledge, 2016. | Includes bibliographical references and index.
Identifiers: LCCN 2016009849 | ISBN 9781138929456 (hardback : alk. paper) | ISBN 9781315681214 (ebook)
Subjects: LCSH: Communication in organizations. | Discourse analysis, Narrative. | Storytelling.
Classification: LCC HD30.3 .C68 2016 | DDC 650.01/4—dc23
LC record available at https://lccn.loc.gov/2016009849

ISBN: 978-1-138-92945-6 (hbk)
ISBN: 978-1-315-68121-4 (ebk)

Typeset in Sabon
by Apex CoVantage, LLC

Contents

List of Contributors	vii

Introduction   1
SANNE FRANDSEN, MARIANNE WOLFF LUNDHOLT
AND TIMOTHY KUHN

PART I
Counter-Narratives and Constitutive Stakeholder Communication   15

1 Communicatively Constituting Organizational Unfolding
through Counter-Narrative   17
TIMOTHY KUHN

2 Counter-Narratives and Organizational Crisis: How
LEGO Bricks Became a Slippery Business   43
MARIANNE WOLFF LUNDHOLT

3 Countering the "Natural" Organizational Self on Social Media   64
TRINE SUSANNE JOHANSEN

4 "Speaking through the Other": Countering Counter-Narratives
through Stakeholders' Stories   83
ASTRID JENSEN, CINDIE AAEN MAAGAARD
AND RASMUS KJÆRGAARD RASMUSSEN

PART II
Counter-Narratives in Changes of Identity and Practices   103

5 Organizational Identity Negotiations through Dominant and
Counter-Narratives   105
DIDDE MARIA HUMLE AND SANNE FRANDSEN

vi *Contents*

6 Fractal Change Management and Counter-Narrative in
Cross-Cultural Change 129
MARITA SVANE, ERIKA GERGERICH AND DAVID M. BOJE

7 Designer or Entrepreneur? Counter-Narratives in
the Professions 155
BIRGITTE NORLYK

8 Rethinking Counter-Narratives in Studies of Organizational
Texts and Practices 171
RASMUS KJÆRGAARD RASMUSSEN

PART III
Counter-Narratives and Narrative Ecologies
of Organizations 193

9 The Fate of Counter-Narratives: In Fiction and in
Actual Organizations 195
BARBARA CZARNIAWSKA

10 Narrative Ecologies and the Role of Counter-Narratives:
The Case of Nostalgic Stories and Conspiracy Theories 208
YIANNIS GABRIEL

Index 227

Contributors

David M. Boje

Barbara Czarniawska

Sanne Frandsen

Yiannis Gabriel

Erika Gergerich

Didde Humle

Astrid Jensen

Trine Susanne Johansen

Timothy Kuhn

Marianne Wolff Lundholt

Cindie Aaen Maagaard

Birgitte Norlyk

Rasmus Kjærgaard Rasmussen

Marita Svane

Introduction

Sanne Frandsen, Marianne Wolff Lundholt and Timothy Kuhn

Narrative is a mode of communication that is essential both to social life and to defining humanness (Fisher 1987). "Narratives connect past, present, and anticipated future, rendering a life-in-time sensible in terms of beginnings, middle, and endings" (McAdams 1996, 298). Through such connections, narratives provide a sense of causality and order in what might otherwise appear to be a random series of events in our daily lives. Their prevalence and utility led MacIntyre (1984) to conclude that "Man [*sic*] is in his actions and practices, as well as in his fictions, essentially a storytelling animal" (216). Narratives, in other words, are powerful sense-making and order-producing devices; for many social theorists, they are at the center of the development of the self (Giddens 1991; Ricoeur, 1991).

The influence of narrative is not, however, limited to explanations of personal identity. Scholars have long relied on narratives for understanding the existence and practice of organization. From such a perspective, narratives do not exist merely *in* organizations, but are instead *constitutive of* the organization; organizations are not best understood as collections of people or sets of contracts but as *storytelling systems* that are performed into existence (Boje 1991; Boyce 1995; Czarniawska 1998). Research in this line of thought has demonstrated the role of narratives in generating organizational-level identities (Chreim 2005), inspiring member identification (Humphreys and Brown 2002), establishing a community memory (Linde 2009), shaping nostalgic and postalgic oriented cultures (Ybema 2004), generating collective sense-making in ambiguous environments (Abolafia 2010), inducing organizational change (Doolin 2003; Dunford and Jones 2000) and maintaining an unmanaged terrain of resistance (Gabriel 1995) among the organizational members. Narrative scholarship has, in other words, been productive and influential in examining organization.

The present volume sees the substantial and well-established narrative tradition in organization studies as a point of departure. Much of the work foregrounding narrative assumes—drawing, often implicitly, from formalist and postformalist models of textuality (the likes of Propp, Todorow, Barthes and Bakhtin)—(a) that narratives produce a relatively linear causality in the sequences of beginnings, middles and endings that compose their

2   Sanne Frandsen et al.

plot and (b) that structural conflicts between characters drive the story line. What tends to be obscured in such analyses are considerations for how some narratives gain dominance over others; how narratives intersect, relate to, challenge and reinforce each other; and how actors 'inside' and 'outside' organizations co-construct narratives.

To address issues such as these, we must complicate our understandings of narratives and organizing. Contemporary organization studies research frames organizing as complicated, where tension, paradox, contradiction, disorder and change are the standard characterizations of organizing—not deviations from some more 'normal' ordered state (Law 1994). Gradually, scholars of narrative have brought this conception of complexity into their work, highlighting the fragmented, subtle, untold and arational character of narration and organization (Boje 2014; Czarniawska 2008; Dailey and Browning 2014; Linde 2009; Tsoukas and Hatch 2001). Another way of saying this is that, drawing on the notion of *counter-narrative*, we wish to tell a different story. To begin down that path, we must first clarify what we mean by the notion of counter-narrative.

Conceptualizing Counter-Narratives

At their base, counter-narratives are "the stories which people tell and live which offer resistance to, either implicitly or explicitly, to dominant cultural narratives" (Andrews 2004, 1). The most common distinction pointed to by those who use the notion of counter-narratives is between a preferred organizational story and an alternate vision, one that seeks to contradict or defy the authoritative version: "counter-narratives only make sense in relation to something else, that which they are countering. The very name identifies it as an oppositional category, in tension with another category" (ibid.). The narratives that counter-narratives counter are variously referred to as "dominant" or "master narratives" (also variably called plotlines, master plots, dominant discourses or simply story lines or cultural texts).

Literature drawing on the concept of counter-narratives has, to this point, examined how individuals or groups who deviate from the cultural norms. With *Damaged Identities, Narrative Repair*, Nelson (2001) focused on the stories of groups (e.g., Gypsies, mothers and nurses) whose identities have been defined by those with the power to speak *for* them, and she considered counter-narrative as being depictive, selective, interpretive and connective. Similarly, in a collection that has become one of the most recognized contributions within this emerging field, *Considering Counter-narratives* (Bamberg and Andrews 2004), the authors pay attention to the use of counter-narratives by individuals to position themselves in relation to dominant and/ or master narratives in society.

This volume, *Organization and Counter-Narratives*, attempts to bring the concept of counter-narratives into an organizational context, since we see counter-narratives as an intrinsic—yet unexplored—aspect of storytelling in

Introduction 3

and around organizations. Focusing on counter-narratives enables us to capture some of the political and social complexities and tensions faced in organizational life. The definition of 'what constitutes a narrative' differs across the chapters, ranging from a sequence of events implying a casual relationship (Lundholt) to a discourse (Norlyk) to any storytelling episodes and narrative performances (Humle and Frandsen). What the chapters in this book share is a view on 'the organization' that emerges from the focus on counter-narratives; the resulting picture is very different from the conception of 'the organization' found in more managerially oriented literature on storytelling. Using a counter-narrative lens to study organizations implies that 'the organization' is seen as (a) constituted in communication and storytelling practices, (b) a site of struggle over meaning and identity and (c) engaging a polyphony of voices, from organizational members (insiders) and those in the organizational environment (outsiders such as nongovernmental organizations [NGOs], the media, consumers and the like). In short, the role and the character of counter-narratives in organizational contexts have been largely in the shadows until now; this book provides an important and necessary nuance to conceptions of narrative and organizing.

A Counter-Narrative Lens on Organization

As is the case with narrative studies generally, there are several possible theoretical camps conducive to organizational analyses based on counter-narrative. In this book, two stand out. The first is the Communicative Constitution of Organization (CCO) perspective (Brummans, Cooren, Robichaud and Taylor 2014), which seeks to explain the existence, recognition, practice, power and modification of organization in explicitly communicative terms. Communication, in a CCO frame, is not merely that which occurs 'inside' a preexisting organizational container, but is the site and surface through which organization—as a verb and a noun—emerges, persists and transforms (Cooren, Kuhn, Cornelissen and Clark 2011; Taylor and Van Every 2000). This perspective has directly inspired several authors in this book (Kuhn; Jensen, Maagaard and Rasmussen; Lundholt and Rasmussen). What the CCO perspective brings to the study of counter-narratives is a vocabulary of "the authoritative text" (Kuhn 2008), "intertextuality" (Koschmann, Kuhn and Pfarrer 2012) and "ventriloquism" (Cooren 2010) that highlight the performative aspects of, and relationships between, dominant narratives and counter-narratives in organizing practice. The remaining authors (Johansen; Norlyk; Humle and Frandsen, Marita, Gergerich and Boje, Czarniawska and Gabriel) share a broadly social constructivist (or construc*tion*ist; see Leonardi and Barley 2008) orientation, where communication, language and stories cannot be reduced to a mirror of 'reality,' but are instead seen as actively constituting organizational realities (see Bruner 1991).

The counter-narrative lens also highlights the struggles over meanings, values and identities that take place in organizing (Mumby 1987). Focusing

4 *Sanne Frandsen et al.*

on counter-narratives implies a critical approach, where the communicative processes and storytelling practices are seen as inherently influenced by power. The binary concept of dominant/master narrative and counter-narrative suggests that the dominant narrative holds the power to shape individuals' and organizations' worldviews, identities and values yet also that this dominant narrative can be destabilized, challenged, negotiated and changed by counter-narratives representing different worldviews and collective identities. Focusing on counter-narratives enables us to see that meaning is always contested, when different organizational actors and stakeholders cross their (narrative) swords in the aim of shaping their collectives' identities, values and interests. Gabriel's, Czarniawska's, and Kuhn's contributions to this book illustrate these struggles over meaning when dominant and counter-narratives clash.

These struggles over meaning described in this volume, however, are more complicated than depicted in much of the counter-narrative literature. The typical view is one of binary opposition, pitting one (dominant) side versus another (insurgent) side. If, as we indicated earlier, organizations and organizing practices are characterized by a multiplicity of interests, values and issues, such a simple conception of opposition is unlikely to be helpful analytically (see Rasmussen for this critique). Fortunately, the chapters in this book all suggest that the organization should be viewed as constructed through ever-present *polyphony*, where counter-narratives both challenge dominant narratives but also are themselves challenged by *other* counter-narratives (see Humle and Frandsen, as well as Jensen, Maagaard and Rasmussen, on this point). Thus, as in the story of Pandora's box, polyphony spreads and finds new fractal ways of evolving both dominant and counter-narratives (see Svane, Gergerich and Boje on this point). The counter-narrative approach foregrounds the multiple voices (and not the single managerial voice of the organization) and highlights the intersection between the different narrators both inside and outside that which analysts identify as 'organization.' The chapters here include, for instance, 'the man on the floor (or in the train),' the press, the customers, the NGOs and the different parties of an organizational merger; in attending to these actors, they encourage analysts to examine the sources of counter-narratives, illustrating how the counter-narrative approach gives voice to those who are part of the ongoing narration of the organization, even if they are not considered 'insiders of' the organization.

Foregrounding polyphony also encourages a consideration of the intentionality assumed in narrative studies. Although it is common to understand counter-narratives as acts of resistance, competition, or contestation deliberately crafted to effect change in some target (e.g., Harter, Scott, Novak, Leeman and Morris 2006; Johnson 2009), several chapters in this volume (including Jensen et al., Rasmussen and Kuhn) draw attention to the notion that counter-narratives can *emerge* from the heterogeneous admixture of human and nonhuman agencies brought together in practices of

Introduction 5

organizing. Such a perspective need not discard the notion that individuals and groups often invent counter-narratives to generate specific effects on sites of power but additionally suggests that there is likely to be a good deal of indeterminacy and unpredictability in the interplay of dominant and counter-narratives in those tension-filled organizing practices (Cooren and Sandler 2014; Harter 2009; Korobov 2004; Kuhn 2014; Trittin and Schoeneborn in press).

Interdisciplinary Insights on Counter-Narratives

This book is the coming together of scholars from different research traditions and disciplinary foundations, but all with the intention of understanding the role of counter-narratives for individuals, professionals and organizations in navigating, challenging, negotiating and replacing established dominant narratives about 'who we are' and 'what we do' as a collective. Counter-narratives became important to us as we found that they could tell us something new about organizational life in an era where traditional forms of organized resistance in the form of unions or consumer boycotts are decreasing (Dean 2016) but where other forms of resistance still propel struggles over meaning and challenge the dominant ways of 'being' in the world. We see counter-narratives emerging on social media in the form of 'shitstorms,' as well as in an increasingly critical business press that exposes scandals and holds corporations accountable for their conduct. And we see that the unmanaged terrain internal to organizations keeps spurring new formations and practices of resistance. *Organization and Counter-Narratives* is an attempt to highlight the value of focusing on counter-narratives in organization studies, displaying the storytelling nature of organization, the struggles of meanings and the polyphony between organizational insiders and their outside environment.

Organization and Counter-Narratives is the outcome of interdisciplinary insight in counter-narratives, drawing on both humanities and social sciences from three perspectives. The first perspective is *counter-narratives as a theoretical concept*. The book seeks to conceptualize counter-narratives and relate the concept to established traditions and current debates within organization and communication studies. The second perspective is *counter-narratives as an empirical object*. The contributions are grounded in empirical investigation of counter-narratives in and around organizations to arrive at theoretical contributions. As such the volume examines counter-narratives in a variety of organizational contexts—public/private, large corporations/entrepreneurial setups and external and internal of the organization—to understand the countering mechanisms and their potential. The third perspective focuses on *counter-narrative as a methodological approach*. Narrative methods for understanding organizational problems are well established. However, little attention has been given to enabling, facilitating and analyzing the productions of counter-narratives. Counter-narratives

6 Sanne Frandsen et al.

may be difficult to grasp for investigation as such narratives are often fragmented, fleeting or subtle, yet the contributions reveal that a methodological focus on the production of counter-narratives provides unique opportunities to locate and exposes tensions in and around organizations for theory development.

Methodological Considerations Using a Counter-Narrative Approach

The chapters in this book are all based on empirical studies of counter-narratives and each of them is illustrative of the methodological challenges and benefits gained when studying counter-narratives in an organizational context. A specific focus on counter-narratives poses methodological questions of how to access and generate counter-narratives as well as how to analyze and give voice to counter-narratives. Czarniawska (in this volume) questions if it is at all possible to 'find' counter-narratives in real organizations and she turns to fiction to illustrate the fate of counter-narratives. The volume does, however, provide evidence that counter-narratives are quite prevalent both in and around organizations if you look carefully.

Counter-Narratives in and around Organizations

With the rise of social media, critical consumers, NGOs and other stakeholders have found new venues for voicing counter-narratives and challenging the established dominant narratives. Johansen, Jensen, Maagaard & Rasmussen and Lundholt have specifically used empirical data from social media platforms to highlight how organizational identity is contested and (re)negotiated in ongoing conversations about 'who the organization is'. The benefit of social media is the ability to observe how the multiple voices come together and intertextually narrate stories of the organization. Also traditional media, newspapers, radio and television, play powerful roles in constructing either a dominant narrative of the organization as seen in Humle and Frandsen, or as an opponent to the dominant narrative, which is the case in Jensen, Maagaard and Rasmussen's chapter. These chapters dissolve the boundaries of internal and external life of organizations and provide empirical evidence of the role of counter-narratives in organizational identity conversations among so-called outsiders and insiders.

Paying special attention to counter-narratives in ethnographic work of organizational members may, however, prove difficult as the counter-narratives may not be publicly voiced or even well articulated among the organizational members sharing the counter-narratives. Often counter-narratives may only be told within specific storytelling communities (as in the case of Humle and Frandsen) and thus not shared with others—let alone the curious fieldworker. Posing direct questions about conflicting views or counter-narratives would rarely bring any relevant empirical material forward. That said, the chapters in this book all build on empirical data conducted through

Introduction 7

interviews *and* observations and are thus a result of "deep hanging out" (Geertz, 1998). Talking to union members (Humle and Frandsen), having informal conversations over lunch or the watercooler (Rasmussen, Svane et al. and Kuhn), shadowing individuals over time (Rasmussen and Svane et al.) or following their training (Kuhn and Norlyk) may provide cues to counter-narratives contesting the dominant narratives of the organization or simply providing an alternative version of them. Such cues may serve as an important base for further inquiry during interviewing or subsequent observations.

Access and Analytical Issues

As Gabriel (1995) argues, counter-narratives are often part of the 'unmanaged' terrain of the organization. Gaining access to such terrains is thus a matter of role negotiation on the part of the researcher. On one hand, being considered to be 'sent from management' might already deem the trust building and leveling with participants impossible. On the other hand, being 'sent from management' might also mean that the fieldworker is used strategically by the participants to give voice to their counter-narratives and to present these to the management or others in power while the participants remain anonymous (Alvesson and Deetz 2000; Søderberg 2006). As such, careful consideration and reflexivity in relation to the role of the researcher are needed to obtain insights to counter-narratives of the field.

Once one moves to the stage of analyzing and writing up the empirical material, new challenges may arise in the quest of understanding counter-narratives in the organizational context. In this book, Czarniawska, as well as Norlyk, provide insight into the dissonance that may be detected in participants' accounts in the narration of their individual identity. Also, Humle and Frandsen, Lundholt and Johansen provide evidence of the ongoing, contradictory and shifting nature of narratives in the struggle among different parties to manage the meaning of the organizational identity. These multiple voices place a certain demand on the researcher to distinguish dominant and counter-narratives from one another, which may not be an easy task in the local context of fluctuating, opposing, inconsistent and perhaps even self-contradictory narratives intersecting both micro-level storytelling practices and macro-level narratives. Humle and Frandsen, Lundholt and Johansen, nevertheless, show with their empirical studies that certain narratives gain authority and thus that the dominant narrative is used intertextually as a backdrop for counter-narratives. The dominant narrative may or may not incorporate these counter-narratives over time (see Kuhn), yet counter-narratives will always emerge in relation to a dominant narrative. Therefore, we may acknowledge Johansen's and Gabriel's argument that counter-narratives in reverse (and ironically) provide legitimacy to the dominant narratives; if there are no counter-narratives, there would be no dominant narratives either.

8 *Sanne Frandsen et al.*

What to Gain from a Counter-Narrative Approach

Despite the methodological challenges of focusing on counter-narratives we also argue that much is to be gained. Turning a blind eye to counter-narratives leaves us with a rather one-dimensional understanding of organizational phenomena of any kind. All the chapters in this volume demonstrate that counter-narratives are an integral part of storytelling practices in and around organizations (as well as in the organizing practices beyond any given organization) and that, accordingly, counter-narratives exercise substantial influence on authority, meaning and identity in organizational life. Advocating for new empirical and theoretical insights on counter-narratives that embrace the complexity and controversy of organizational life, our hope is that this volume appeals to those who identify broadly with narrative, constructivist or CCO approaches to understanding organization. We welcome those who are familiar with these traditions—and new generations of scholars who only just have found their ways to narrative research—to join us on an explorative journey into the organizational world of counter-narratives.

The Organization of the Book

With these considerations in mind, *Organization and Counter-Narratives* initiates this explorative journey with various theoretical and empirical contributions.

Timothy Kuhn presents a vision of counter-narrative-inspired organizational development that expands the potential utility of counter-narratives in organizational analysis in "Communicatively Constituting the Unfolding of Organization through Counter-Narrative." The chapter reveals that counter-narratives are not necessarily diametrically opposed to the master narrative, to the authoritative text; in fact, they are likely to emerge together and find their meanings in struggles over authorship of a collective's trajectory. This chapter, therefore, demonstrates that counter-narratives are highly relevant concepts for those who wish to develop explanations of organizational persistence and change, topics that broaden considerably counter-narratives' conceptual purchase in organization studies.

Marianne Wolff Lundholt examines the evolvement of counter-narratives in organizational crises in the chapter "Counter-Narratives and Organizational Crisis: How LEGO Bricks Became a Slippery Business." Considering Greenpeace's campaign against the partnership between Shell and LEGO A/S in 2014, the chapter indicates that in order to understand the interrelation between intertextuality and counter-narratives, it is necessary to go beyond the traditional understanding of intertextual relations. Moreover, the chapter points to the fact that organizations should pay careful attention to their own texts (i.e., organizational strategies) and actions when diagnosing organization's crisis vulnerabilities.

Introduction 9

Trine Susanne Johansen explores digital processes of organizational identity construction in the intersection between organization and market in her chapter "Countering the 'Natural' Organizational Self on Social Media" by using narrative as a theoretical and a methodological lens. The purpose is to understand the ways in which online interactions produce counter-narratives that contrast, challenge and contradict organizational self-narration in light of marketplace skepticism and cynicism. The study identifies three strategies of counter-narrativizing (authenticity, legitimacy and irony) based on juxtaposing pairs of opposites. Moreover, it suggests counter-narration to be a natural consequence of organizational self-narration pointing to an understanding of counter-narratives as key contributing factor in organizational identity construction.

Astrid Jensen, Cindie Aaen Maagaard and Rasmus Kjærgaard Rasmussen explore the interaction of master and counter-narratives in interpretations of an abstract company policy in "'Speaking through the Other': Countering Counter-Narratives through Stakeholders' Stories." The authors show how personal narratives are used by stakeholders to ventriloquize a managerial master narrative as a response to critical counter-narratives about Corporate Social Responsibility (CSR). The chapter contributes to an understanding of ventriloquism as a narrative activity by which positions are made concrete through temporal structures involving specific people and specific actions. Using the concept of ventriloquism in a dialogic perspective on the interaction of master and counter-narratives, the authors demonstrate how counter-narratives influence the dynamics by which managerial control of the master narrative is maintained.

Didde Maria Humle and Sanne Frandsen study the role of dominant and counter-narratives in organizational identity formation processes in their chapter "Organizational Identity Negotiations through Dominant and Counter-Narratives." Based on a case study of the highly contested organization E-rail—a European rail service, which faces persistent criticism from media, politicians and customers—the chapter concludes that the counter-narratives of the ticket inspectors make room for multiple and sometimes even opposing understandings of organizational identity to coexist. These multiple understandings of organizational identity make it possible for organizational members to perform and pursue different story lines while simultaneously establishing and maintaining a sense of continuity and stability around their organization and work.

Marita Svane, Erika Gergerich and David M. Boje present a quantum storytelling framework for analyzing and theorizing cross-cultural change of fractal narratives and counter-narratives in their chapter "Fractal Change Management and Counter-Narrative in Cross-Cultural Change." The antenarrative process of fore-caring inquiry is suggested as an approach to managing cross-cultural fractal change. Their contribution lies in developing an understanding of the subterranean 'fractal' patterns between antenarratives out of which narratives and counter-narratives interplay is affected. The

10　*Sanne Frandsen et al.*

authors develop a fractal analytic theory of and methods for understanding this dynamic interplay in its cross-cultural sociality. The two cases they develop are, first, the cross-cultural aspects of a merger and, second, the cross-cultural dynamics of homeless and home-full in American society.

Birgitte Norlyk contributes with an interdisciplinary framework of narrative, discourse and identity with the chapter "Designer or Entrepreneur? Counter-Narratives in the Professions." Norlyk explores the professional counter-narrative of a group of professional designers taking part in a course on business and entrepreneurship. The chapter illustrates how designers' discourse, metaphors and framing devices contribute to a professional counter-narrative that supplies designers with a means of resistance in their meeting with the dominant master narrative of business and entrepreneurship. Based on thematic narrative analysis, the analysis identifies four main themes that constitute designers' counter-narrative of artistic integrity: experiences of violence and force, experiences of conflicts of identity, experiences of the enemy and experiences of entrapment. The chapter concludes by relating counter-narratives to the emergence of hybrid identities in the professions.

Rasmus Kjærgaard Rasmussen's chapter "Rethinking Counter-Narratives in Studies of Organizational Texts and Practices" examines the potential of the counter-narrative framework as an analytical device in organizational analysis by re-rethinking master narratives as authoritative texts. Departing from a case with two competing master narratives, rather than a master opposed by a counter, the chapter demonstrates how organizational power struggles can be conceptualized as discursive struggles between master narratives-as-authoritative texts.

Barbara Czarniawska provides an excursion into the world of fiction with an illustration of three cases of counter-narratives in organizational settings in her chapter "The Fate of Counter-Narratives: In Fiction and in Actual Organizations." The first novel is Joyce Carol Oates's *Mysteries of Winterthurn* (1984), in which the detective finds the proper solution of murder puzzles—but to no avail, as it counters the established institutional thought order. The second is a novel by Joseph Heller, *Something Happened*, written in the late 1960s (1966/1975), when this institutional order should have been modernized but had not and when organizations vastly improved but had not. The third is David Lodge's *Nice Work* (1988), in which a postmodern researcher obtains access to a company and tries to launch her narrative, which runs counter to that of the manager. The result is a proper dialogue between the two protagonists, which could be a model for meetings of narratives and counter-narratives in actual work organizations.

Yiannis Gabriel argues in the chapter "Narrative Ecologies and the Role of Counter-Narratives: The Case of Nostalgic Stories and Conspiracy Theories" that narratives and counter-narratives depend on each other, need each other and co-create each other. By examining two particular types, nostalgic stories and conspiracy theories, Gabriel proposes that narratives and counter-narratives are elements of narrative ecologies and proposes a number of distinct narrative ecologies that foster different configurations of narrative patterns.

The publication of *Organization and Counter-Narratives* originates from research initiated by the Center for Narratological Studies, University of Southern Denmark—an interdisciplinary research center founded in 2003. The aim of the center is to examine the role of narratives in different communicative contexts. Currently the research group is interested in counter-narratives in and around organizations. In November 2014, the center hosted a seminar with outset in this topic with Timothy Kuhn and David Boje as keynote speakers. The seminar became the groundwork for the publication of this volume.

References

Abolafia, M. Y. 2010. "Narrative Construction as Sensemaking: How a Central Bank Thinks." *Organization Studies* 31: 349–367.

Alvesson, M. and S. A. Deetz. 2000. *Doing critical management research*. Thousand Oaks, CA: Sage.

Andrews, M. 2004. "Opening to the original contributions: Counter-narratives and the power to oppose." In *Considering counter-narratives: Narrating, resisting, making sense*, edited by M. G. W. Bamberg and M. Andrews, 1–6. Philadelphia: John Benjamins.

Bamberg, M. G. W. and M. Andrews. (eds.). 2004. *Considering counter-narratives: Narrating, resisting, making sense*. 351–371. Philadelphia: John Benjamins.

Boje, D. 1991. "The Storytelling Organization: A Study of Story Performance in an Office-Supply Firm." *Administrative Science Quarterly* 36: 106–126.

Boje, D. M. 2014. *Storytelling organizational practices: Managing in the quantum age*. New York: Routledge.

Boyce, M. E. 1995. "Collective Centering and Collective Sense-Making in the Stories and Storytelling of One Organization." *Organization Studies* 16: 107–137.

Brummans, B. H. J. M., F. Cooren, D. Robichaud and J. R. Taylor. 2014. "Approaches to the communicative constitution of organizations." In *The Sage handbook of organizational communication*, edited by L. L. Putnam and D. K. Mumby, 173–194. (3rd ed.). Los Angeles: Sage.

Bruner, J. 1991. *Acts of meaning*. Cambridge, MA: Harvard University Press.

Cooren, F. 2010. *Action and agency in dialogue: Passion, incarnation and ventriloquism*. Philadelphia: John Benjamins.

Cooren, F., T. Kuhn, J. P. Cornelissen, and T. Clark. 2011. "Communication, Organization, and Organizing: An Overview and Introduction to the Special Issue." *Organization Studies* 32: 1149–1170.

Cooren, F., and S. Sandler. 2014. "Polyphony, Ventriloquism, and Constitution: In Dialogue with Bakhtin." *Communication Theory* 24: 225–244.

Chreim, S. (2005). The Continuity–Change Duality in Narrative Texts of Organizational Identity*. *Journal of Management Studies*, 42(3), 567–593.

Czarniawska, B. 2008. *A theory of organizing*. Northampton, MA: Edward Elgar.

Dailey, S., and L. D. Browning. 2014. "Retelling Stories in Organizations: Understanding the Functions of Narrative Repetition." *Academy of Management Review* 39: 22–43.

12 *Sanne Frandsen et al.*

Dean, J. 2016. *Crowds and party*. London: Verso.

Doolin, B. 2003. "Narratives of Change: Discourse, Technology, and Organization." *Organization* 10: 751–770.

Dunford, R., and D. Jones. 2000. "Narrative in Strategic Change." *Human Relations* 53: 1207–1226.

Fisher, W. R. 1987. *Human communication as narration: Toward a philosophy of reason, value, and action*. Columbia: University of South Carolina Press.

Gabriel, Y. 1995. "The Unmanaged Organization: Stories, Fantasies and Subjectivity." *Organization Studies* 16 (3): 477–501.

Geertz, C. 1998. "Deep Hanging Out." *New York Review of Books*, 22(October): 69–72.

Giddens, A. 1991. *Modernity and self-identity: Self and society in the late modern age*. Stanford, CA: Stanford University Press.

Harter, L. M. 2009. "Narratives as Dialogic, Contested, and Aesthetic Performances." *Journal of Applied Communication Research* 37: 140–150.

Harter, L. M., J. A. Scott, D. R. Novak, M. Leeman, and J. F. Morris. 2006. "Freedom through Flight: Performing a Counter-Narrative of Disability." *Journal of Applied Communication Research* 34: 3–29.

Humphreys, M., and A. D. Brown 2002. "Narratives of Organizational Identity and Identification: A Case Study of Hegemony and Resistance." *Organization Studies* 23 (3): 421–447.

Johnson, L. 2009. "Counter-Narrative in Corporate Law: Saints and Sinners, Apostles and Epistles." *Michigan State Law Review* 847: 847–874.

Korobov, N. 2004. "Narratives as drawn-upon and narratives as occasioned: Challenges in reconciling an emic and etic analysis." In *Considering counter-narratives: Narrating, resisting, making sense*, edited by M. Bamberg and M. Andrews, 191–199. Philadelphia: John Benjamins.

Koschmann, M., T. Kuhn, and M. Pfarrer. 2012. "A Communicative Framework of Value in Cross-Sector Partnerships." *Academy of Management Review* 37: 332–354.

Kuhn, T. 2008. "A Communicative Theory of the Firm: Developing an Alternative Perspective on Intra-Organizational Power and Stakeholder Relationships." *Organization Studies* 29 (8/9): 1227–1254.

Kuhn, T. 2014. "Extending the Constitutive Project: Response to Cooren and Sandler." *Communication Theory* 24: 245–251.

Law, J. 1994. "Organization, narrative, and strategy." In *Toward a new theory of organizations*, edited by J. Hassard and M. Parker, 248–268. London: Routledge.

Leonardi, P. M., and S. R. Barley. 2008. "Materiality and Change: Challenges to Building Better Theory about Technology and Organizing." *Information and Organization* 18: 159–176.

Linde, C. 2009. *Working the past, narrative and institutional memory*. Oxford: Oxford University Press.

MacIntyre, A. 1984. *After virtue: A study in moral theory* (2nd ed.). Notre Dame, Ind.: University of Notre Dame Press.

McAdams, D. P. 1996. "Personality, Modernity, and the Storied Self: A Contemporary Framework for Studying Persons." *Psychological Inquiry* 7 (4): 295–321.

Mumby, D. K. 1987. "The Political Function of Narrative in Organizations." *Communication Monographs* 54: 113–127.

Nelson, L. H. 2001. *Damaged identities, narrative repair*. Ithaca: Cornell University Press.

Ricoeur, Paul. *Narrative and Interpretation*. New York: Routledge, 1991.

Søderberg, A. M. 2006. "Narrative Interviewing and Narrative Analysis in a Study of a Cross-Border Merger." *Management International Review* 46 (4): 397–416.

Taylor, J. R. and E. J. Van Every. 2000. *The emergent organization: Communication as its site and surface*. Mahwah, NJ: Lawrence Erlbaum.

Trittin, H., and D. Schoeneborn. 2015. Diversity as Polyphony: Reconceptualizing Diversity Management from a Communication-Centered Perspective. *Journal of Business Ethics* 1–18.

Tsoukas, H., and M. J. Hatch. 2001. "Complex Thinking, Complex Practice: The Case for a Narrative Approach to Organizational Complexity." *Human Relations* 54: 979–1013.

Ybema, S. 2004. "Managerial Postalgia: Projecting a Golden Future." *Journal of Mangerial Psychology* 19 (8): 825–841.

Part I

Counter-Narratives and Constitutive Stakeholder Communication

1 Communicatively Constituting Organizational Unfolding through Counter-Narrative

Timothy Kuhn

Scholars of organization have long been interested in understanding the unfolding of—the emergence, formation and alteration of—organizations. Some explain emergence, formation and alteration by referring to members' cognitive processes (Jelinek and Litterer 1994), whereas others draw attention to the imposition of environmental and structural forces on organizations (e.g., Deephouse and Suchman 2008). In contrast, those who ground their analyses in narratives and counter-narratives see organizational unfolding as a characteristic of ongoing communication (Clegg, Kornberger and Rhodes 2005; Taylor and Van Every 2000). Communication, for these scholars, is about neither message transmission or the expression of actors' interiorities, visions common in the management and organizational studies fields; it is, instead, "the ongoing, situated, and embodied process whereby human and non-human agencies interpenetrate ideation and materiality toward realities that are tangible and axial to organizational existence and organizing phenomena" (Ashcraft, Kuhn and Cooren 2009, 26). This definition, unwieldy as it is, suggests that communication is always simultaneously symbolic and material and that it communication generates meanings that *constitute* (rather than merely represent) organizations and organizing processes. And if we take a step further to understand communication as a struggle over meanings regarding an organization's unfolding (Kuhn and Burk 2014; Peterson and Langellier 2006; Mumby 1987) we start to see how the narratives that define organization are the ongoing and inevitable products of efforts to promote some interests over others (Boje 1995; Fontana and Frey 2000; Humphreys and Brown 2002).

One version of this struggle over meanings is that it pits a dominant projection of organizational reality against alternatives that oppose the dominant version. Several authors of the chapters in this volume define counter-narratives in a manner similar to this, and for many aims, such an oppositional model makes sense. Yet, in the study of formal organizations, narratives that are directly, fundamentally and diametrically opposed to a dominant narrative are uncommon. Counter-narratives produced by protest groups, for instance, seldom contest the basic premises that undergird a corporation's right to exist and pursue its profit-maximizing ends; more frequent are

18 *Timothy Kuhn*

efforts to contest particular organizational initiatives or to insert additional (moral) considerations into managerial decision making. In this chapter, therefore, I present counter-narratives as ever-present components of organizational constitution that always saturate and infuse (i.e., are continually present in) overarching narratives of organization. Counter-narratives, from this perspective, are vehicles to aid in comprehending organizational unfolding, but counter-narratives do not merely pit a center against a periphery, a hub of power against a site of local resistance. Instead, I shall frame counter-narratives as a conjunction of symbolic-material resources that can come together to generate challenges to an organization's trajectory.[1]

To examine counter-narratives from such an alternative perspective, I describe organizing practices in a high-tech "start-up accelerator," a 12-week program that aids early-stage technology ventures in becoming viable businesses. I focus on one team of entrepreneurs, in particular, and note the multiple sources of influence over what their start-up was to become. One of these sources of influence, as I describe in the following, is mentors, experienced entrepreneurs or topical specialists who volunteer to assist entrepreneurs and who are matched to start-up team by the directors of the accelerator. An important challenge frequently noted by entrepreneurs who participate in accelerators is "mentor whiplash," the presence of a wide array of advice and opinion from these sources of assistance. Brad Feld, the titular leader of the start-up community in Boulder, Colorado, where the study is based, suggested that

> if you ask five mentors the same question you'll get seven different answers. This is especially true early in any relationship, when the mentors are just getting to know you and your company. . . . As the business grows, there are more points of stimuli, more agendas, more exogenous factors, and more potential whiplash. If you don't build your own muscle around collecting, synthesizing, dealing with, and decided [*sic*] what to do with all the data that is coming at you, then you are going to have massive problems as your company scales up.
>
> (Feld 2013)

Similarly, Steve, one of the founders of the start-up on which this chapter focuses, suggested that mentor influence is "like being in a tornado, always being turned around. And it's your [the entrepreneur's] job to figure out which direction to go." Both Feld and Steve are addressing the trajectory of the developing firm and asserting the founder's right to control it. I contend that those who seek to understand counter-narratives should look for instances such as these: instances where emergence, formation and alteration are occurring in and around a nascent organizational narrative, where challenge occurs not from a diametrically opposed antagonist but is encountered in the practices that define the organization itself.

This chapter pursues such a path. It begins by describing constitutive communication scholarship from the standpoint of narrative and then, drawing

Communicatively Constituting Organizational Unfolding 19

on the notion of the authoritative text, suggests that counter-narratives are simultaneously common and key to understanding development and change in organizations. The chapter then illustrates these claims through a case study of one start-up firm, tracing the emergence of the firm's authoritative text with respect to the challenges and incursions made by counter-narratives encountered in practice. Finally, the chapter draws conclusions for scholarship on organizational trajectories and (counter-)narratives.

Communication as Constitutive of Organization and the Centrality of Narrative

If a key concern for organization theorists is the unfolding of organization, we need theories that account for the existence, persistence, and trajectory of organizations. One body of thought, relatively recently developed, addresses these issues by placing communication practices in the forefront of its descriptions. This work, which generally falls under the moniker "Communication as Constitutive of Organization" (CCO), sees the organization not as a pregiven and monolithic entity; instead, it reframes organizations as ongoing and interconnected communicative processes. Accordingly, scholars working in this tradition emphasize the continually (re)negotiated and (re)accomplished character of that which we recognize as "an" organization. It is a move away from seeing communication as one of many processes occurring *within* orgs, to seeing communication *as* organization.

A set of six "premises" presented in Cooren, Kuhn, Cornelissen and Clark (2011) provides a concise introduction to this mode of thinking; more thorough overviews of this work are available elsewhere (e.g., Ashcraft et al. 2009; Brummans, Cooren, Robichaud and Taylor 2014). First, for Cooren et al., CCO thinking studies communicational events, and finds both organization and organizing practice in those events. Second, Cooren et al. hold that CCO thinking should be as inclusive as possible about what is meant by (organizational) communication, suggesting that analysts should move well beyond the textual/verbal messaging activity of actors, and understand communication practices, as well as participants, as broadly as possible. Third, they hold that CCO scholarship acknowledges the co-constructed or co-oriented nature of (organizational) communication, which means that actors' intentions are only loosely coupled to the unfolding of communication, and therefore that "ambiguity, indeterminacy, and heterogeneity across agents (of all sorts) is to be expected in organizing" (2011, 1152). Communicative practice, in other words, is not driven by an actor's agency; instead, it proceeds as a result of a myriad of forces interacting in the production of a phenomenon. Their fourth premise is related to the third: that who or what is acting always is an open question. This assertion implies that agency cannot be limited, or reduced, to capacities of humans but is always a hybrid or conjoint capacity—and one that is empirically variable. Fifth is that CCO scholarship never leaves the realm of communicational events, a

20   Timothy Kuhn

move that denies common distinctions like subject–object, micro–macro, and structure–action in the interest of transcending them to understand how we might place the (re)production of reality in communication—and, as mentioned earlier, nowhere else. And finally, Cooren et al. argue that this approach favors neither organizing nor organization, suggesting that "CCO scholarship refuses to choose between studying how people get organized and how organizations come to be reenacted and reproduced through these activities" (1153). Taken together, these six premises present a dramatically different conception of communicating and organizing than is typically encountered in the organization studies literature, but one that has been demonstrating its novelty and utility over the past two decades or so (Schoeneborn, Blaschke, Cooren, McPhee, Seidl and Taylor 2014; Taylor, Cooren, Giroux and Robichaud 1996).

With respect to the topic of this volume, Taylor and Van Every's foundational CCO work is particularly relevant. Although their work is tremendously wide ranging, they may be best known for their portrayal of organization as

> an imbricated assemblage of hierarchically embedded transactions, mediated by accounts and crowned by the one all-important constitutive transaction that constitutes the organization as an entity, and thereby a legally recognized person who relates to all its members, whatever their rank. At that point, the organization has been authored.
>
> (Taylor and Van Every 2014, 27)

Organization, as both noun (the "thing" we call the organization) and verb (the process of organizing), is thus always communicative. For Taylor and Van Every, one of the most significant outcomes of the ongoing process of communicative constitution is the generation of a narrative that depicts a collective-level intention; it presents a story about the collective. That narrative is *useful* in organizing: it becomes the basis of accounts that members provide to one another (as well as to those outside what are taken to be the boundaries of the organization) and presents a vision of right and wrong.

Narrative, as depicted by Taylor and Van Every, is rather similar to what I have called the *authoritative text* (Kuhn 2008, 2012; see also Koschmann, Kuhn and Pfarrer 2012). This notion suggests that, as texts emerge from (and are inserted into) organizing practices, collectives coalesce around a limited number of statements—not always, and perhaps least important, written documents—that condense the complexity of an organization's practices into a representation of an abstracted whole. Taken together, these statements comprise a dominant narrative of "what we are (and are not)," "where we're going" and "how we're going to get there" (what I shall truncate as a conception of the "we").

The text is authoritative in that it directs attention and disciplines actors by compelling some level of consistency between distributed practices and the narrative of the "we." In other words, it outlines responsibilities for managing problems encountered in practice, and it exercises influence over

Communicatively Constituting Organizational Unfolding 21

practice as it is appropriated (Cooren 2004; Law 1994; Vásquez and Cooren 2013). For instance, Coll's (2012) detailed account of ExxonMobil highlights its Operations Integrity Management System (O.I.M.S.), a detailed policies and procedures document that both drew on, and subsequently shaped, figurative elements such as the firm's beliefs about proper action, attitudes about risk, relations between functions, evaluations of choices and ambitions for growth. The O.I.M.S was not, in Coll's telling, merely a set of formal guidelines; it was a fusion of texts that represented ExxonMobil's practice as a whole.

Although it is possible to think of the authoritative text as a preexisting, order-producing and ontologically "real" element of the organizing scene, I see such a move as unhelpful. From this sort of perspective, the aim would be to "operationalize" the authoritative text and defend its independently verifiable existence. I see the authoritative text, however, more as an analytical device than a construct operating in the scene. It is a conceptual resource useful in identifying the configuration of elements involved in organizing—a configuration created through narrative.

In portraying this configuration, I (via Taylor and Van Every 2014) deployed the notion of *assemblage* earlier. This term is frequently the translation from French of a term originally used by Deleuze and Guattari but developed by Michel Callon and those extending his work; many argue that a more accurate translation is the English neologism *agencement*. *Agencement*, for Callon and his followers, highlights not the fixed and stable elements composing a whole but the ongoing process of creating arrangements that comprise a practice (Cochoy 2014; Cochoy, Trompette and Araujo in press; Phillips 2006). Those arrangements, moreover, consist of a myriad of agencies:

> The notion of *agencement* . . . demands that a panoply of entities be flexibly taken into account and described in detail, whether they are human beings or material and textual elements. The term is also designed to facilitate the study of a variety of forms of action these forces are capable of generating. . . . *agencements* are arrangements endowed with the capacity to act in different ways, depending on their configuration.
> (Caliskan and Callon 2010, 8–9)

And even though it may be analytically relevant to suggest that some of the elements of the arrangement are stable, the focus here is always on the connections that comprise agency—and, thus, always on the practice (Gherardi in press).

The authoritative text is, then, not an object; it is not the *end* of analysis. Instead, the authoritative text is a vehicle for the examination of the practice of organizational (re)constitution and the struggles over meaning marking an organization's trajectory. It is an analytical tool that allows a researcher to identify the *connections between (human and nonhuman) participants evident in a practice* that are brought together to enact the "we" in cases of organizing.

22   Timothy Kuhn

Counter-Narratives and the Authoritative Text

One of the central features of my characterization of the authoritative text is that it should be understood as a site of struggles over meaning. The authoritative text is not merely a formal mission statement or a portrayal of organization's identity or culture; it is a broader concept that emphasizes relations of power and legitimacy, clarifies roles and responsibilities, and provides an overall sense of what an organization *is* and the trajectory it seeks to pursue (Kuhn 2008). The textual metaphor suggests that its production is the ongoing result of a process of authorship—and that authorship is where a multiplicity of actors vie to inscribe their visions of the whole into the conception of the "we" while simultaneously contesting the writing efforts of others.

Counter-narratives are those that contend for authorship by reinterpreting or challenging a plot line (Abolafia 2010); they disrupt canonical stories, dominant identities and master narratives, replacing them with alternatives that—at least from the perspective of one set of interests—provide better, healthier, more effective or more sustainable practices (Harter 2009; Lindemann-Nelson 2001). If authoritative texts are narratives about the "we," counter-narratives would be understood as confronting or influencing the authoritative text in organizing practice, an encounter that *could* take the form of dramatic resistance to a dominant narrative, but are more likely to be observable as subtle changes that alter the authoritative text in a gradual fashion. The challenge might be seen when actors make connections between the authoritative text and new texts (i.e., those of comparison groups), when a new version of understanding the "we" is introduced into practice, when the organization experiences a challenge to one of its textual foundations, when a text from another domain is introduced or when the authoritative text receives comment from the social surround.

If organizations are to be understood as *agencements*, as heterogeneous agencies bound together in practice, the authoritative text is that which establishes an order—it *configures* elements in the conduct of practice while also establishing a narrative for the sorts of moves that will count as authoritative in establishing the "we." Communication, seen in this light, is the practice of connecting, identifying, naming, knowing, bounding and assigning meaning to elements in the *agencement* (indeed, communication can be understood as key to making the distinctions identifying those elements, or substances, in the first place). The themes of the authoritative text provide criteria for subsequent contributions to organizing. Studying organizing implies analyzing the processes of communication that bring sets of elements together, differentiates them from a surround, and makes them act in particular ways. Agency, in turn, is not something "possessed" or "owned" by any element on its own; agency is a reference to action, realized only in and through interactive events in the marshaling of multiple elements of an *agencement* in the performative and relational generation of action (Callon 2008; Law 2002). Encountering new texts, reappropriating existing texts

Communicatively Constituting Organizational Unfolding 23

and facing commentaries that force reflections on the "we" are not merely the result of human intention, but are likely to be the product of a myriad of human and nonhuman participants. The authoritative text, then, is not under the control of any human agent, no matter the authority granted to the person through formal organizational channels.

Agencements and the practices they imply thus include human intentionality but are not reducible to it. Instead, all action should be understood as the product of a multiplicity of agencies, and analysts should eschew granting any single element ontological priority outside of practice (Cooren 2010). To expand on the point about confrontation made earlier in this section, counter-narratives can be seen as produced through a *conjunction* of forces coming together to influence (e.g., prod, alter, disrupt or challenge) the authoritative text. The key task in understanding counter-narratives, then, is to find the moments in a stream of organizing in which opportunities to shape the conception of the "we"—the trajectory of the organization— occur, and then to locate the forces that combine to present the potential for the saturation of, or incursion into, the authoritative text. The overarching aim, of course, is not merely to identify those moments and their sources but to use this to develop understandings of the unfolding of the firm.

If counter-narratives alter the *agencement* via modifying the authoritative text, we might specify how such challenges address either the *what* or the *how* of the statement of the "we." Accordingly, I suggest two analytically distinct types of counter-narratives: procedural and compositional. *Procedural* counter-narratives are those that challenge the authoritative version of "how we'll get there," in the sense that they suggest that the path presently being followed is either somehow inadequate or that there exists a superior route—or, even more radically, that the aims being pursued are inappropriate. In contrast, a second type, *compositional*, are counter-narratives that challenge the makeup of the organization—those influencing the configuration of elements comprising the *agencement*. As will likely be evident, these broad distinctions mask a good deal of practical overlap in complex organizing practices. The important point, however, is that these categories provide lenses to examine how counter-narratives mitigate closure of authoritative texts; they are evidence of, and they foster, the opening of an *agencement* to ongoing renegotiation.

To illustrate the value of a perspective on counter-narrative informed by CCO theorizing, in the next section I present a case of a team of entrepreneurs launching and building a high-tech start-up firm. By framing their nascent firm as an *agencement* that makes a promise of future success, I show how writing the firm's authoritative text was a lengthy process marked by ambiguity, sporadic development and struggle—and display that the moments of potential counter-narrative influence can provide unique insight on this process. The guiding question for the study is this: *How does an entrepreneurial start-up develop a narrative of what we are (and are not), where we're going, and how we're going to get there, in light of a multiplicity of*

24 *Timothy Kuhn*

counter-narratives? In other words, how does it generate an authoritative text that configures people, ideas, objects, spaces and communication practices that produce a sense of what the emerging firm *is* and is *going to be*?

Boomtown and the Case of "Peercurement"

Since the fall of 2014, I have been studying a "start-up accelerator" called Boomtown in Boulder, Colorado, as part of an ongoing research project. In this section, I first describe start-up accelerators, and Boomtown specifically. And, although I observed several developing organizations throughout my observation period, I focus my attention on one such firm to illustrate the value of the perspective outlined earlier.

Among economists and politicians, entrepreneurship is routinely heralded as a key source of job creation and economic development (Audretsch 2002; Lazear 2005; Valliere and Peterson 2009; but also see Shane 2009). Consequently, and increasingly, many bodies—governments, universities and venture capitalists, to name a few—encourage individuals to embark on the process of creating a start-up business. The process of launching a firm is one that involves a high degree of effort on the part of entrepreneurs and, because between 75% and 90% of start-up endeavors fail in the first four years (Dalkian 2013; Gage 2012) and because many entrepreneurs leave other jobs to work exclusively on the start-up, it involves significant personal risk. Recently, "accelerators" have sprung up around the world (Kempner 2013; Miller and Bound 2011) to foster the success of start-up ventures. These accelerators are, according to Cohen,

> programs of limited duration—lasting about three months—that help cohorts of startups with the new venture process. They usually provide a small amount of seed capital, plus working space. They also offer a plethora of networking opportunities, with both peer ventures and mentors, who might be successful entrepreneurs, program graduates, venture capitalists, angel investors, or even corporate executives. Finally, most programs end with a grand event, a "demo day" where ventures pitch to a large audience of qualified investors.
>
> (2013, 19)

Accelerators, in other words, endeavor to aid in the development of successful start-ups and, in turn, tend to see themselves at the vanguard of economic and community development (e.g., Feld 2012).

As Cohen and Hochberg (2014) note, however, there is very little research on start-up accelerators. They suggest this lack could be the result of these being rather new phenomena, as well the absence of data sets on these sites and their processes. In one sense, then, this study can be understood as responding to a gap in the literature. Beyond that—and more importantly— understanding start-ups is key to gaining insight into organizational and economic processes. Because they are the sites in which nascent firms are developing, start-ups provide the potential for insight into the cultural and economic forces that influence the structuring and trajectory of firms—and, in turn, of the economies that valorize and invest in them (Hoffman and Radojevich-Kelley 2012). The resources presented in an accelerator include lessons—not all explicitly stated *as* lessons—regarding how successful firms "look," so accelerators could be useful sites for examining the discursive resources shaping beliefs about the necessary configuration of elements in the *agencement*. Accordingly, this study is less about the accelerator than it is about the development of the firms created in the accelerator context.

Background on Boomtown

The accelerator that was the context for this study, Boomtown, focuses specifically on technology-oriented start-ups. The Denver–Boulder region (Boulder is only about a 30-minute drive from Denver and is considered one of the outer suburbs of the metropolitan area, an area with a population of roughly 3.3 million) has become something of a hotbed of high-tech entrepreneurship, and the founders of Boomtown have tried to capitalize on the region's mounting interest in high-tech start-ups.

Funded by venture capital firms and a bank, and modeled on established accelerators such as TechStars and Y Combinator, Boomtown provides $20,000 of seed capital to each firm accepted into its cohort in exchange for a 7% equity stake in the business. The cohorts it has hosted have ranged from 8 to 11 start-ups, and each start-up typically consists of two or three members (usually the founders). The program is akin to a semester at a university, as Boomtown presents the cohort, over the 12-week session, with a series of educational opportunities: classroom-like instruction, meetings with mentors from the surrounding community (all with experience as successful entrepreneurs or with expertise in areas relevant to the teams; there are 92 mentors listed on the Boomtown website), occasions for interaction with venture capitalists and graduates of the program, and resources for each team to hone its business case.

The cohort I observed was only Boomtown's second class, the first being held in the spring of the same year. The selection process is competitive: in its most recent cohort, Boomtown received roughly 200 applications and accepted only 12 teams—a rate that one of the co-directors claimed "is more stringent than getting in to an Ivy League university." On the cohort's first day, Boomtown's three codirectors (Tony, Steve and Juan) began by assigning teams to tables in a space that measured approximately 20 meters by 12 meters (see Figure 1.1); this was the space marked for the accelerator's teams, whereas the rest of the space was available as a coworking space: one that was open to freelance and project-based workers—those who frequently work out of their homes and who have no other office space—to inhabit for a monthly fee.

26 *Timothy Kuhn*

Figure 1.1 The cohort space at Boomtown, displaying the close proximity between start-up teams (one team occupied each two-table row).

Note: Not captured in the picture are one row of tables to the left of the frame, and a row of tables on the right, also outside the frame, comparable to those on the left.

At one end of the start-ups' room was a large TV used for projecting presentations and other data; it functioned much like the front of a university classroom and was where presenters stood when addressing the cohort of entrepreneurs. Installed shortly after this photo was taken was a "countdown clock": Immediately above the TV, in red LED numbers, it told entrepreneurs the days, hours and minutes remaining until Demo Day. I positioned myself at the rear of this room (the vantage point in Figure 1.1) and, at one of the tables near me, sat the team that is the focus of this analysis. There were only two members as the session began: Steve,[2] the chief executive officer (CEO), and Alex, the chief technology officer (CTO), and both appeared to be relatively young—in their mid-twenties, I estimated. In our first conversation, Alex mentioned how a novel use of Internet technology facilitated their ability to interact with the kernel of an idea, leading eventually to their arrival in Boomtown: only a few months prior, he said, "Steve posted a message on a Reddit forum with the idea for the company, asking how tough it would be to create computer code for the idea." Alex was one of a handful of Reddit users who replied; after Steve interviewed several respondents, he asked Alex to join him in pursuing the idea. Shortly afterward, Steve heard of Boomtown (along with a few other accelerators) and applied. They were accepted into the cohort, and although Steve was living in New Jersey and Alex in Texas, they decided to quit their jobs and move to Boulder for the 12 weeks of the program. Steve also mentioned that his sister, Natasha, would soon be moving from New York City to join them in founding the company.

The Emergence and Articulation of the Authoritative Text

Business Model Artifacts

When applying for the Boomtown program, as well as on entering, Steve and Alex had not yet created *an* organization. They had a business idea, what they thought was a clever name—CompraNous, a name combining words for *buying* and *we* in Spanish and French, respectively, with the twist that *nous* in English is pronounced "new," implying novelty—a draft webpage and the members mentioned here. The plan for their business was a version of crowdfunding applied to small suppliers; the tagline they used was "an online platform that helps investors fund small business inventory." Small suppliers often encounter challenges generating capital sufficient to bring their products to retail locations, but they also are often unattractive to banks. Steve reasoned that a large set of small funders—people who often either didn't invest in traditional financial vehicles or whose funds were more modest than would be reasonable for longer-term investments—could provide the capital that would enable them to manufacture and ship their products, and that this sort of distributed microfinancing could support those suppliers while also providing a quick return (they were planning on a 7% to 10% return in the space of two months, on average) to those funders.

With this model of the business in Steve's and Alex's minds, one of the first activities in the Boomtown course was to complete a "Value Proposition Canvas" (see Figure 1.2), along with an exercise that forced them to approach potential customers to assess user interest and possible obstacles. The Value Proposition Canvas, first, was a textual object that, as deployed in the session, summoned Steve and Alex to generate explicit claims regarding the value their business would create for customers—and, accordingly, it forced them to articulate assumptions about their intended customers, their "pain points," other solutions to customers' pain and how the features of their plan would create a customer experience that would address those pains in a superior manner. The teams completed this in two-hour-long sessions marked by persistent yet generative interrogation by the session's leader (one of the mentors on Boomtown's roster) and then posted these on the walls of their sections of the room.

Steve later told me that they modified their Value Proposition Canvas several times over the course of the program (often making addendums via sticky notes) and held that its continual presence in their workspace encouraged them to reflect on the choices made in authoring it. Moreover,

28 *Timothy Kuhn*

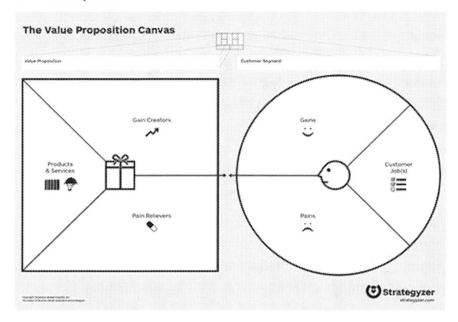

Figure 1.2 Value Proposition Canvas
Source: http://www.businessmodelgeneration.com/canvas/vpc.

its presence allowed a quick introduction to their business model, using a common language, to both other teams in the cohort and to visitors (e.g., mentors, venture capitalists) entering the space. Another entrepreneur interviewed for this study anthropomorphized the value proposition canvas by suggesting that it played an important role in his team's trajectory:

> [the materials on the wall] are a shrine, kind of an homage to what you want to be, may have been, could have been. It's just a way to visualize where you came from—and a lot of people use that as a kind of ethics, or gauge, or morals, just to always view where you've come from, where you're going, or just to look into the past. . . . I think the wall can be considered a mentor, too, you know—you can get whiplash from looking at what you used to be.

The Value Proposition Canvas, then, became a key element of the configuration of elements characterizing the start-up; it focused attention on the production of value, with value defined in terms of solving a customer problem in a manner superior to any alternatives. Moreover, its meaning was not fixed: though it was considered a touchstone of sorts by entrepreneurs, its contents were abstract enough to appeal to different audiences and guide decision making on a wide variety of topics.

The second experience in the first days of the program was an exercise forcing the teams to identify potential customers, interview them, and present a customer "persona" to the rest of the cohort. Steve and Alex made several assumptions about customers in constructing the Value Proposition Canvas, and this exercise provided an opportunity to test those assumptions. They decided that university students would make a good market for investing small sums that merchandisers could use to bring their products to market, so Steve made a trip to the local university campus to gauge students' interest. He handed out $5 vouchers for students to use as they began investing in merchandisers' products on the site (in a format reminiscent of Kickstarter, where users can choose from among several funding offers and choose to invest in one or more) and reported that he was hopeful that they would garner a good deal of interest.

Statement of Purpose

A second, and related, element of the authoritative text was ComraNous's conception of the reason for its existence. For many Boomtown teams, a statement of its purpose was something articulated when they completed the Value Proposition Canvas and customer personas, as they identified "pain points" in customers' lives they could address. Steve suggested that CompraNous was different in that it was motivated by something more substantial:

> There are a lot of companies that exist for the sake of being a company, and then what you'll see is almost cookie-cutter. [You ask them] "How is this different from any other company?" and then their CEOs will have a difficult time explaining, and I think it's hard to fake this passion, fake this being driven by trying to solve what we consider to be a big important problem. Everybody always says "we need to solve a pain point," but I think that's paying lip service to the accepted methodology. It's not saying "I've encountered this terrible, awful problem in my life, and I recognize this as a problem for society as a whole, and I'm going to confine my efforts to make this a better place. No, they want to say "what's a pain point I can solve, give me a pain point, I've going to solve it."

Steve continued by arguing that CompraNous was driven by an "MTP," a Massive Transformative Purpose (Ismail, Malone and van Geest 2014) that not only distinguished the firm from other start-ups but also provided a motivation for the team and a ground for subsequent action:

> It means that everybody you bring on, everybody who comes in, everybody who's tangentially related, even the customers or the businesses you work with, it gives you a personality. And for us, what the MTP of CompraNous is, is *to make the world rich*. It's simple. And it's crazy.

30 *Timothy Kuhn*

And it's massive. And it's impossible. But, at the same time, it illustrates exactly what we want to do. And it's to make the world rich, not to make the 1% of the world rich.

By drawing the notion of the MTP, Steve displayed that CompraNous's authoritative text was the emerging and ongoing product of a wide array of influences. He also suggested its centrality to organizing processes in suggesting that it provides a personality, a statement of distinctiveness about the "we" that guides and directions action and decision.

Locale

A final component of Peercurement's developing sense of the "we" related to space was its Boulder location. As mentioned earlier, Alex and Steve had moved to Boulder to participate in Boomtown, and they enjoyed living in the area a great deal—and Steve, at least, vowed to never return to New Jersey after living in Colorado for the 12 weeks of the program. The problem was that theirs was a financial services business, and Boulder is far removed from the US financial services capital, New York City (NYC). My fieldnotes captured Steve's claim about Boulder, from a conversation in the Boomtown space four months after his program ended:

Colorado is great for start-ups generally, and is very good for finding talent (because there are many technically skilled people in the area looking for work), but he said that Peercurement needs to have a headquarters in New York because that's where financial services companies are—that "you can go to a networking event there, and someone can introduce you to 12 other people all in the same lending space." The issue, he says, is one of legitimacy: Unless your company is located in NYC, it's not going to be taken seriously. So they're renting space in a coworking space in NYC, which—for $300 a month—allows them to have a[n] NYC mailing address, along with a place to take meetings whenever they're in town.

Being situated in this cultural-geographic locale thus provides benefits and drawbacks to the firms inhabiting it (see Kuhn 2006). These can be understood to be components of Peercurement's authoritative text, components that participate in—and shape—ongoing organizing practices.

The *agencement* recognizable as CompraNous was composed of the specific people founding the company, ideas, artifacts, its location, computer code, and (the hope for) economic and social capital. It presented itself as possessing an innovative approach to funding merchandising and, concomitantly, an innovative and effective investment vehicle for small investors (specifically targeted, at the beginning, at college students, though this was to change soon, as described in the following). The development of this investment opportunity was the result of a commitment to working against wealth inequality, to "make the world rich." It was located in Boulder but also had a presence in New York, signaling simultaneously a distinction from the typical financial technology firm and a recognition of the requirements of for firms in this sector. It was not, therefore, a marketing scheme, a vehicle to further enrich the already-wealthy, or one of the many other New York–based start-ups seeking to profit from small investments. These conceptions of the "we" became authoritative in the sense that they guided and directed subsequent practice—including practices in which the start-up encountered counter-narratives, as described next.

Procedural and Compositional Counter-Narratives at Peercurement

The previous section described the contents of CompraNous's emerging authoritative text, a text authored primarily by its founders. This section shows how counter-narratives shaped the development of the embryonic organization; to do so, I return to the categorization, introduced above, of procedural and compositional counter-narratives. To reiterate, *procedural* counter-narratives challenge the dominant (and, of course, still-developing) conception of goals and the means by which they will be achieved; *compositional* challenge the configuration of agencies making up the *agencement*.

Procedural Counter-Narrative: Mentor Whiplash

On my first visit following the team's customization of the artifacts mentioned in the preceding section, I noticed CompraNous's Value Proposition Canvas posted on the wall and talked with Alex about both it and the exercise in which they developed a customer persona. He mentioned that, given his focus on technological activity, he "struggled to see the logic or reasons for them"; he then directed my attention to the number of users on the website. When we began talking, I noted that his screen count displayed ten users; when he checked no more than 15 minutes later, the number was zero. Alex was clearly disappointed but framed the result as needing to figure out their user group—he mentioned that they "had also thought about housewives, 20-somethings just out of school, and even 14 to 17 year olds as their target market, since the idea behind the site is to use it as an investment device," and that these groups would want to realize a return from small, short-term investments—a return comparable to that currently available only to larger investors (such as 10% in a quarter). Two days later, I noted the following in field notes:

> As I was leaving for the day, I saw Alex waiting by the elevator. He mentioned that they had "pivoted" sharply. They were moving away from their model of marketing to individual users, since they realized they'd

32 *Timothy Kuhn*

> need an awful lot of users, maybe 10,000. They were going after "value customers" and, while I didn't fully understand their move, he noted that they would see a small set of individuals and firms as the foundation of their business model. In this new vision, CompraNous would make a very small margin on each deal, but that they'd "have to do lots of deals." Tony and Juan encouraged and helped them craft this change, and Tony suggested a new name: He proposed "Peercurement," implying peer-to-peer purchasing, or procurement, of goods. Steve walked by a few minutes later; he joined us and he talked very excitedly about this pivot.

The upshot of this conversation was that the company began pursuing a very different strategy than what Steve and Alex originally expected. Based on the advice of the codirectors—advice that was generally seen as authoritative in the setting—the company would no longer focus on attracting a large number of small investors like students, but would instead try to interest several well-placed merchandisers along with high-profile users. Steve and Alex were in agreement, at least to the audience of an outsider, that this was the right direction—it was not what they had planned, but the shift in their conception of what the "we" was, they agreed, necessary. The name change and the value proposition "pivot" provide evidence of the struggle over authorship of the developing authoritative text. It suggests that the narratives about the firm and its trajectory are continually circulating in the practices in the accelerator.

Several weeks later, I learned of another form of agency shaping the Peercurement *agencement*. Steve informed me that the team had been in contact with another Boomtown mentor, a lawyer who had experience working with the US Securities and Exchange Commission (SEC)—a crucially important regulatory agency that could, with a single decision, judge Peercurement's model to be an illegal form of investment and, therefore, prevent it from operating in the United States. Steve reported that he was enthused by this meeting because the lawyer "gave his blessing to [their] idea." This idea was the *original* (i.e., prepivot) notion of attracting a large number of small investors who would commit relatively small sums of money to fund small merchants to aid them in producing goods and getting them to market. Steve relayed that the lawyer noted that he had never encountered an idea like theirs before—thereby suggesting the novelty they sought—but was confident that it would pass muster with the SEC. Steve also mentioned that this lawyer might be willing to be an early-stage investor and potentially to be part of the pitch they would give on Demo Day; this was important to the team because the lawyer possessed the gravitas of an older and more experienced businessperson ("He's been doing this stuff for 30 years," Steve said). Several weeks after that, the lawyer did just that: He endorsed their business plan to a crowd of approximately 600 venture capitalists and community members at Demo Day, and mentioned to the audience that he had just decided to become an early investor in Peercurement.

Communicatively Constituting Organizational Unfolding   33

On the topic of mentor influence, the lawyer suggested some slight changes to the business plan, inserting a (perhaps necessary) legal rationality for developing authoritative text and providing confidence that the configuration of elements marking the *agencement* was likely immune from SEC interference. But, in contrast to the Boomtown codirectors' advice, the lawyer largely reinforced (i.e., reinscribed) the choices the team had already made. The lawyer did, additionally, suggest a possible alternate business model (having to do with large, accredited investors only, a second pivot that would have represented a third, and very different, version of the firm's business) that could be pursued should the SEC render the primary value proposition—Steve and Alex's original strategy—illegal. He recommended that the team hold this idea as a potentiality, one to be considered only if necessary, so it might be considered a latent procedural counter-narrative to be held in reserve, one that could provide a sense of security for the founders.

What is particularly interesting for the category of procedural counter-narratives was that this encounter with the lawyer laid in front of the team a choice: They could pursue the strategy change offered by Tony and Juan (and on which Steve and Alex had been working for a few weeks), or they could switch back to their original strategy. The decision was theirs, but it was shaped by the lawyer's assurance of the SEC's approval, the authority of the Boomtown codirectors and the financial resources accompanying it, the drives of the other teams in the space, the acknowledgment of the work necessary to make either strategy materialize, the projection of the future financial value of the firm and their own statement of their desires at the start of the program encoded in the value proposition canvas now hanging on the wall. Steve and Alex thus chose to revert to their original model, but, as *agencement* thinking demonstrates, all choices are sociomaterial hybrids rather than individualized cognitive processes: the opportunity for choosing came via other agencies marking the *agencement*; the potential for choice (as well as the move itself) was shaped by the configuration of these forces.

These instances provide two examples of the influence mentors and advisors exerted over the entrepreneurs. The entrepreneurs frequently talked about the experience of the "mentor whiplash" mentioned in the Introduction to the chapter, a term referencing the challenge of being pushed in many mutually exclusive directions simultaneously by the many mentors circulating through Boomtown. The notion suggests an ongoing struggle over meaning, a competition in which participants vie to author the firm's trajectory. Entrepreneurs generally felt that these mentors had the teams' best interest in mind but also acknowledged that the "whiplash" placed the onus on the start-up team to decide how, or whether, to incorporate the long list of advice.

The presence of mentor whiplash indicates the ongoing potential for change in the story of the "we" created by the textual efforts of others to author the trajectory of the firm. Boomtown featured an ever-present possibility

34 *Timothy Kuhn*

for teams to encounter counter-narratives—for texts to be inserted in, or removed from, the developing authoritative text through the vehicle of the mentors. Although the official stance was, as reflected in Brad Feld's statement in the introduction, that the presence of so much advice and opinion was useful for entrepreneurs, the degree of agency possessed by the teams with respect to the mentors is open to debate. Some advice was connected with systems or specializations the teams could not fully understand (e.g., the legal system), some was connected with the promise of funding—or, in the case of Tony and Juan, the *authority* of existing funding via the accelerator, and some were linked with "gurus": mentors whose reputation made it rather challenging for teams to ignore the advice. Seeing agency as situated *in* the entrepreneurs, then, misses important contingencies and connections between the *agencement*'s configuration of elements.

Compositional Counter-Narrative 1: Distinctive Bodies in the Agencement

The next week, Natasha (Steve's sister) arrived from New York City after completing another job and immediately expressed support for the "pivot" the company had made—though she was less certain about the name change. On her second day in the accelerator, she used the small space to secure the attention of all the teams. She was marked in several ways: she was clearly new to the space, and she was the only woman among the 23 entrepreneurs in the cohort. I noticed that she had been talking with a team at an adjacent table—this was my first introduction to her, and she seemed very outgoing, personable and humorous and possessed a loud voice. The following is from my field notes:

> As Natasha reached for a business card (one with CompraNous written on it), Alex mentions that they're going to be changing the name. Members of the other teams ask about the existing name, and suggest that it's a problem for anyone searching for the business online—and that if one would hear the name in conversation, someone will search under compra new—that's even if the English speaker would know what *compra* is and how to spell it. Natasha replies that their original choice was made largely because they searched for names for which they could get a free Internet address, and that CompraNous was one of the few available when they started the process.

The point of this episode is not about the name per se, but to direct attention to materiality in the site: The small setting enabled quick (and fleeting) interactions like this on a regular basis, allowing other members to participate in the authoring of each firm's developing authoritative text. The presence of a female body attracted attention; Natasha was well aware of this, and

Communicatively Constituting Organizational Unfolding   35

she used it strategically. I asked her about her reflections on being the only woman in Boomtown, acknowledging that the high-tech sector was generally seen as male dominated, and she replied:

N: I actually kinda like it. I just feel like I can own it, I'm very comfortable with it, and I've been able to spin it to my advantage in lots of ways. . . . and there are a lot of benefits to being a girl [*sic*].
TK: Here [in Boomtown]?
N: Yeah—well, in the tech world. But, actually, just as an entrepreneur. I don't know what the numbers are, but there are definitely more male entrepreneurs than female entrepreneurs. But if you can, like, *own* it, and learn to use it to your advantage—I know it sounds bad, but you can't help using it to your advantage.
TK: Are you talking about sexuality, or a way of thinking . . .?
N: No, let's put it this way: if you're a really important investor, and you have a choice to speak to a 25-year-old guy, or a 25-year-old girl, unfortunately, you're probably going to pick the girl, whether you realize it or not, it's just your preference. . . . So, because of that, I've had access to really interesting conversations, I've had invitations to meetings, all sorts of things I wouldn't have gotten if I wasn't a girl.

One of the marks of distinction for Peercurement, then, was its gender (sex, to be more precise) diversity. And, directly relevant to her claim in this interview, Natasha had obtained a meeting later that day with a potential investor (a man) that other start-ups could not secure (and about which others were jealous). Clearly, then, the presence of other teams, the physical space, and bodily differences were key to the textual constitution of what Peercurement was to become.

This distinctive element of Peercurement's sense of its "we" was not, however, highlighted in its explicit statements about itself. Gender diversity as a source of competitive advantage only emerged later and was rarely discussed as an element of the authoritative text—until, that is, it disappeared.

Specifically, Natasha did not last long as a member of Peercurement. About a week before Demo Day—a week before the official end of the Boomtown program—she left the team over what Steve called "leadership differences" that had been present between the siblings since their youth. In an interview eight months after the conclusion of Boomtown, Steve depicted Natasha's departure as a firing—one that he made and one he did not regret, even though it might have cost them that potential investor mentioned above. During that interview, Steve noted that Peercurement had hired 12 more employees (many of them interns rather than salaried employees), and Steve had discovered the importance of having women on the team. After agreeing with Natasha's point about women having greater access to conversations with investors ("you'd rather talk to the pretty girl than some husky dude"),

36 Timothy Kuhn

Steve admitted that Peercurement lacked an important component, one that was not a concern for most other Boomtown firms:

> We're looking for a female salesperson. We have one female [intern] in the company right now—that's not good. We need more.

Steve then asked if I knew of any female university students who might have the potential to fill this gap. The lack of female bodies came to be seen as a challenge to Peercurement's sense of distinctiveness, not to mention its ability to attract funding. Thinking of bodies in textual terms, this lack can be understood as a counter-narrative that challenged the previous distinctiveness enjoyed by Peercurement. The lack could have been handled by altering the authoritative text (through a vision of merit against gender diversity) but, instead, led the founders to recognize a need to alter, or rebalance, the composition of the firm.

Compositional Counter-Narrative 2: Rich versus King

A final element Steve and Alex mentioned was one of ambivalent desirability about taking funding from early-stage investors—about the value of money and those who provide money, as elements in the *agencement*, along with those elements' relationships with other agencies. In a follow-up interview two months after the end of the Boomtown program, Steve told me that he had an offer for a $500,000 investment from a venture capital (VC) firm that had seen them at Demo Day but that he was going to turn it down because

STEVE: They wanted too much of my company—they wanted 30% for half a million [dollars]. And it's like we don't need that much money right now—where we are, we can do a lot of growth, we can get really far on much less money than that. . . . Tony, from Boomtown, has been pressuring me like hell to take the money. . . . they're our shareholders, so we told them, and they're also our advisors still, so we keep them close and informed. . . . [this VC firm] also wanted board control—they wanted the sun and the moon, so we just said no. I believe in Peercurement at the end of the day.

TK: And you think that it's going to get you more, down the road, than that.

STEVE: And I think that if we demonstrate any kind of traction—we got that offer when we were essentially pre-revenue; what's it going to be when we have 10,000 users? . . . and if we had accepted that deal, they would have owned more of the company than Alex.

He also mentioned that Alex was more positively inclined toward the offer, but that the two of them had discussed the importance of growth toward their long-term goal and decided to turn it down.

Communicatively Constituting Organizational Unfolding 37

This discussion is an instance of a previous conversation I had with Steve about the discourse of "being rich or king." This distinction is a common trope among start-ups (see Wasserman 2012), and refers to entrepreneurs' motivations regarding the benefits of their business. It invokes a distinction between developing the business just enough to sell it to another company or investor (to "cash out," or "make an exit") versus building it into an established firm that will persist over time and which the entrepreneur will manage.

In a subsequent interview, Steve made it clear that he was planning to make his money from the firm in the future but was convinced that a slow (and non-capital-intensive) approach was appropriate for building the business into something more substantial and valuable than this VC firm recognized:

> [W]hen I look at what they wanted us to do—in our talk, they were like, "you're going to have to hire accountants, you're going to have to do this, have to do that," what they *wanted* us to do is not what I did. But they would have really pressured us to do that, "now you've got the money, spend the money, we want to see growth. I mean, we're sick of you bootstrapping, this slow growth BS, we want to see growth, we want to see that curve, you know, January, today! Not June, not July, today." And it just, it wasn't there. We could have done that, but it wasn't there at the time. But having the time to bootstrap it and build it out a little more now, and not giving up 30% of your company, or complete control, 60%, or 66% of my board, that's crazy. So there was no way. And it was tempting, and I look back, and I think, thank god I didn't do the easy, greedy, thing, of just taking the money.

Moreover, the effort to convince Peercurement to accept this VC offer came from the Boomtown leadership as well. Steve noted that Tony had the interests of the funding of the accelerator in mind when encouraging them to accept the deal:

> [I]t became very clear when the money was on the table, that the advice they were giving was advice for Boomtown, and not advice for Peercurement. I understand. You've got your own bag, you've got to run it, you're raising more funds for the next two classes, you've got to have some success stories. I get it. But it's also short-sighted. Tony needs results today because he's going to go talk to investors tomorrow. I need results 2–3 years from now.

Rejecting this funding, then, was the result of Steve (in particular) drawing on Peercurement's authoritative text to select a slower-growth trajectory for the firm, one that turned away from the lure of this offer.

38 *Timothy Kuhn*

Summary: The Unfolding of the Authoritative Text

The authoritative text, as argued earlier, should not be understood as a naturally occurring entity that develops in (and, worse, prior to) a firm's organizing practice, one that lies in wait for the analyst to "uncover" it. Rather, the authoritative text is best understood as an *analytical tool*, a device useful for gaining insight into the configuration of elements that guides and directs a firm's configuration of agencies bound together in practice. It not only expresses the "we" (what we are and are not, where we're going, and how we're going to get there); it also leads the firm to become *what it's going to be*.

In the case of Peercurement, the authoritative text displayed the firm's uniqueness through its narrative of its novel business model (and its changing conceptions of its customers), its (temporary) gender diversity, its novel location, and its desire to create a lean firm viable over the long term (and immune from SEC regulation). This narrative changed over time as the firm encountered potential counter-narratives, such as when Tony and Juan suggested the "pivot" noted earlier, when the lawyer gave his approval to the original idea (and when he suggested the potential alternative) or when Natasha resigned (or was fired). The conception of the "we" in the authoritative text also enabled Steve to turn down a large VC investment opportunity because the offer would threaten the narrative he and the team had created (i.e., the narrative informed the decision, even in the face of strong pressure). Clearly, not all of these were intentional efforts to author the authoritative text, but each challenged Peercurement's procedures and composition and, in so doing, induced activity that shaped the trajectory of the firm.

Discussion

The unfolding—the trajectory—of organizations is a longstanding interest in organization studies, and the aim of this chapter has been to illustrate how organizational narratives are ongoing products of a wide array of influences. In describing the emerging authoritative text of a start-up firm operating in an accelerator called Boomtown (and after that program as well), I also provided evidence of counter-narratives encountered by the firm in the course of its ongoing organizing and showed that these counter-narratives need not be starkly or diametrically oppositional; instead, they position themselves as challenging the configuration of elements marking an *agencement*. As Gabriel (this volume) notes—and as Feld (2013), addressing mentor whiplash, would likely agree—it is only through encountering counter-narratives that master narratives (i.e., authoritative texts) recognize themselves as such. This is likely especially the case in start-ups, where the collective "we" is a central focus of organizing effort. Nascent organizations, then, can be excellent sites for the investigation of organizational trajectory.

Communicatively Constituting Organizational Unfolding   39

Counter-narratives, accordingly, turn out to be an axial element of the ongoing process of organizing. The struggles over meaning seen in the Peercurement case have the potential to shape CCO theorizing by showing how constitution is the ongoing, and somewhat precarious, product of the multiple bids to author the authoritative text that circulate in routine organizing (Kuhn 2012). These counter-narratives are not merely the product of humans drawing on elements of the surrounding discursive repertoire but are generated out of conjunctions of sociomaterial elements and actions. The authoritative text, in turn, is not developed as a configuration device intentionally; it is as much a response to events and conditions as it involves human choice. Such an insight is at the core of the attractiveness of a CCO vision: because it places the genesis and persistence of "the" organization in communication practices (and nowhere else), it provides a unique vantage point from which to examine the emergence and trajectory of organization.

The chapter also contributes to both CCO and counter-narrative thinking by suggesting the value of employing the concept of *agencement* to describe that which becomes recognized as the organization, attending to the configuration of heterogeneous agencies bound together in practice. The recognition of this configuration leads to an understanding of both *procedural* and *compositional* counter-narratives: challenges to goals, methods and elements pursued by the *agencement*. Attention to these challenges display that nascent organizations' conceptions of what they are and what they're going to be— inscribed into authoritative texts—are the result of ongoing and challengeable efforts on the part of conjoined human and nonhuman agencies that articulate a version of value attractive to a market (Caliskan and Callon 2010). And, perhaps of even more value to the study of organizing, the chapter showed how counter-narratives provide potential challenges to organizational strategies; those challenges can generate openness to change or a rejection of the possibility of change. In other words, organizational emergence, formation and alteration (i.e., unfolding), as ongoing change in narratives, are ever present. Though the notion of change is not likely to be surprising to leaders of start-up accelerators (Deering, Cartagena and Dowdeswell 2014), it can point to the centrality of a struggle over meanings at the very founding of a firm, a struggle that can shape the trajectory of the firm well into its future.

In conclusion, this chapter has presented a vision of counter-narrativeinspired organizational development that expands the potential utility of counter-narratives in organizational analysis. These counter-narratives are not necessarily diametrically opposed to the master narrative, to the authoritative text; in fact, they are likely to emerge together and find their meanings in struggles over authorship of a collective's trajectory. This chapter, therefore, demonstrates that counter-narratives are highly relevant concepts for those who wish to develop explanations of organizational persistence and change, topics that broaden considerably counter-narratives' conceptual purchase in organization studies.

40 Timothy Kuhn

Notes

1. Interestingly, both the standard conception and my alternative are based on spatial metaphors (core periphery and incursion by saturation), but my articulation of this alternative leads to the claim that temporality matters in the analysis of counter-narratives: *when* analysts attend to them influences their understandings of counter-narratives' influence over organizational trajectories.
2. Other than Boomtown, all names in the chapter—of persons and organizations—are pseudonyms.

References

Abolafia, Mitchel Y. 2010. "Narrative Construction as Sensemaking: How a Central Bank Thinks." *Organization Studies* 31 (3): 349–367.

Ashcraft, K. L., T. Kuhn and F. Cooren. 2009. "Constitutional amendments: 'Materializing' organizational communication." In *The academy of management annals*, edited by A. Brief and J. Walsh, 1–64. New York: Routledge.

Audretsch, David B. 2002. "The Dynamic Role of Small Firms: Evidence from the U.S." *Small Business Economics* 18 (1–3): 13–40.

Boje, D. 1995. "Stories of the Storytelling Organization: A Postmodern Analysis of Disney in 'Tamara-Land'." *Academy of Management Journal* 38: 997–1035.

Brummans, Boris H. J. M., François Cooren, Daniel Robichaud and James R. Taylor. 2014. "Approaches to the communicative constitution of organizations." In *The Sage handbook of organizational communication*, edited by L. L. Putnam and D. K. Mumby, 173–194. Los Angeles: Sage.

Caliskan, Koray, and Michel Callon. 2010. "Economization, Part 2: A Research Programme for the Study of Markets." *Economy and Society* 39 (1): 1–32.

Callon, Michel. 2008. "Economic markets and the rise of interactive agencements: From prosthetic agencies to habilitated agencies." In *Living in a material world: Economic sociology meets science and technology studies*, edited by Trevor Pinch and Richard Swedberg, 29–56. Cambridge, MA: MIT Press.

Clegg, Stewart R, Martin Kornberger, and Carl Rhodes. 2005. "Learning/Becoming/ Organizing." *Organization* 12 (2): 147–167.

Cochoy, Frank. 2014. "A theory of 'Agencing': On Michel Callon's contribution to organizational knowledge and practice." In *The oxford handbook of sociology, social theory, and organization studies: Contemporary currents*, edited by Paul Adler, Paul du Gay, Glenn Morgan and M. Reed, 106–124. Oxford, UK: Oxford University Press.

Cochoy, Frank, Pascale Trompette, and Luis Araujo. 2016. "From Market Agencements to Market Agencing: An Introduction." *Consumption Markets & Culture* 19 (1): 3–16.

Cohen, Susan. 2013. "What Do Accelerators Do?: Insights from Incubators and Angels." *Innovations* 8 (3/4): 19–25.

Cohen, Susan G., and Yael V. Hochberg. "Accelerating Startups: The Seed Accelerator Phenomenon." Retrieved from http://papers.ssrn.com/sol3/Papers.cfm?abstract_id=2418000

Coll, Steve. 2012. *Private empire: ExxonMobil and American power*. New York: Penguin.

Cooren, Francois. 2004. "Textual Agency: How Texts Do Things in Organizational Settings." *Organization* 11 (3): 373–393.

Communicatively Constituting Organizational Unfolding 41

Cooren, F., Timothy Kuhn, Joep P. Cornelissen, and Timothy Clark. 2011. "Communication, Organization, and Organizing: An Overview and Introduction to the Special Issue." *Organization Studies* 32 (9): 1149–1170.

Dalkian, Glen. "90% of Tech Startups Fail." http://www.wamda.com/2013/02/90-percent-of-tech-startups-fail-infographic

Deephouse, David L. and Mark C. Suchman. 2008. "Legitimacy in organizational institutionalism." In *The Sage handbook of organizational institutionalism*, edited by R. Greenwood, Christine Oliver, Roy Suddaby and Kerstin Sahlin, 49–76. Los Angeles: Sage.

Deering, Luke, Matt Cartagena and Chris Dowdeswell. 2014. *Accelerate: Founder insights into accelerator programs*. Boulder, CO: FG Press.

Feld, Brad. 2012. *Startup communities: Building an entrepreneurial ecosystem in your city*. New York: Wiley.

Feld, Brad. 2013. "The positive benefit of mentor whiplash." In *Feld thoughts*. Boulder, CO. http://www.feld.com/archives/2013/07/the-positive-benefit-of-mentor-whiplash.html

Fontana, Andrea, and James H. Frey. "Interviewing: The Art of the Science." In *Handbook of Qualitative Research*, edited by N. K. Denzin and Y. S. Lincoln, 361–76. Thousand OAks, CA: Sage, 1994.

Gage, Deborah. 2012. "The Venture Capital Secret: 3 Out of 4 Start-Ups Fail." *Wall Street Journal* September 19, 2012. http://online.wsj.com/article/SB1000087239 63904437202045780004980476429190.html

Gherardi, S. "To Start Practice Theorizing Anew: The Contribution of the Concepts of Agencement and Formativeness." *Organization* (advance online publication) Available at: http://org.sagepub.com/content/early/2015/09/18/1350508415605 174.abstract.

Harter, Lynn M. 2009. "Narratives as Dialogic, Contested, and Aesthetic Performances." *Journal of Applied Communication Research* 37 (2): 140–150.

Hoffman, David Lynn, and Nina Radojevich-Kelley. 2012. "Analysis of Accelerator Companies: An Exploratory Case Study of Their Programs, Processes, and Early Results." *Small Business Institute Journal* 8 (2): 54–70.

Humphreys, Michael, and Andrew D. Brown. 2002. "Narratives of Organizational Identity and Identification: A Case Study of Hegemony and Resistance." *Organization Studies* 23 (3): 421–447.

Ismail, Salim, Michael S. Malone and Yuri van Geest. 2014. *Exponential organizations: Why new organizations are ten times better, faster, and cheaper than yours*. New York: Diversion Books.

Jelinek, Mariann and Joseph A. Litterer. 1994. "Toward a cognitive theory of organizations." In *Advances in managerial cognition and information processing*, edited by Chuck Stubbart, James R. Meindl and Joseph F. Porac, 3–41. Greenwich, CT: JAI Press.

Kempner, Randall. 2013. "Incubators Are Popping up Like Wildflowers . . . But Do They Actually Work?" *Innovations* 8 (3/4): 3–6.

Koschmann, Matthew, Timothy Kuhn, and Michael Pfarrer. 2012. "A Communicative Framework of Value in Cross-Sector Partnerships." *Academy of Management Review* 37 (3): 332–354.

Kuhn, Timothy. 2006. "A 'Demented Work Ethic' and a 'Lifestyle Firm': Discourse, Identity, and Workplace Time Commitments." *Organization Studies* 27 (9): 1339–1358.

42 Timothy Kuhn

Kuhn, Timothy. 2008. "A Communicative Theory of the Firm: Developing an Alternative Perspective on Intra-Organizational Power and Stakeholder Relationships." *Organization Studies* 29 (8–9): 1227–1254.

Kuhn, Timothy. 2012. "Negotiating the Micro-Macro Divide: Communicative Thought Leadership for Theorizing Organization." *Management Communication Quarterly* 26 (4): 543–584.

Kuhn, Timothy and Nicholas Burk. 2014. "Spatial design as sociomaterial practice: A (Dis)organizing perspective on communicative constitution." In *Language and communication at work: Discourse, narrativity, and organizing*, edited by F. Cooren, E. Vaara, A. Langley and H. Tsoukas, 149–174. Oxford: Oxford University Press.

Law, John. 1994. "Organization, narrative, and strategy." In *Toward a new theory of organizations*, edited by John Hassard and Martin Parker, 248–268. London: Routledge.

Law, John. 2002. "Objects and Spaces." *Theory, Culture and Society* 19 (5–6): 91–105.

Lazear, E. M. 2005. "Entrepreneurship." *Journal of Labor Economics* 23 (4): 649–680.

Lindemann-Nelson, H. 2001. *Damaged identities, narrative repair*. Ithaca, NY: Cornell University Press.

Miller, Paul and Kirsten Bound. 2011. *The startup factories: The rise of accelerator programmes to support new technology ventures*. London: NESTA.

Mumby, Dennis K. 1987. "The Political Function of Narrative in Organizations." *Communication Monographs* 54 (2): 113–127.

Peterson, Eric E., and Kristin M. Langellier. "The Performance Turn in Narrative Studies." *Narrative Inquiry* 16 (2006): 173-80.

Phillips, John. 2006. "Agencement/Assemblage." *Theory Culture and Society* 23 (2–3): 108–109.

Schoeneborn, D., S. Blaschke, F. Cooren, R. D. McPhee, D. Seidl, and J. R. Taylor. 2014. "The Three Schools of CCo Thinking: Interactive Dialogue and Systematic Comparison." *Management Communication Quarterly* 28 (2): 285–316.

Shane, Scott. 2009. "Why Encouraging More People to Become Entrepreneurs Is Bad Public Policy." *Small Business Economics* 33 (2): 141–149.

Taylor, James R., Francois Cooren, Helene Giroux, and Daniel Robichaud. 1996. "The Communicational Basis of Organization: Between the Conversation and the Text." *Communication Theory* 6 (1): 1–39.

Taylor, James R. and Elizabeth Van Every. 2014. *When organization fails: Why authority matters*. New York: Routledge.

Taylor, James R., and Elizabeth J. Van Every. *The Emergent Organization: Communication as Its Site and Surface*. Mahwah, NJ: Lawrence Erlbaum, 2000.

Valliere, Dave, and Rein Peterson. 2009. "Entrepreneurship and Economic Growth: Evidence from Emerging and Developed Countries." *Entrepreneurship and Regional Development* 21 (5): 459–480.

Vásquez, Consuelo, and Francois Cooren. 2013. "Spacing Practices: The Communicative Configuration of Organizing through Space-Times." *Communication Theory* 23 (1): 25–47.

Wasserman, Noam. 2012. *The founder's dilemmas: Anticipating and avoiding the pitfalls that can sink a startup*. Princeton, NJ: Princeton University Press.

2 Counter-Narratives and Organizational Crisis

How LEGO Bricks Became a Slippery Business

Marianne Wolff Lundholt

Introduction

> Children are our major concern and the central focus of our company. We are determined to leave a positive impact on society and the planet that children will inherit. Our unique contribution is through inspiring and developing children by delivering creative play experiences all over the world. A co-promotion like the one with Shell is one of many ways we are able to bring LEGO bricks into the hands of more children and deliver on our promise of creative play.
>
> (Knudstrop, October 8, 2014)

In the preceding press release, the CEO of the LEGO Group, Jørgen Vig Knudstorp, explains the strategic decision behind LEGO's collaboration with the oil company Shell dating back to the 1960s. However, due to a three-month campaign run by Greenpeace, Knudstorp concludes the press release with the announcement that LEGO will not renew its co-promotion contract with Shell signed in 2011, in which co-branded LEGO toy cars are sold at Shell stations in selected countries in a deal valued at £68 million. The Greenpeace campaign was a reaction to Shell's recently announced plans to drill in the Alaskan arctic. In August 2014, Shell submitted a new offshore drilling plan to US authorities to explore for oil in the arctic in 2015, off the coast of northwest Alaska. As a response Greenpeace declared a global sanctuary in the arctic with the intention of banning offshore drilling in the area. In order to draw attention to the initiative, Greenpeace created a three-month-long campaign against the partnership between Shell and LEGO, where LEGO toys were sold at Shell gas stations around the world.

According to Knudstorp, the "LEGO brand and everyone who enjoys creative play, should never have become part of Greenpeace's dispute with Shell" (Knudstorp, October 8, 2014). Several media outlets concluded that Greenpeace humiliated and 'won the battle' over LEGO by running a campaign against LEGO's agreement with Shell. So why did LEGO end up in this undesirable and seemingly unpredictable situation? In this chapter, I examine the dimensions of such organizational tensions and thereby develop

44 Marianne Wolff Lundholt

an increased understanding of the process and content of organizational counter-narratives in a situation of organizational crisis.

As pointed out by Andrews (2004, 1), "counter-narratives only make sense in relation to something else, that which they are countering. The very name identifies it as a positional category, in tension with another category." The paper aims at examining not only ways in which counter-narratives may destabilize an organization, as illustrated in the LEGO case, but also how a deep knowledge of their dimensions may help better predict the evolvement of a crisis.

The chapter is concerned with the following two research questions:

1. How do organizational texts[1] produce counter-narratives resulting in organizational crises?
2. How can an increased understanding of the dimensions of counter-narratives help in foreseeing a potential crisis?

The research questions will be related to the conflict evolving in 2014 among the three organizations Shell, LEGO and Greenpeace.

In order to increase our understanding of the potential of counter-narratives' ability to help predict the evolution of organizational crisis, we need to understand the offspring of such crisis. Theories within crisis communication are mainly focused on external threats (environmental scanning) and internal factors (diagnosing the vulnerabilities of a specific organization). Environmental scanning strategies involve "watching the environment for changes, trends, events, and emerging social, political, or health issues" (Coombs 2015, 45). Diagnosing an organization's crisis vulnerabilities concerns reflection on an organization's specific industry, size, location, operations, personnel, and risk factors—all of which could lead to different kinds of crisis. Within this field of crisis communication, little attention has been paid to organizations' own texts (i.e. organizational strategies) and actions as a source of potential organizational vulnerability.

The chapter begins with a reflection on the relevance of a narrative approach to organizational crisis communication. What are the mechanisms in narrative texts and how is meaning established through its various components?

When applying narrative theory within an organizational context, communication is considered as constitutive of the organization. As will be illustrated, this carries along an openness to interpretations. This openness is explained further in the subsequent section, where the transtextual nature of counter-narratives is explored.

The next section includes a reflection on crisis management related to counter-narratives and their narrativization processes in order to increase our understanding of the dimensions of counter-narratives in crisis situations. The chapter concludes with a reflection on the predictability of organizational crisis and a conclusion, in which theoretical implications are considered.

Why a Narrative Approach to Organizational Crisis Communication?

Although Bamberg (2004) states that narrative is not a privileged discourse genre when compared to other genres in everyday interactions (354), the narrative format stands out as it is "simply there like life itself" (Barthes 1977, 79). The consideration of narrative as a natural part of human nature is further emphasized by MacIntyre, who states that "man is in his actions and practices, as well as in his fictions, essentially a story-telling animal" (MacIntyre 1984, 216). MacIntyre's philosophy that social life is a narrative is also shared by Roland Barthes, who explains that "the history of narrative begins with the history of (hu)mankind; there does not exist, and has never existed, a people without narratives" (1966, 14). Communication scholar Walter Fisher goes even further as he claims that "all forms of human communication need to be seen fundamentally as stories" (1987, xiii). According to this narrative paradigm, narrative is considered unavoidable and fundamental to human sense-making.

To understand the authority of narrative, a deeper understanding of its constituents is needed. A useful set of terms is Ryan's (2004) distinction between 'narrative' and 'narrativity.' Having narrativity means "being able to evoke [. . .] a script" (9) whereas "[t]he property of 'being' a narrative can be predicated on any semiotic object produced with the intent of evoking a narrative script in the mind of the audience" (ibid.). Thus, unlike other genres, narrative is capable of igniting some kind of causality which may be inferred by the reader connecting events. With the definition of narrative as "a perceived sequence of non-randomly connected events" (Toolan 2001, 6), Toolan captures the relation between sequence and causality which can be traced all the way back to Aristotle. Polkinghorne explains that "Narrative meaning is created by noting that something is a 'part' of some whole and that something is the 'cause' of something else" (1988, 6). Temporality and causality are both at the core of Bamberg's understanding of narrative as he explains that "narratives order characters in space and time and, therefore, as a format, narrative lends itself not only to connecting past events to present states [. . .] but also to revealing character transformations in the unfolding sequence from past to future. In other words, narratives, as a particular speech genre, may be able to offer something to the presentation of selves (and others) that other speech genres don't do so eloquently and directly" (354). Although Bamberg refers to 'speech genre', it seems reasonable to turn his observation on the connection between past, present and future to narrative in general. The representation of specific events—otherwise represented as lists or chronicles—brought into one meaningful whole is, according to Polkinghorne, the definition of a plot:

> When a human event is said not to make sense, it is usually not because a person is unable to place it in the proper category. The difficulty stems, instead, from a person's inability to integrate the event into a plot whereby it becomes understandable in the context of what

46   *Marianne Wolff Lundholt*

has happened . . . Thus, narratives exhibit an explanation instead of demonstrating it.

(1988, 21)

Polkinghorne defines plot as the basic means by which specific events, otherwise represented as lists or chronicles, are brought into one meaningful whole (1988). More recently, Kukkonen depicts plot as "that feature of narrative which facilitates the mental operations that translate story events into a meaningful narrative" (Kukkonen 2014, 707). A plot thus entails a suggested connection between events. Thus, a narrative can simply put events closely together and thereby exhibit explanations (Czarniawska 2004). The nature of narratives as open to interpretation is also emphasized by Czarniawska (1997): "some kind of causality may be inferred, but it is crucial to see that narrative, unlike science, leaves *open* the nature of the connection (18). This mechanism may help explain why events that might not seem to be interrelated still are translated into meaningful narratives as illustrated with the LEGO case, where Knudstorp states that the LEGO brand should never have become part of Greenpeace's narrative of Shell's drilling.

Narrative as a Communicative Constituent of Organization

The consideration of organizational activity as narratives takes its outset in the view that organizations are constituted in and through human communication (referred to as the CCO approach—Communicative Constitution of Organization) (see Cooren et al. 2011; Fairhurst and Putnam 2004; Taylor et al. 1996; Taylor and Van Every 2000), where communication is considered the means by which organizations are established, composed, designed, and sustained (1150). As a consequence, organizations are portrayed "as ongoing and precarious accomplishments realized, experienced, and identified primarily—if not exclusively—*in* communication processes (ibid.). Following this idea of communication as constitutive of organization, Cooren (2001) states that "any organizational form is structured ultimately as a narrative" and "any organizational activity can be anticipated prospectively and understood retrospectively as a narrative" (181). In this sense, the theoretical outset carries along an extended notion of narrative going beyond the traditional study of narrative as a way of understanding human interactions (Fenton and Langley 2011, 1174). Following this perception, "[a] CCO perspective of organizational sensemaking considers organizations not as a given, but as emerging in, and indeed constituted by or incarnated in local episodes of communication. What this means is that organizations are constantly (re)produced, (re)incarnated, and (re)embodied in local interactions, and thus subject to change and renewal" (Cooren et al. 2011, 1158). At the core of this methodological framework lies the assumption that organization documents and texts are constitutive in themselves. Cooren et al. (2011) remind us that "any performance will never be reducible to the way it was

Counter-Narratives and Organizational Crisis 47

intended or meant by its producer [. . .] meanings that emerge (in ongoing fashion) from communication are unlikely to be isomorphic with the original intentions" (1152). In this view, meaning is negotiated, translated and/or debated. Within the CCO frame, translation has been applied to explain "the articulation or organization of multiple interests within a same project without referring to any shared meaning or goals" (Cooren 2001, 92–93). In what follows, some of the multiple interests among Greenpeace and LEGO are examined.

Transtextuality Interrelating Climate Change, Arctic Drilling and Social Acceptance

When considering the various actions initiated by Greenpeace to draw attention to the partnership between Shell and LEGO, it is interesting to note that Greenpeace has used LEGO's own products and strategies in their campaign. One example is the constructed illustration of the LEGO platform from the LEGO arctic product range which is partly covered by oil—published in a 14-page report developed by Greenpeace titled 'Lego is keeping bad company'

Figure 2.1 LEGO arctic product range
Source: *Lego is keeping bad company* (Greenpeace 2014, July 1, 9).

48 *Marianne Wolff Lundholt*

(Greenpeace 2014, July 1) explaining the main motives behind the campaign:[2] Here the original arctic product range makes critical commentary on the partnership between LEGO and Shell.[3] Another example is the film *LEGO: Everything is NOT awesome* (Greenpeace 2014, July 8) initiating the campaign. Here polar bears and LEGO figures are drowning after what seems to be an Arctic oil spill. By using 120 kilograms of LEGO bricks covered in oil to depict a pristine Arctic and with an evocative cover version of the theme song "Everything Is Awesome," originating from *The LEGO Movie*, the film instantly became a viral hit as it attracted more than 7.5 million views.

Figure 2.2 Greenpeace placed in a LEGO brick
Source: *Lego Is Keeping Bad Company* (Greenpeace 2014, July 1, front page)

The interrelation between texts, as exemplified earlier, takes on what the French narratologist Genette referred to as a "transtextual relationship," that is, "all that set the text in a relationship, whether obvious or concealed, with other texts" (Genette 1997, 1). In other words, with the term *transtextuality* Genette points at the mechanism where one text prompts readers to be acquainted with other texts. He puts forward five types of transtextual relationships (1997): intertextuality, paratextuality, architextuality, metatextuality and hypertextuality.

When analyzing the three-month-long campaign run by Greenpeace against the partnership between Shell and LEGO, the use of transtextual features is a recurring strategy applied by Greenpeace in an attempt to convince their stakeholders that "[i]n addition to driving climate change, Arctic oil drilling also poses a huge threat to the Arctic itself" (*Lego Is Keeping Bad Company*, Greenpeace 2014, July 1, 12) and that "LEGO makes itself complicit with Shell's destructive activities by allowing the oil giant to use this partnership to buy social acceptance" (ibid.). As will be illustrated, transtextuality and other related features such as spoofing (Berthon and Pitt 2012) enable Greenpeace to obtain a discursive interrelatedness between climate change/Arctic drilling (Shell) and social acceptance hereof by LEGO.

The word *spoof* means to trick or deceive and is often used to refer to a type of satire in which an original work is parodied by creating a similar but altered work. In the report *Lego Is Keeping Bad Company*, Greenpeace places itself at the center of a LEGO brick with the image shown in Figure 2.2.

Mission	Inspire and develop the builders of tomorrow
Aspiration	Globalize and innovate the LEGO system-in-play
Promises	**Play Promise** Joy of building. Pride of creation — **Partner Promise** Mutual value creation / **Planet Promise** Positive impact — **People Promise** Succeed together
Spirit	Only the best is good enough
Values	Imagination - Creativity - Fun - Learning - Caring - Quality

Figure 2.3 The LEGO Brand Framework (LEGO, 2014)

The intertextual relation not only alludes to LEGO's main product, that is, the LEGO brick, but also to its own documents, namely, the LEGO's brand framework where text has been inserted into a LEGO brick (Figure 2.3).

Furthermore, *Lego Is Keeping Bad Company* also copies other visual effects from the LEGO Responsibility Report by using similar colors, graphics and setup. This interrelatedness between Greenpeace and LEGO is furthermore obtained through metadiscursivity in the following headlines:

- Lego is keeping bad company *Lego Is Keeping Bad Company* (Greenpeace 2014, July 1, front page)
- No more playdates with Shell (Ibid., 2)
- Shell needs nice playmates (Ibid., 3)
- Lego is Shell's number one playmate (Ibid., 4)
- Lego is too good for Shell (Ibid., 10)
- Shell is bad company (Ibid., 11)

The choice of wording (i.e., *playdates, playmates*, good vs. bad company) alludes to LEGO's main stakeholder, that is, the child, by using a discursive realm associated with childhood. Here Shell is portrayed as the villain, exposing LEGO to a bad company, while at the same time Greenpeace positions itself in a parental role forbidding LEGO to *play* with Shell. In addition, Greenpeace establishes an oppositional and conflicting relation between LEGO and Shell by putting forward its visions in a comparative discourse as pollution being constructed both as a figure of speech and used literally: "A first step to stopping Shell from polluting one of the most pristine places on the planet is to stop Shell polluting our children's minds."

Intertextuality (i.e. a relationship of co-presence between two texts or among several texts for example in quotes or allusions) is also applied in

50 *Marianne Wolff Lundholt*

Lego Is Keeping Bad Company where the LEGO Group Responsibility Report 2013 is quoted several times:

- *"Children—and their parents—should continue to have very high expectations of us"* (LEGO Group Responsibility Report 2013, 10)
- *"The LEGO Group firmly believes that only the best is good enough"* (Ibid., 35)
- *"LEGO's vast consumption of paper for toy boxes has been minimised in recent years and will be 100% environmentally certified by 2015"* (Ibid., 126)

These statements quoted in direct speech from the LEGO Group Responsibility Report are, according to Genette's understanding of transtextuality, an intertextual relation, as one text alludes to the other through quotations (Genette 1997, 1–2). The quotations are recontextualized in the sense that they are transferred from one discourse to another within the Greenpeace report and are thereby embedded in a new context transforming the original meaning (Linell 1998, 144–145).

It is worth noticing that the quotations listed earlier are not explicitly embedded in the text but are placed at the bottom right corner in a yellow LEGO brick (creating paratextuality) as illustrated in Figure 2.4.

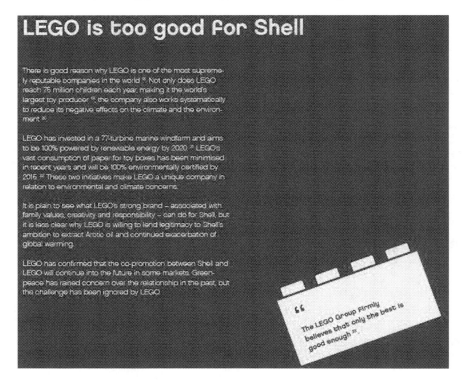

Figure 2.4 LEGO is too good for Shell
Source: *Lego Is Keeping Bad Company* (Greenpeace 2014, July 1, 10)

Counter-Narratives and Organizational Crisis   51

Although there is no explicit link between the quotation and the text in Figure 2.4, the two texts are interrelated and establish what Genette would refer to as a "textual transcendence of the text" (1997) creating a relationship between the involved texts. As illustrated in the following, the relationship also involves a counter-relation.

Narrative Cohesion and Intertextual Counter-Relation

As already touched upon, a basic element of narrative is its ability to exhibit a meaningful whole and entail a suggestion of connection between events. The proximity between the texts exhibits a meaningful whole as the reader infers a causal relation. The narrative cohesion which is at the root of this causal link ignites what Sperber and Wilson (1986) refer to as 'narrative implicature'—a concept derived from Grice's understanding of implicature, referring to what is suggested in an utterance but not strictly implied (Grice 1989). Toolan (2013) explains the concept of narrative implicature as follows: "the reader of narrative assumes the general cooperativeness of the teller, and draws on powers of inferencing to fill out the sense of the information conveyed by the teller where these seem calculatedly incomplete or indirect" (28). In other words, the quote in the yellow LEGO brick is embedded intertextually in the meaning construction through the inference of causality established by the process of narrative implicature:

Transtextual relation/Proximity of texts

⬇

Narrative implicature/Inference of causality

⬇

Meaning transformation

However, in the preceding example there is more at stake than an allusion or embedding. The recontextualized text (i.e. the quotes from the LEGO Group Responsibility Report) creates a sense of what could be referred to as a 'counter-relation' because the textual interaction between the interconnected texts generates friction. This friction evolves as the statement "only the best is good enough" is ascribed a new meaning when embedded in the Greenpeace report—what Gabriel (in this volume) explains as a situation where a narrative *travels*, that is, crosses boundaries, "moving from one organization to another, from one discourse to another, and from one narrative space to another." In other words, Greenpeace's recontextualization (defined by Linell (1998, 144–145) as "the dynamic transfer-and-transformation of something from one discourse/text-incontext . . . to another") of the

52 *Marianne Wolff Lundholt*

LEGO statement results in a transformation of meaning as the quote ends up serving Greenpeace's intent of proving that LEGO's words are inconsistent with its actions. This transformation of meaning is supported by the context (the aim of the Greenpeace Report) and the surrounding text where Greenpeace questions LEGO's willingness to lend legitimacy to Shell's drilling plans.

The example illustrates that the construction of inferences through narrative text comprehension in the situation of transtextuality may involve or generate a power dimension. This dimension is constituted by the recontextualization process which may give rise to an asymmetric power relation between the old text/original source (the LEGO Group Responsibility Report) and the new text/source (the Greenpeace Report) evolving into a counter-relation between the interrelated texts. As Greenpeace is facilitating the recontextualization of the quote from the LEGO Group Responsibility Report, an unequal encounter (as termed by Fairclough 2015) emerges; Greenpeace becomes the powerful participant in control of the meaning construction.

This insight reveals a need to take the process of recontextualization and the transformation of meaning to a level beyond classic intertextuality theory and focus on chronology (Fairclough's concept of 'intertextual chains' encapsulating the predictability of the transformation occurring among series of types of texts (1992, 130) and the 'past-in-the-present,' where the past is the object of a retrospective commentary (Fairclough 1992; Keenoy and Oswick 2003; Kristeva 1986). In order to grasp the complexity arising in situations of such 'intertextual counter-relations,' the concepts of counter- and master narratives seem to bring about an applicable frame for increasing our understanding of the meaning transformation as their very existence emerges from such asymmetric counter-relations:

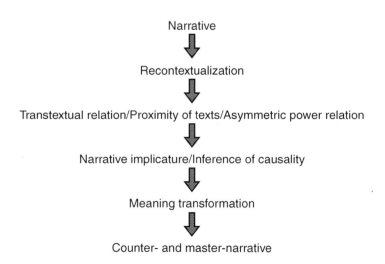

Counter-Narratives and Organizational Crisis 53

As has been stated by several contributors to this publication, there exists a reciprocal relation between the counter-narrative and the master narrative—one cannot exist without the other. With reference to Bamberg's understanding of counter-narratives as a concept that only makes sense in relation to something else, that which they are countering, Johansen in this volume observes that counter-narratives are intertextual by nature. Consequently counter- and master narratives are relational and thus transtextual in a Genettian sense as they are interconnected by nature whether covert or overt. Kuhn (in this volume) depicts the reciprocal relation as follows:

> Counter-narratives are those that contend for authorship by reinterpreting or challenging a plot line (Abolafia 2010); they disrupt canonical stories, dominant identities and master narratives, replacing them with alternatives [. . .]
>
> (p. 22)

Citing Bamberg and Andrews' (2004) understanding of counter-narrative as only making sense in relation to that which they are countering and as a positional category in tension with another category (Bamberg and Andrews 2004, x), Jensen, Maagaard, and Rasmussen (in this volume) characterize master narrative against the backdrop of the definition of counter-narrative: "their [master narratives'] very status as "master' depends on there being implicit variations, alternative ways of interpreting and telling that are to be controlled, suppressed or silenced—*mastered*" (87).

According to these definitions of the concept, the existence of a master narrative—and eventually counter-narratives—evolves in the present case when the LEGO Group Responsibility Report is quoted and thereby recontextualized in the Greenpeace report establishing a transtextual relation. As such it is the asymmetric power relation and the recontextualizer's (Greenpeace') counter-intentions that evolve into a master/counter-narrative relation.

Before elaborating on the relation between recontextualization/transtextual relations and counter-/master narratives in an organizational crisis situation, we need to understand the nature of such crisis.

Crisis Management and the Mitigation of Crisis

As has been generally agreed upon, "the best way to manage a crisis is to prevent one" (Coombs and Holladay 2012). Crisis management theory offers a wide variety of theory on how to handle crisis issues but pays only little attention to the prevention of crisis. In order to better prevent crises we need to understand what crises are made of and how they are produced. According to Coombs (2015) a crisis is perceptual, which means that if "stakeholders believe an organization is in crisis, a crisis does exist, and stakeholders will react to the organization as if it is in crisis" (3).

54 Marianne Wolff Lundholt

In a press release published by Knudstorp on July 1, 2014, LEGO resisted Greenpeace's protests:

> The Greenpeace campaign focuses on how Shell operates in a specific part of the world. We firmly believe that this matter must be handled between Shell and Greenpeace. We are saddened when the LEGO brand is used as a tool in any dispute between organizations. We expect that Shell lives up to their responsibilities wherever they operate and take appropriate action to any potential claims should this not be the case. I would like to clarify that we intend to live up to the long term contract with Shell, which we entered into in 2011 (Trangbæk, 2014).

However, as already mentioned at the beginning of the chapter on October 8, 2014, Knudstorp clarified that the company will not renew its co-promotion contract with Shell when the current deal ends.

Considering the online reach of the events, the extent to which social media have amplified the impact of the organization and the concern for the reputation, the crisis can be categorized as what Owyang (2011) refers to as a 'social media crisis' (also quoted in Coombs 2015, 22), that is, events that can harm an organization and arise in or are amplified by social media with specific focus on reputational concerns. Seen within an organizational context, social media increase risk dynamics as the social media platforms expand the spectrum of reputation risks (Aula 2010, 45). As pointed out by Page and Bronwen (2011), Web 2.0 technologies have given users with relatively low technical skills platforms to upload and manipulate texts with unprecedented ease (Page and Bronwen 2011, 2).

The social media platforms challenge conventional reputation management in three ways, according to Aula (2010). First, social media are not just a channel for distributing corporate communications but rather an arena for participation in which organizations interact with the public creating an impression of the organization. Second, strategic reputation management should concentrate on ethics rather than pursuing short-term interests—an organization cannot just look good; it has to be good. Third, social media have the effect of presenting a collective truth as users create and search for information, gain knowledge, and make interpretations based on communication about an organization which they share with other users (45–46).

Aula (2010) draws particular attention to the risk associated with unverified user-generated information about the organization (both true and false), users putting forth ideas about organizations that conflict with an organization's own idea of what it is or what it wants to be, users' opinions on ethical business practices or the transparency of operations and finally the reputation risk resulting from an organization's own

Counter-Narratives and Organizational Crisis 55

communication activities, including their reaction to claims presented in the social media (45).

Coombs (2015) categorizes three overall types of social media crisis:

1. **Organizational misuse** social media crisis (when an organization violates the norms of behavior in a particular social media channel)
2. **Dissatisfied customer** social media crisis (when dissatisfied customers for example use an organization's hashtag to complain, and the original intention was to provide customer service)
3. **Challenges** (when stakeholders perceive that an organization's behaviors and/or policies are inappropriate or irresponsible).

   i. An organic challenge (when an organization loses touch with changes in stakeholder values and interests)
   ii. An expose challenge (when stakeholders prove an organization's words are inconsistent with its actions)
   iii. The villain challenge (when a stakeholder seeks to portray the organization as a villain that needs to reform its evil ways) (Coombs 2015, 23–24)

These types of social media crisis can increase our understanding of various ways in which counter-narratives may disrupt master narratives and thereby expose the dimensions of certain types of organizational counter-narratives. In 'organizational misuse,' the master narrative is disrupted by an organization's unethical use of a social media channel (for example capitalizing on a charity or natural disaster to generate more 'likes' or buying followers). The dimensions of the counter-narrative in this strategy thus consist of ethical organizational behavior in tension with unethical behavior. 'Dissatisfied customer' involves tension between an organization's original intentions of a specific post and customers' reactions to it. 'Challenges' are transtextual by nature as they concern conflicts between stakeholders' expectations to organizations and organizations' actual behavior or policies. These expectations are typically constructed from Corporate Social Responsibility (CSR) strategies and reports as is also the situation in the LEGO case which falls into this final category: LEGO's stakeholders prove that the organization's words are inconsistent with its actions by the establishment of a transtextual relation between LEGO's responsibility report and its partnership with Shell. Thus LEGO's decision of choosing what Matten and Moon (2004) refer to as 'an explicit CSR approach,' where their CSR strategies are articulated to the stakeholders via their responsibility report—rather than 'an implicit CSR approach,' where CSR strategies are not communicated explicitly—provides a good foundation for the evolvement of expose challenges (and thus counter-narratives) when being recontextualized as the very nature of challenge crisis involves conflicts. In the expose challenge, such counter-narratives consist of internal conflicts between an organization's own intentions and actions, whereas the

56 *Marianne Wolff Lundholt*

villain challenge counter-narrative consists of a conflict between a villain (destroyer) and a hero (savior).

Seen from an overall perspective, the general dispute between Shell and Greenpeace can be categorized as a 'villain challenge' as Greenpeace seeks to portray Shell as a villain, whereas the conflict between Greenpeace and LEGO can be considered an 'expose challenge,' as Greenpeace intends to illustrate a conflict (established through the use of transtextuality) between LEGO's own responsibility strategy (e.g., intentions of building a better world) and their actions (lend legitimacy to Shell's drilling plans, as framed by Greenpeace). The partnership between Shell and LEGO is depicted by LEGO as "one of many ways we are able to bring LEGO bricks into the hands of more children and deliver on our promise of creative play" (Knudstorp, October 8, 2014). However, in the narrative constructed by Greenpeace in *Lego Is Keeping Bad Company* LEGO is considered a partner used by Shell to condone environmental destruction in the Arctic and the strategy is depicted as a "carefully thought-out strategy by Shell to buy friends who can make its conduct look acceptable and misleadingly associate it with positive values" (*Lego Is Keeping Bad Company*, 2). Here it is evident how internal documents become subjects to a contested terrain serving Greenpeace' strategic goals:

> *Goal: to ensure the ability of the earth to nurture life in all its diversity*
>
> *Mission statement: to expose global environmental problems, and to force the solutions which are essential to a green and peaceful future*
> (Greenpeace, 2014)

When Greenpeace accuses LEGO of putting sales above its commitment to the environment and children's futures, it seeks to invoke its mission statement, namely, to expose global environmental problems by recontextualizing LEGO's responsibility report.

Counter-Narratives and Recontextualization

According to Cooren (2001), making sense of a conflict is coextensive with the creation of a narrative structure linking different actors through a process of translation. Moving beyond Greimas's actantial model (see Humle and Frandsen, in this volume) enables Cooren (2001) to depict the *ongoing* narrative processes taking place in organizing processes according to the CCO perspective: "By showing how Greimas's model can be applied simultaneously to many different organizing processes, I have opened up its linear approach and shown how heterogeneous effects always contaminate and undermine organizational homogeneity" (196). In that sense,

Counter-Narratives and Organizational Crisis   57

recontextualization can be read as simultaneous narrativization processes, which can be illustrated in Figure 2.5, following Cooren (2001):

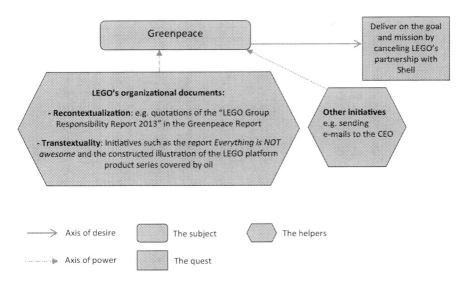

Figure 2.5 The narrativization process in the counter-narrative

This model discloses how the subject (i.e. Greenpeace) seeks to achieve a specific quest (i.e. to cancel LEGO's partnership with Shell) through the use of helpers (i.e. LEGO's own responsibility report). As illustrated in the model, these helpers constitute the main ingredients in the establishment of counter- (and master) narratives, that is, recontextualization and transtextuality. It is, however, the subject (in this case Greenpeace) that is in charge of the recontextualization process and thereby ignites an asymmetric relation as LEGO's organizational documents are embedded in the subject's documents transforming meaning. This meaning transformation emerges through what Linell refers to as the ambiguous nature of contexts as "they are partly outside of the discourse or text, but at the same time the discourses and their relevant contexts constitute each other. All this means that discourses and their contexts presuppose and imply each other, and that a piece of discourse cannot be taken out of a given matrix of contexts without changing its interpretations, or its potential of being interpreted in specific ways" (1998, 144).

Thus, the impact of the ambiguous nature of contexts can to some extent be illustrated through the narrativization model which provides an overview of a situation where an organizational text (the LEGO Group Responsibility Report) intended to increase the image of the organization turned out to be a 'helper' in an opponent's quest to cancel a valuable

58 *Marianne Wolff Lundholt*

business agreement. The *intended* process by LEGO can be illustrated in Figure 2.6:

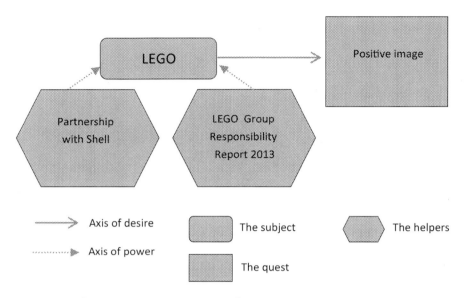

Figure 2.6 The narrativization process in the master narrative

This case seems to suggest that by comparing the two models, it is clear how counter- and master narratives are interdependent. If we return to Jensen, Maagaard and Rasmussen's definition of the concepts of counter- and master narratives as a 'master' depending on alternative interpretations and Kuhn's understanding of counter-narratives as reinterpretations or challenges of a plot line, the case implies that two narrativization processes need to be in place in order for a counter- and master narrative to emerge: two different subjects serving two contradicting quests recontextualizing one or more helpers (this observation also corresponds with Humle and Frandsen's finding, in this volume, that one defining feature of counter-narratives is the creative recasting or replacement of actantial positions against the ones prescribed by dominant narratives). In the LEGO case, the helpers are internal documents igniting challenge crises.

Conclusion and Theoretical Implications

Returning to the first research question, that is, "How do organizational texts produce counter-narratives resulting in organizational crisis?" some theoretical implications of the study emerge. The contemplations on how proximity leads to the construction of meaning, and reflections on the point of narratives' openness to interpretations in an organizational context provide a useful foundation for understanding the mechanisms behind the establishment of meaning. To explain how proximity and openness to interpretation become key players in the formation of counter-narratives, a turn to strategies that help grasp the interrelation that occurs when texts are closely linked seems to provide a useful framework for understanding their role. The examples from the Greenpeace campaign illustrate that particularly one strategy was applied repeatedly, namely, that of transtextuality. However, the traditional understanding of intertextual relations does not enable an explanation of the friction that arises in the LEGO case, namely how does a commentary on a text turn into a *critical* comment when recontextualized?

To understand this transformation of meaning we need to understand the mechanisms involved in the recontextualization process. The findings suggest that the proximity of texts exhibits an inference of causality realized through narrative cohesion. Due to the principle of cooperativeness, narrative implicature generates a meaning transformation. To catch the evolvement of the critical part, we need to turn our attention to the asymmetric power relation that occurs when another subject (following Cooren's [2001] model) recontextualizes a text to serve their quest. This process generates meaning transformation and the evolvement of a master and a counter-narrative.

The question is, what we can learn about the nature of counter-narratives based on this knowledge? As stated counter- and master narratives are intertextual by nature and counter-narratives are characterized by their reinterpretion or challenge of a master narrative. To fully understand the nature of these two concepts, we need to turn to the narrativization process behind recontextualization, which illustrates how the role of the recontextualizer, or what Cooren refers to as the subject, generates friction when undergoing a narrativization process with the quest and the helpers. It is in this very process where one document is recontextualized and ending up serving a new subject (and thereby a new quest), that the counter- and master narratives come into existence. When only one narrativization process exists, there is no conflict and thereby neither a counter- nor a master narrative, as one only comes into existence through the other.

To return to the research question and the link between organizational texts, counter-narratives and organizational crisis, there is a clear connection between the expose and villain challenges, the role of organizational texts and the evolvement of counter-narratives. This connection is strengthened by the fact that not only counter-narratives but also challenge crises are transtextual by nature. The reinterpretation that Kuhn in this volume mentions in his understanding of counter-narratives is eventually brought about by the subject position in the narrativization process depicted by Cooren (2001).

As this research has taken outset in a case depicted primarily as expose challenges, the focus has been on the conflicts between inconsistencies between words and actions. It would be interesting to extend the research

60 *Marianne Wolff Lundholt*

to look beyond this particular crisis category and examine whether counter-narratives are established by different means in other cases.

Practical Implications

Returning to the research question, "How can an increased understanding of the dimensions of counter-narratives help in foreseeing a potential crisis?" some practical implications of the study emerge.

It seems reasonable to draw the conclusion that when diagnosing the vulnerability of an organization regarding potential crises organizations need to pay careful attention to the ways in which their own documents may be recontextualized by its stakeholders, as this may ignite potential counter-narratives particularly those concerning CSR strategies as such documents according to Podnar is "the process of anticipating stakeholders' expectations" (2008, 75). Such texts are particularly vulnerable due to the risk that stakeholders may not feel that their expectations are met and therefore may use them to recontextualize the organization and thereby transform meaning causing an expose or villain challenge.

As illustrated, the combination of an explicit CSR approach and social media generates a fruitful platform for the evolvement of counter-narratives. With Web 2.0, stakeholders have easy access to sharing unfulfilled expectations. The changing media landscape that has come along with this new era is a landscape signifying a "transfer of control" of the internet, and ultimately the central platform for communication, from the few to the many" (Brown 2009, 1–2). As noticed by Voit (and referred to in Coombs (2015, 19)), social media share five common characteristics: participation, openness, conversation, communities and connectedness (Voit n.d.)—all characteristics concerned with the involvement of stakeholders in the communication processes. This supports Brown's observation that a shift from considering customers as audiences to a perception of customers as active participants in conversations is needed (2009, 23). Thus, when Knudstorp states that the LEGO brand should "never have become part of Greenpeace's dispute with Shell" and that the dispute must be "handled between Shell and Greenpeace," it is simply not within his power to control the outcome due to the substantial reach of the campaign via the social media platforms: consider the numerous e-mails sent to the CEO and the film *Everything Is NOT Awesome*, which attracted more than 7.5 million views, was liked by nearly 61,000 Facebook members, shared on Facebook nearly 119,000 times and has received more than 2,500 comments, not including the large number of threads attached to these comments (some of the comments have additionally generated more than 100 comments). Thus with the changing media platform, stakeholders have numerous possibilities for recontextualizing organizations to support their own quests.

The narrativization model can thus be applied as a tool to better identify the vulnerabilities of a specific organization. This suggests that in the process of deciding on strategic initiatives, the following question would be relevant: "What would be a potential quest among the organization's stakeholders?" The answer should not only be sought among external conditions but should also be considered in relation to the organization's own documents.

Does this mean that organizations should avoid an explicit CSR approach in order to evade the vulnerability that such documents may evoke? As Boje (2001) rightly notices, "[e]ach organizational text opens different lines of inter-relatedness to preceding and anticipated texts" (74). This means that texts naturally invite for transtextual relations. Thus, the case seems to suggest that rather than aiming at overcoming interrelatedness, organizations should rather concentrate on scanning partnerships and other strategic initiatives for potential expose or villain challenges in order to better foreseeing potential crisis situations and thereby be better prepared.

Notes

1. The concept of "organizational texts" follows Kuhn's understanding of texts as "the 'substances' upon and through which conversations form" (2008, 1233).
2. Greenpeace activists also targeted the Legoland theme park in Windsor, England, dressing up as LEGO figures. The activists also got children to build giant LEGO animals outside Shell's London headquarters "in playful protest of their favorite toy's partnership with the oil company planning to drill the Arctic" (http://www.greenpeace.org/international/en/news/Blogs/makingwaves/save-the-arctic-lego-dumps-shell/blog/50917/). In various cities, miniature LEGO people held small protests against their LEGO bosses' partnership with Shell, and LEGO climbers held a protest banner at a Shell gas station in Legoland in Billund, Denmark.
3. It should be noted that Greenpeace also applied other mechanisms. As an example, on their website Greenpeace encouraged stakeholders to send an e-mail to Knudstorp encouraging the company to end its deal with Shell. According to Greenpeace, this resulted in more than one million e-mails.

References

Abolafia, M. Y. 2010. Narrative Construction as Sensemaking: How a Central Bank Thinks. *Organization Studies* 31 (3): 349–367.

Andrews, M. 2004. "Counter-narratives and the power to oppose." In *Considering counter-narratives: Narrating, resisting, making sense*, edited by M. Bamberg and M. Andrews, 1–6. Amsterdam: John Benjamins.

Aula, P. 2010. "Social Media, Reputation Risk and Ambient Publicity Management." *Strategy & Leadership* 38 (6): 43–49.

Bamberg, M. 2004. "Considering counter-narratives." In *Considering counter-narratives: Narrating, resisting, making sense*, edited by Michael Bamberg and Molly Andrews, 351–371. Amsterdam: John Benjamins.

Bamberg, M. and M. Andrews. (eds.). 2004. *Considering counter-narratives: Narrating, resisting, making sense*. Amsterdam and Philadelphia: John Benjamins.

Barthes, R. 1966. "Introduction to the Structural Analysis of the Narrative." Occasional Paper, Centre for Contemporary Cultural Studies, Birmingham: University of Birmingham.

62 *Marianne Wolff Lundholt*

Barthes, R. 1977. "Introduction to the structural analysis of narratives." In *Image, music, text*, edited by R. Barthes, (Stephen Heath, Trans.). 79–124. New York: Hill and Wang.

Berthon, P. R., and Pitt, L. F. 2012. "Brands and burlesque: Toward a theory of spoof advertising". AMS Review, 2(2–4), 88–89.

Boje, D. 2001. *Narrative methods for organizational and communication research*. London: Sage.

Brown, R. 2009. *Public relations and the ocial web: How to use social media and web 2.0 in communications*. Philadelphia, PA: Kogan Page.

Czarniawska, B. 1997. *Narrating the organization: Dramas of institutional identity*. Chicago and London: University of Chicago Press.

Czarniawska, B. 2004. *Narratives in social science research*. London: Sage.

Coombs, W. T. 2015. *Ongoing crisis communication: Planning, managing, and responding* (4th ed.). Thousand Oaks, CA: Sage.

Coombs, W.T., and S. J. Holladay 2012. *The handbook of crisis communication*. Oxford: Wiley-Blackwell.

Cooren, F. 2001. "Translation and Articulation in the Organization of Coalitions: The Great Whale River Case." *Communication Theory* 11 (2): 178–200.

Cooren, F., T. R. Kuhn, J. P. Cornelissen, and T. Clark. 2011. "Communication, Organizing and Organization: An Overview and Introduction to the Special Issue. Organization Studies." *Organization Studies* 32 (9): 1149–1170.

Fairclough, N. 1992. *Discourse and social change*. Cambridge: Polity Press.

Fairclough, N. 2015. *Langauge and power*. London and New York: Routledge.

Fairhurst, G. T. and L. L. Putnam. 2004. Organizations as Discursive Constructions. *Communication Theory* 14 (1): 5–26.

Fenton, C. and A. Langley. 2011. "Strategy as Practice and the Narrative Turn." *Organization Studies* 32 (1171): 1171–1196.

Fisher, W. R. 1987. *Human communication as narration: Toward a philosophy of reason, value, and action*. Columbia: University of South Carolina Press.

Genette, G. 1997. *Palimpsests: Literature in the second degree* (Channa Newman and Claude Doubinsky Trans.). Lincoln, NB: University of Nebraska Press.

Greenpeace. (2014). Greenpeace Core Values. Retrieved from http://www.greenpeace.org/international/en/about/our-core-values/

Greenpeace. (2014, July 8). Everything is NOT awesome. Retrieved from https://www.youtube.com/watch?v=qhbliUq0_r4

Greenpeace. (2014, July 1). Lego is keeping bad company. Retrieved from http://www.greenpeace.org/canada/Global/canada/report/2014/06/Lego-Is-Keeping-Bad-Company.pdf.

Greenpeace. Greenpeace Report. (2014, October 9). Retrieved from http://www.greenpeace.org/international/en/news/Blogs/makingwaves/save-the-arctic-lego-dumps-shell/blog/50917/.

Grice, H. P. 1989. *Studies in the way of words*. Cambridge MA: Harvard University Press.

Keenoy, T. and C. Oswick. 2003. "Organizing Textscapes." *Organization Studies* 25 (1): 135–142.

Klement, P. 2008, April. "Communicating Corporate Social Responsibility." *Journal of Marketing Communications* 14 (2): 75–81.

Knudstorp, J. V. (CEO of the LEGO Group) 2014, October 8. http://aboutus.lego.com/en-gb/news-room/2014/october/comment-on-the-greenpeace-campaign-and-the-lego-brand

Counter-Narratives and Organizational Crisis   63

Kristeva, J. 1986. "Word, dialogue, and the novel." In *The Kristeva reader*, edited by T. Moi, 35–61. New York: Columbia University Press.

Kuhn, T. 2008. "A Communicative Theory of the Firm: Developing an Alternative Perspective on Intra-Organizational Power and Stakeholder Relationships." *Organization Studies* 29 (8/9): 1227–1254.

Kukkonen, K. 2014. "Plot." In *The living handbook of narratology*, edited by Peter Hühn, John Pier, Wolf Schmid and Jörg Schönert, 706–720. Hamburg: Hamburg University Press. 706–720.

LEGO Brand Framework: http://aboutus.lego.com/en-us/sustainability/our-approach

Lego Group Responsibility Report 2013: http://aboutus.lego.com/da-dk/lego-group/annual-report

Linell, P. 1998. "Discourse across Boundaries: On Recontextualizations and the Blending of Voices in Professional Discourse." *Text* 18 (2): 143–157.

MacIntyre, A. 1984. *After virtue: A study in moral theory*. Notre Dame, Indiana: University of Notre Dame Press.

Matten, D., and J. Moon. 2004. "A conceptual framework for understanding CSR in Europe." In A Habisch, J. Jonker, M. Wegner and R. Schmidpeter (Eds.), *CSR across Europe*, 3339–60. Berlin: Springer.

Nelson, H. L. 2001. *Damaged Identities, Narrative Repair*. Cornell: Cornell UP.

Owyang, J. 2011. "Social Business Readiness: How Advanced Companies Prepare Internally." http://www.web-strategist.com/blog/research/ [December 11, 2015].

Page, R. and T. Bronwen. (eds.). 2011. *New narratives: Stories and storytelling in the digital age*. Lincoln: University of Nebraska Press.

Podnar, K. 2008. "Guest Editorial: Communicating Corporate Social Responsibility." *Journal of Marketing Communications* 14 (2): 75–81.

Polkinghorne, D. E. 1988. *Narrative knowing and the human sciences*. Albany: Suny Press.

Ryan, M. 2004. *Narrative across media: The languages of storytelling*. Lincoln: University of Nebraska Press.

Sperber, D. and D. Wilson. 1986. *Relevance: Communication & cognition*. Blackwell: Oxford.

Taylor, J. R., F. Cooren, N. Giroux, and D. Robichaud. 1996. "The Communicational Basis of Organization: Between the Conversation and the Text." *Communication Theory* 6 (1): 1–39.

Taylor, J. R. and E. J. van Every. 2000. *The situated organization: Case studies in the pragmatics of communication research*. New York: Routledge.

Taylor, J. R. and E. J. Van Every. *The Emergent Organization: Communication as Its Site and Surface*. Mahwah, NJ: Lawrence Erlbaum, 2000.

Toolan, M. 2001 (org. 1981). *Narrative, a critical linguistic introduction*. London: Routledge.

Toolan, M. 2013. "Coherence." In *The living handbook of narratology*, edited by Peter Hühn, John Pier, Wolf Schmid and Jörg Schönert, Hamburg: Hamburg University. URL = http://www.lhn.uni-hamburg.de/article/coherence [view date: 11 Dec 2015].

Trangbæk, Roar Rude. 2014. (July 1). Comment on Greenpeace campaign using the LEGO® brand. Retrieved from http://www.lego.com/en-gb/aboutus/newsroom/2014/july/lego-group-comment-on-greenpeace-campaign.

Voit. n.d.: http://www.uk.sagepub.com/upm-data/9690_023494Ch1.pdf http://brickfanatics.co.uk/ben-saunders-becomes-face-of-lego-city-arctic/

3 Countering the "Natural" Organizational Self on Social Media

Trine Susanne Johansen

> "Is it still possible to claim with credibility that Arla milk takes you closer to nature when it undergoes an industrialization process before it reaches the consumer's table? And when the farm sector and the cows' milk production also are highly industrialized? Do Arla's . . . initiatives outweigh the industrialization of the sector?"

Organizational identity is in a constant state of flux (Gioia and Patvardhan 2012). It is continuously created, disrupted, changed and rebuilt, not only among organizational members but also in the intersection between an organization and its market (Handelman 2006; Hatch and Schultz 2002; Johansen 2012). A market that is increasingly inhabited by engaged, empowered and critical consumers who challenge and question organizational claims, as the chapter's opening blog quote might suggest. Using narrative as a theoretical and a methodological lens (Rhodes and Brown 2005), this study conceptualizes and explores digital processes of organizational identity construction in the intersection between organization and market. A narrative perspective on the organizational identity flux allows researchers to explore identity constructing practices of multiple constituents inside and outside the organization (Brown 2006; Czarniawska 1997; Johansen 2012; Johansen and Andersen 2012). Consumer counter-narratives, as reflections or manifestations of critical and cynical views on the commercialization or marketization of society (Odou and de Pechpeyrou 2011), are a central part of such narrative practices (Johansen and Andersen 2012). The presence and importance of counter-narratives are potentially augmented by digitalization as it empowers consumers by transforming them into active co-creators of organizational messages, meanings and brands (Cova and Pace 2006; Fournier and Avery 2011; Prahalad and Ramaswamy 2004). However, little attention has been afforded to understanding online consumer counter-narratives and the role they play in the processes of organizational identity construction. The present study seeks to remedy this oversight by exploring how one organization's identity is constructed in and by consumer counter-narratives on social media in light of marketplace skepticism

Countering the "Natural" Organizational Self on Social Media 65

and cynicism. The purpose is to explore the ways in which interactions between organization and consumers, as well as between consumers, produce counter-narratives that contrast, challenge and contradict organizational self-narration. Therefore, the chapter seeks to answer the research question, "What role do counter-narratives play in consumers' online construction of organizational identity?"

The study draws on counter-narratives surrounding the Scandinavian-based dairy cooperative Arla Food's and its international strategy "Closer to Nature." The strategy was designed to create a unified identity for the organization, which had continuously grown through mergers and acquisitions and, as a result, was represented by multiple identities manifested in a large number of product brands. Launched in 2008, "Closer to Nature" alluded to the organization's products stemming from a natural ingredient (milk) alongside its intentions to use as many natural ingredients as possible (e.g., no genetically modified organism [GMO] ingredients, no artificial coloring and no artificial aromatics) and a greater emphasis on environmentally friendly production and packaging (e.g., reductions in CO_2 emissions). The strategy was supported by an integrated, corporate branding campaign, which ran until 2014, across different media platforms including web, print and television. "Closer to Nature" is chosen as the focal point for the study as it allows for the exploration of counter-narratives within a demarcated period (2008–2014). In addition, the campaign spurred much debate in one of the organization's Scandinavian home countries, where it was profiled in the media, reported to the food safety authority for deceptive advertising and caused public debate. This debate suggests "Closer to Nature" to be a potentially fruitful opportunity for exploring counter-narratives as part of identity constructing practices. The study is guided by dialogical reflexivity whereby new insights are generated from the interplay between existing theories and empirical findings (Alvesson and Kärreman 2007, 2011). Consequently, the chapter opens by presenting extant literature to shed light on the organizational identity flux. Then, it proceeds by empirically exploring counter-narratives as a backdrop for entering into dialogue with, and reflecting on, the extant literature.

Introducing the Organizational Identity Flux

The study is informed by identity research located within organization studies and communication studies, as well as marketing and consumer studies. From organization studies comes the idea that the identity of an organization emerges from narrative practices and processes as dynamic, fragmented and intertextual (e.g., Boje 1995; Brown 2006; Czarniawska 1997; Johansen 2012). From communication studies comes an increased focus on and interest in consumer and stakeholder dialogue and engagement (e.g., Foster and Jonker 2005; Johansen and Andersen 2012; Johansen and Nielsen 2011). And from marketing and consumer studies emerge ideas of the marketplace

66 Trine Susanne Johansen

as a site of brand-, organization- and consumption-centered conversations in which consumer empowerment is paramount (e.g., Andersen and Johansen 2014; Prahalad and Ramaswamy 2004). These three areas are combined in a multidisciplinary framework to theoretically ground and guide the study.

One strand of organization studies literature suggests that organizational identity is continuously created, disrupted and rebuilt. These creation and re-creation processes not only involve organizational members but also the organization's external constituents (Coupland and Brown 2004; Handelman 2006; Johansen 2012). In a narrative theoretical lens, these processes take a narrative form, as stories are a preferred way of creating and negotiating meaning in social interaction (Brown 2006). Consequently, an organization's identity is seen as "a continuous process of narration where both the narrator and the audience are involved in formulating, editing, applauding, and refusing various elements of the ever-produced narrative" (Czarniawska 1997, 49). The quote implies that multiple authors partake in the identity construction processes. As pointed out by Coupland and Brown (2004, 1325), organizational identities can be seen as "authored in conversations between notional 'insiders', and between notional 'insiders' and 'outsiders.'" Organizational identity is seen as emerging from the narratives, that is, "specific, coherent, creative re-descriptions of the world" (Humphreys and Brown 2008, 405), told by employees and consumers, as well as other external constituents (see also Humle and Frandsen, this volume). However, the stories that contribute to organizational identity narration come in many shapes and sizes. Some, like corporate self-presentations, are coherent and come complete with plot and chronology (Brown 2006). Others are only partial stories. They are fragmented, nonlinear, incoherent and unplotted. In short, they are ante-stories (Boje 2001). Investigations into narration processes need to take both the complete and the incomplete stories into account in order to address the dynamic, fragmented and intertextual nature of organizational identity construction (Johansen 2010, 2014).

A defining feature of organizational identity narration is intertextuality, that is, the "relation each text has to the texts surrounding it" (Bazerman 2004, 84). Intertextuality suggests that different narrative elements are woven together through their telling and retelling (see also the discussion on intertextuality in Kuhn, this volume). In other words, each story or story fragment is part of a complex, changing narrative web (Boje 1995, 2001; Brown 2006; Johansen 2012). The web is constantly expanding. As Boje (2001, 74) suggests, "[e]ach day organizations add more texts to an intertextual world. Each organizational text opens different lines of interrelatedness to preceding and anticipated texts. And each line of utterance opens up dialogue with texts of other times and places." It follows that identity-constructing stories can either seek to continue or challenge preceding stories: "The very fabric of organization is constantly being created and re-created through elaboration, contestation and exchange of narratives . . . The fabric is both a patchwork quilt of narrative episodes stitched together through shared

Countering the "Natural" Organizational Self on Social Media 67

conversations, and rippled, with stories variously borrowing threads from each other, continuing and extending some, and seeking to unravel others." (Brown 2006, 735)

The challenging and contradicting stories can be thought of as counter-narratives, that is, as versions of actors or events that contradict or are in conflict with the dominant or official version on offer by an organization (Johansen and Andersen 2012). Counter-narratives are thus intertextual by nature in that they "only make sense in relation to something else, that which they are countering. The very name identifies it as an oppositional category, in tension with another category" (Bamberg and Andrews 2004, x). It follows that counter-narratives are marked by an interest in hegemony and power (Bamberg 2004) mirroring Brown's (2006, 742) claim that inside and outside voices compete "constantly with one another for dominance and narrative control, each seeking to impose its understanding of an organization's identity, and to variously delete, over-write, and undermine others." As identity constructing narratives, counter-narratives can be both coherent and incoherent.

Interaction is of interest to communication research in connection with its growing emphasis on strategic options and opportunities for constituent involvement (Johansen and Nielsen 2011; Nielsen and Thomsen 2009). This involvement emphasis resonates with a technologically motivated shift towards privileging interaction-based, or dialogical, communication understandings in lieu of transmission-based understandings. Dialogue refers to two-way communication processes where conflicting interests and concerns are addressed (Foster and Jonker 2005). Involvement based on dialogue suggests that organizations should not only attempt to influence, or persuade, their constituents; they should also be willing to be influenced by them when it comes to identity matters. The relational nature of identity suggests that organizations and constituents engage in mutual identity construction in order to manifest themselves as legitimate societal and market actors (Johansen and Nielsen 2011). Here, the organization integrates itself into an open source market where the traditional roles of sender and receiver—or narrator and audience—converge (Johansen and Andersen 2012).

Multiple studies within marketing, branding and consumption have highlighted the reciprocal and dynamic nature of identity in relation to brands, organizations and consumers (Arnould and Thompson 2005; Cova and Pace 2006). The consumer is seen as an engaged, active co-creator both of his or her own identity and of the branded identities of organizations (Hatch and Schultz 2010; Prahalad and Ramaswamy 2004). Mirroring the interaction focus of communication studies, co-creation is perceived as a dialogical process "where people and organizations together generate and develop meaning" (Ind and Coates 2013, 86). However, the dialogical process of co-creation is not said to take place in a power-neutral or value-free marketplace. The brand/consumer interface is influenced by consumer cynicism and skepticism toward commercialization and marketization (Odou and

68 Trine Susanne Johansen

de Pechpeyrou 2011). The marketization of society transforms citizens into consumers (Smith and Higgins 2000), leads to disillusionment and disappointment, and causes consumers to react with cynicism towards the consumerist ideology by participating in a "global anti-consumerist project" (Odou and Pechpeyrou 2011, 1800). Cynicism is manifested in various acts of consumer resistance, for example, brand hijacks and boycotts (Handelman 2006; Kozinetz and Handelman 2004). Moreover, it is visible in books (e.g., *No Logo*), magazines (e.g., *Adbusters*), documentaries (e.g., *SuperSize Me*) and online forums (Handelman 2006) that become sites for the telling and retelling of counter-narratives (Johansen and Andersen 2012) infused with struggles of hegemony and resistance.

The organization–market interface is influenced by new technologies and virtual platforms (Fournier and Avery 2011), which open up not only for interactions between organizations and their brands and consumers but also for interactions between consumers in relation to organizations and brands. The democratization of communication technology also allows for consumer resistance to spread virally, for example, as 'shit storms,' which can hit and engulf an organization at a moment's notice. In the digital world, consumers hijack commercial messages, play with them, turn them into parodies and counter them (Fournier and Avery 2011). As such involvement and interaction, envisioned as a positive outcome of technological developments in communication studies, have a potential negative manifestation as well. Such negative manifestation may result in organizational crisis as pointed out by Lundholt in this volume. The critical and cynical market environment creates a potentially hostile or troublesome arena for organizational identity construction as anticommercialization and anticonsumption sentiments spill over into organization, identity and brand counter-narratives.

In sum, the study draws on a multidisciplinary framework inspired by organization, communication, marketing and consumer studies. Although the disciplines have different foci, they share an interest in what happens in the intersection between organization and market. In addition, they suggest that this intersection is characterized by the duality of collaboration and contestation as consumers, along with other constituents, engage with organizations through the retelling and counter-telling of organizational stories creating complex intertextual identity webs. These webs are forever unfolding, suggesting organizational identity to be in a constant state of flux. Exploring organizational identity counter-narratives may shed additional light on how this identity flux can be understood.

Exploring Organizational Identity Counter-Narratives

Centered on the Scandinavian-based dairy cooperative Arla Foods and its global strategy "Closer to Nature," the study explores digital counter-narratives through nonparticipant netnography (Cova and Pace 2006) focused on two types of archival material (Belk, Fischer and Kozinets 2013): first, interactions between Arla Foods and consumers, for example, organizational weblogs and e-mail discussions, and, second, interactions among consumers, that is, consumer-generated content, for example, spoof sites and the like. Based on this initial choice, empirical material has been collected across as many digital platforms as possible. A broad search strategy was used to locate as much material as possible to secure a solid foundation for the analysis. First, official communication from Arla Foods was retrieved based on material collected for a previous research project (Johansen 2010). Besides official brochures, the material consisted in internal leaflets, weblog posts by Arla Foods employees and e-mail correspondences between employees and consumers. Second, a broad Internet search was conducted to locate other sources and locations where Arla Foods and "Closer to Nature" were discussed. The search produced additional material in the form of blog posts from other, nonorganizational-controlled blogs along with comments to these posts. These additional materials contain comments from employees and consumers and were posted between November 2008 and September 2014. The combined archival material retrieved comprises the data corpus to be analyzed. Although the goal has been to generate as large a corpus as possible, the intention is not to comprehensively map all the counter-narratives produced in relation to "Closer to Nature." Rather, the aim is to demonstrate and explore the dynamic and intertextual nature of social media counter-narratives in order to understand their importance for organizational identity construction in the intersection between organization and market.

Intertextual Analysis

The analytic aim is to shed light on identity-centered counter-narratives by exploring them as intertextual networks of meaning. An intertextual approach makes it possible to address the multiple forceful and subtle voices that are present in a text (Solin 2004). It allows the researcher to identify "a crowd of authors, actors and readers engaged in carnivalesque scenes of dynamic textual production, distribution and consumption." (Boje 2001, 76) Intertextuality is a well-suited strategy for analyzing counter-narratives as they become meaningful in relation to that which they are countering. This relational meaning can be uncovered though intertextual analysis where "each text is theorized as a network of fragments that refer to still other narrative texts" (Boje 2001, 74). Moreover, intertextuality implies "a web of complex inter-relationships ensnaring each story's historicity and situational context between other stories" (Boje 2001, 91). Thus, intertextual analysis can uncover "how texts selectively draw upon orders of discourse—the particular configurations of conventionalized practices (genres, discourses, narratives etc.) which are available to text producers and interpreters in particular social circumstances" (Fairclough 1992, 194). Intertextual analysis highlights how narratives and counter-narratives are inscribed in wider discourses; that is, it "draws attention to the dependence of texts upon society

70   Trine Susanne Johansen

Production	Distribution	Consumption
What voices are present? Who gets quoted? Who is referenced?	What themes are situated as relevant by the different authors? What are the parodies, ironies and metaphors?	Who are the intended audiences? What interpretive matrix/script does the authors construct for audiences to consume?

Figure 3.1 The Analytic Strategy

and history in the form of the resources made available within the order of discourse" (Fairclough 1992, 195). This dimension is characterized as constitutive intertextuality (or interdiscursivity) contrasted with manifest intertextuality (Fairclough 1992). To Boje (2001) this translates into horizontal and vertical intertextuality, where the former addresses the text within a chain of preceding and proceeding texts and the latter extends beyond a text's location in linear time into local and global contexts. The applied analytic strategy is inspired by a matrix of questions developed by Boje (2001, 77) combining the horizontal and vertical dimensions in a three-step analysis. Each of the overlapping and interdependent steps is carried out with inspiration from questions suggested to be relevant by Boje (2001; see Figure 3.1).

The first step identifies utterances addressing "Closer to Nature" and produces "an intertextual system of quotes and interpretations" (Boje 2001, 78). The second step addresses how different utterances are distributed in space and time (horizontal intertextuality). And the third step focuses on how the utterances are embedded in wider consumption patterns located in cultural and societal contexts (vertical intertextuality). The analysis explores the counter-narratives constructed in relation to "Closer to Nature" and presents the outcome of the analytic process in the form of different voices and strategies. However, since counter-narratives make sense in relation to that which they are countering (Bamberg and Andrews 2004), the analysis first establishes a backdrop for exploring counter-narratives by briefly mapping the strategic self-narrative offered by Arla Foods in connection with the campaign. The strategic organizational self-narrative refers to the intentional narrative told by organizational insiders in order to present and promote a specific, coherent redescription of their organization (Johansen 2012).

Analyzing "Closer to Nature"

"Closer to Nature" was anchored in a number of strategic initiatives and embedded in an integrated corporate branding campaign. It was reflected in an adapted mission statement in which the word *natural* was added: "Our

Countering the "Natural" Organizational Self on Social Media 71

mission is to offer modern consumers *natural*, milkbased food products that create inspiration, confidence and well-being." The use of the words *natural* and *nature* was frequent in all communication materials, as illustrated by the voice-over in an animated film: "At Arla we work with milk. It is a natural raw material made by nature."[1] The terminology was frequently accompanied by images of green fields, grazing cows and milk. Viewing Arla Foods's self-narrative as a backdrop, the following analysis explores the online debates it spurred. An initial glance at the corpus reveals that both employees and consumers are active participants in the narrative construction of Arla Foods and "Closer to Nature." The counter-narratives produced by consumers are intertwined in different versions of the self-narrative (re)told by different employees. In the following, these multiple voices are addressed before strategies of counter-narrativizing are introduced.

Voices

Multiple voices are identified in and across the texts that make up the corpus. These voices belong to both identifiable organizational insiders and outsiders, mostly employees and consumers. Among the voices stemming from inside the organization are those of the vice president of Corporate Marketing, the director of Corporate Communication, the Corporate Social Responsibility (CSR) advisor, the local director of Communication, the local marketing responsible for Milk, the manager of Arla Forum (consumer dialogue center), a cooperative farmer and the girlfriend of a cooperative farmer.[2] The outside voices are potentially more difficult to identify. However, they include one politician, several scholars and those who can be labeled consumers in general or generic terms, that is, someone who has the ability to consume the organization's products, meanings and values, such as when the following discussant takes on a consumerist voice:

> Wherein lies the argument for me as a consumer, what is it that makes me want to pull more Arla products of the shelves after having seen this film?

In addition to the identifiable individual voices, Arla Foods, as an organization, is assigned a collective, unified presence by allowing it to, for example, 'dream' and 'launch':

> Arla is dreaming its way back to the good old days with its new logo which has just "hit the streets."

> Arla has launched an international campaign to bring the dairy giant "Closer to nature."

That the organization is given its own voice by the discussants mirrors Cheney's (1992) claim that although it is recognized that the narrative practices reside with individuals, many stories are told on behalf of the

72 Trine Susanne Johansen

organization. To this end, Heath (1994, 22) suggests the "organization does not speak or act, individuals speak for it." Therefore, the organizational voice "consists of all the statements and actions made by members of an organization, by the organization as a single entity, or by a person who represents the organization" (Heath 1994, 21).

The collective organizational presence is established not only by assigning Arla Foods agency but also by commenting on the rhetoric used by some of the different employees who participate in the online discussions both indirectly by referencing Arla Foods and directly by commenting on what has been said by the employees:

> But respect for their [Arla's] willingness to enter into dialogue—just too bad, that they continue in newspeak-mode.

By referring to the organization as entering into dialogue, it is assigned a voice in its own right. And it is praised for attempting interaction with its market. However, the corporate voice is also criticized and is said to be in contrast to a personal or human voice:

> Here, towards the end, you have gained a human voice, that is nice. However, the point of departure was the cool corporate voice, which expressed a thematic interest in dialogue, but emanated anything but.

In other words, Arla Foods is not perceived to be genuinely interested in actual dialogue. This suggests that although dialogue between organization and market is considered paramount, it is not necessarily readily achieved as organizational practices risk producing pseudo-dialogues that only mimic dialogical communication (Johansen and Andersen 2012).

All voices active in the online debates are also frequently referenced and quoted by the other participants in the blog threads. Referencing and quoting take place across the different blogs resulting in narrative repetition (Dailey and Browning 2014) whereby the stories are retold on different platforms. In particular, the repetition of employee stories helps to construct a collective corporate voice and a coherent organizational identity self-narrative by reinforcing the official interpretation of "Closer to Nature." Discussants also practice self-referencing by referring to or quoting their own comments or posts on the different blogs. Most references and quotations stem from the voices of those insiders and outsiders participating as discussants. However, additional voices are included, for example, a reference to the Cluetrain manifesto[3] and references to other advertising and branding campaigns used to contrast "Closer to Nature."

In sum, diverse texts are interwoven starting with the launch of the "Closer to Nature" campaign and continuing on different online platforms bringing a number of constituents together. Each constituent has an individual, that is, uniquely identifiable, voice. Some voices are present to a larger extent

Countering the "Natural" Organizational Self on Social Media   73

than others, for example, two outside voices who participate in discussions not only on their own blogs but also on other sites as well as the marketing responsible for milk and the vice president for corporate marketing from Arla Foods. In addition, the constituents quote, reference and address each other—both to agree and disagree—connecting the different posts and voices in and across blogs. In quoting and referencing, the discussants add their own interpretations and meanings to the texts they are incorporating into their own. Thereby, the discussants do not merely repeat or retell stories, as suggested by Dailey and Browning (2014), but make them their own. This points to complex strategies of counter-narrativizing, which are explored next.

Strategies of Counter-Narrativizing

Narrativizing is "the activity of engaging in narratives" (Bamberg 2004, 359). Therefore, counter-narrativizing refers to engaging in counter-narratives. When narrativizing different counter versions of Arla Foods and "Closer to Nature," the outside voices make use of different strategies, that is, ways in which countering takes place. Three different, yet overlapping, strategies are identified. These are labeled *authenticity, legitimacy* and *irony*.

Authenticity refers to a strategy employed by outside voices in relation a perceived discrepancy between the reality of the increased industrialization and mass production of the dairy and farm sectors and the representation of the sectors in the campaign imagery, as one voice remarks:

> It is also because fewer cows are put out to pasture and therefore we see fewer scenarios like the ones in the ending of your film.

The discrepancy or misalignment between reality and imagery is central to the countering in many of the comments offered; for example,

> The communication has become too transparent, and Arla ends up telling a story that is difficult to believe. Because it is detached from reality.

Authenticity as a strategy of counter-narrativizing is thus linked to how Arla Foods represents dairy farming in its marketing communication messages. It is visible in comments that contrast the commercial, glossy images of cows grazing on green pastures with their actual living conditions where a majority of all milk cows never leave the stable; for example,

> Does the final image of the cow in the pasture in Arla's film give a credible picture of milk production? The answer is: no, it does not. It gives a picture of how Arla would like the consumer to believe that it looks.

How Arla Foods communicates is furthermore addressed in relation to how the various organizational insiders participate in the online debates. While

74 Trine Susanne Johansen

Arla Foods is praised for taking part in the online discussions, it is also criticized as in the preceding examples that reference "newspeak-mode" and a "cool corporate voice." In addition, the positive response to the organization's social media communication is contrasted with a negative response to the official campaign communication:

> One cannot deny that they apparently make an effort to stay updated (and participate) on social media. That is good. However, their film and slogan are still wide of the mark.

Outside voices frequently address the campaign's credibility based on whether or not it correctly and truthfully represents dairy farming in a modern, industrialized society. Hence, the communication of Arla Foods is central:

> Arla ends up telling a story that is difficult to believe. Because it is disconnected from reality. It is like picturing old people on the cookie package in an attempt to give the illusion that a grandmother has baked them.

These and similar comments point to a perceived misalignment between the images of the advertising and branding universe created by Arla Foods in the "Closer to Nature" campaign images and the lived experience of the consumer. It is suggested that a decoupling has taken place between advertising and reality. As one of the discussants argue, the advertising images of cows grazing "create an illusion." The authenticity strategy parallels arguments relating to the credibility of green advertising, that is, the use of pleasant nature imagery and claims (see, e.g., the discussion in Hartmann and Apaolaza-Ibáñez 2009). Thus, realism, or the lack of, is a central element, as one outside voice says: "Closer to reality, please." Within a branding context, authenticity is a question of whether or not "the brand is justifiably, what it says it is. . . . You see what you get with an authentic brand" (Fournier and Avery 2011, 198). In short, the strategy of authenticity involves questioning if there is alignment between the frontstage and backstage (Goffman 1959) operations of the organization. Such alignment calls for transparency, as Holt (2002, 86) points out, "to be authentic, corporations cannot simply act as ventriloquists but, rather, must reveal their corporate bodies, warts and all, to public scrutiny." It is the "warts" that the outside voices are looking for in relation to the advertised images.

Another main strategy employed by outside voices is questioning or attacking the *legitimacy* of Arla Foods's claim to naturalness. The legitimacy strategy reflects the idea that organizations have to align their identities to societal norms and practices to gain the support of constituents (Glynn 2008; Johansen and Nielsen 2011). Arla Foods's self-narrative, as represented in the "Closer to Nature" slogan, is questioned in some of

Countering the "Natural" Organizational Self on Social Media 75

the headlines from the blog posts; for example, "Arla has gotten closer to nature, or what?" and "Arla: Closer to Nature??" Organizational outsiders continue questioning the legitimacy of the self-narrative, as in the opening quote of the chapter:

> Is it still possible to claim with credibility that Arla milk takes you closer to nature when it undergoes an industrialization process before it reaches the consumer's table? And when the farm sector and the cows' milk production also are highly industrialized? Do Arla's . . . initiatives outweigh the industrialization of the sector?

The legitimacy strategy creates a binary opposition between natural and unnatural. That Arla Foods and the dairy industry are unnatural is, for example, linked to the use of industrial produced fodder (instead of natural food sources such as grass and hay):

> If your basic milk production—and derived products, cheeses for instance—were to be close(r) to nature, then the cows should be eating as much grass as they could. They are not. They are eating industrially produced fodder. It is possible to discuss advantages and disadvantages. But it is nevertheless unnatural.

In addition, it is addressed in relation to farming in general and to mass-production characteristic of industrialization; for example,

> [I]ndustrialization is and remains something which is in contrast to what is natural.

> Nature is that which has not been cultivated, farmed, tamed.

In that sense, unnatural becomes unreal. This sentiment is mirrored in discussions on the "Closer to Nature" slogan, it is, for example, suggested that "it is unnatural that Arla trademarks the natural." Thus, the legitimacy of Arla Foods's claim to naturalness is challenged based on its perceived organizational characteristics as well as the characteristics of the industry to which it belongs (Glynn 2008); for example,

> It is because farming is becoming increasingly industrialized, because Arla is one of the most industrialized in the farm sector—and undoubtedly the most industrialized in the dairy sector.

As pointed out by Fournier and Avery (2011), brands that exemplify or epitomize a product category, or an industry, often attract unwanted attention, as this quote might suggest.

The strategy of legitimacy is countered by inside voices who disagree with the distinction between industrial and natural or, rather, oppose the labeling

76 Trine Susanne Johansen

of industrial as unnatural, as illustrated in a comment from the local marketing responsible for milk:

> Yes, we have large dairies. You call it industrialization. We call it large-scale operations, and do not think that it is in opposition to naturalness, because we are doing the same, as dairymen have done always, at large as well as small dairies, just at a larger scale.

In addition to the emphasis on dairy production, other insiders, here exemplified by the girlfriend of an Arla farmer and a farmer, address naturalness in relation to dairy farming:

> We are as bloody close to nature that you would not believe it! Do you even know how hard it is to produce milk??? How sensitive and "natural" cows and their entire environment are? I doubt it.

> As a producer for Arla and as an owner of Arla I would like to back the argument that we are natural.

The debate on whether or not dairy production is to be considered natural is tied in with the authenticity of the images of cows grassing in green pastures provided by Arla Foods as part of the campaign. Legitimacy as a strategy of counter-narrativizing is similar to authenticity in that it works by juxtaposing. Where authenticity is about the contrast between the reality of dairy farm industrialization versus the imagery of dairy farm idyll, legitimacy is about the fundamental, ontological contrast between that which is industrial and that which is considered natural.

A third strategy employed by outside voices is *irony*. This strategy is visible in the way some of them rephrase the "Closer to Nature" slogan, for example, "closer to pointless," "closer to reality," "closer to morality" and "closer to the factory." Such paraphrasing mirrors cultural jamming activities where consumers change or play with advertising copy (Fournier and Avery 2011; Handelman 2006; Holt 2002). Others introduce the idea of green washing, or greening, as a way of labeling the campaign. Green washing is normally defined as "intentionally misleading or deceiving consumers with false claims about a firm's environmental practices and impact" (Nyilasy, Gangadharbatla and Paladino 2014, 693). However, in the comments it has a slightly different meaning. Here it is used in a more literal sense with an ironic undertone as it is contrasted with the notable use of the color green in the campaign images:

> And the question is then if Arla is "greening" the dairy production more than is good. I believe they are.

> A big truck is thundering across green fields, and splashing about flowers and other cute creatures. It's a brand new way—also for Arla: the green side of life.

Countering the "Natural" Organizational Self on Social Media   77

The use of greening and the paraphrases of "Closer to Nature," as part of an ironic strategy, have an affinity to the strategy of authenticity as both operate based on opposites that play with the slogan and the green imagery used in the marketing communication campaign. However, compared to the explicit critique that is found in the authenticity strategy, the irony strategy is implicit, and playful, in its critique.

Based on the notions of distribution and consumption rooted in the idea of vertical and horizontal intertextuality, the analysis of the online discussions on "Closer to Nature" point to three strategies of counter-narrativizing. The strategies of authenticity, legitimacy and irony suggest that consumption and distribution are marked with duality. There is a constant play with the contrast between the green color used in the advertising images and the term *greening* as something that signals painting a glossy picture of reality. In addition to the contrast between reality and imagery, and the authenticity of the imagery of cows in green pastures versus the reality of dairy cows, the strategies juxtapose industry and nature, or industrial and natural. Hereby, the juxtaposing of opposites can be seen as a defining characteristic of counter-narrativizing strategies. The strategies—and their embedded juxtapositions—have implications for conceptualizing and understanding the ways in which counter-narratives shape organizational identity construction on social media. These implications are addressed in the reflections that follow through dialogue with extant literature.

Reflecting on Counter-Narratives and the Organizational Identity Flux

The analysis suggests that the organizational self-narrative is the dominant story countered by a resistant story with different articulations—and visible in different strategies—supporting Bamberg and Andrews's (2004) argument that counter-narratives only become meaningful in relation to what they are countering. Nevertheless, "what is dominant and what is resistant are not, of course, static questions, but rather are forever shifting placements" (Bamberg and Andrews 2004, x). Consequently, there is interplay between dominant and resistant narratives, which highlights the fluctuating state of organizational identity. In addition, it may be possible to reverse the argument; that is, without counter-narrative, there is no master narrative. In other words, by countering a particular story or version of reality, the original narrative is given legitimacy by the outside voices. As they continuously question Arla Foods's claim to naturalness, they simultaneously reinforce the claim. Therefore, narrative and counter-narrative are mutually constitutive. However, whether or not the organizational self-narrative is the dominant narrative can be questioned. The labeling of Arla Foods's narrative as that which is being countered may therefore potentially be misleading in the sense that the counter-narrative of industrialization as unnatural dominates the discussions. When it comes to narratives of organizational identity then, we may question what is

78 Trine Susanne Johansen

dominant and resistant suggesting that issues of hegemony and power (Boje 2001; Brown 2006) are not only highly relevant but also highly complex. In addition, it gives credibility to the idea of critical and skeptical consumers as empowered co-creators thereby marking a convergence of narrator and audience (Johansen and Andersen 2012). The analytic outcome thus points to the blurred lines between narrative and counter-narrative also identified by Humle and Frandsen, in this volume, as well as to the potential challenges embedded in operating with a fixed dichotomy (see the discussion in Rasmussen, this volume).

Second, as addressed by Heath (1994), an organization's voice stems from those who speak on its behalf. This is highlighted in the analysis where several inside voices construct or contribute to the strategic self-narrative of Arla Foods. In addition, it is recognized by the outside voices that the insiders represent the organization and speak on its behalf. Consequently, the organizational self-narrative is polyphonic. Besides the multiple inside voices, the organization is also attributed a collective organizational voice (Heath 1994), for example, the reference to the "cool corporate voice." In doing so, outside voices potentially construct an opposition between the human, or humane, voices of those employees and farmers who participate in the discussions and the organization as a distant, nonhuman actor. Organizational outsiders emphasize the importance of dialogue praising the organizational members for their willingness to participate and engage with the critical voices. However, the level or form of engagement is questioned in comments relating to the answers provided by the organizational insiders leading to a questioning of whether actual dialogue is taking place. The complexity of voices identified in the analysis suggests that counter-narratives can be explored not only with reference to the contents of the story told but also with reference to how various tellers construct themselves and each other in oppositional roles. Here, the concept of ventriloquism (see, e.g., Maagaard et al., this volume) could be of relevance in shedding light on the multiple voices and tellers.

Third, it has been suggested that social media, such as blogs, enable criticism to "travel fast and far" (Fournier and Avery 2011, 200). Addressed in light of the issue of voice, it can furthermore be suggested that online discussions may represent an uneven playing field for organizations as employees, despite their widespread presence, may quickly be outnumbered by outside voices. An important point to note in connection with the discussions is that counter-narratives seemingly are articulated by a few, key outside voices. That is, the same individuals participate in different discussions on different platforms. Therefore, it is not possible to generalize the critical voices to consumers as such and suggest that the consumer per se is critical. Indeed, the online discussions do also reveal a few consumer voices that counter the counter-narrative in support of Arla Foods. One such example comes from a discussant who directs the following question at the critical discussants:

> Do you raise the same demands for realism and "soberness" in other brands' advertising universe?

Countering the "Natural" Organizational Self on Social Media   79

The discussant thus suggests that those questioning the credibility of Arla Foods and the "Closer to Nature" campaign are harsher in their critique than is warranted. Nevertheless, the negative, resistant voices may still point to useful insights into how consumer critique manifests digitally instead of solely acknowledging online forums as sites where cynicism is present (Handelman 2006). Moreover, it also helps to shed light on how resistant, adversarial narratives, that is, counter-narratives, contribute to organizational identity construction. There is, of course, a potential danger in suggesting that critique is a general form of expression. Critique, nevertheless, can be seen as important to our understanding of identity. As suggested by Heding, Knudtzen and Bjerre (2009) and Holt (2004), successful brands are often contested; the more successful a brand is, the more likely it is to attract the attention of antibrand movements. In other words, criticism—and counter-narratives—may be a by-product of success.

Finally, it is possible to ask, "How do the various voices construct counter-narratives and how do the counter-narratives construct organizational identity?" The discussions can be said to construct or produce narratives through different counter-narrativizing strategies that create plots casting actors, in particular, Arla Foods and its employees, in particular roles. These roles, in turn, offer different identity positions for the involved actors. A derived discussion relates to whether it is justifiable to explore the organizational identity of Arla Foods with reference to "Closer to Nature." In what way is the strategy, payoff and campaign linked to the organization's identity as such? As the analysis shows, "Closer to Nature" spurred multiple different versions, or redescriptions, of the organization, for example, as industrialized, unreliable and unnatural, pointing to the focus being not only on "Closer to Nature" but also on the organization behind the campaign. In challenging the commercial claim to "naturalness," organizational outsiders are not only challenging the advertising imagery's representation of reality; they are also countering the organization's authenticity and legitimacy as a "natural" organization.

Concluding Remarks

The chapter has sought to theoretically and methodologically address the organizational identity flux in light of counter-narrative practices on social media in the form of blogs. Concrete examples of counter-narrativizing show how three different strategies (authenticity, legitimacy and irony) are used. These strategies are marked or defined by juxtapositions. In addition, the analysis suggests counter-narration as a natural consequence of organizational self-narration pointing to understanding counter-narratives as contributing to constructing organizational self both vertically and horizontally. Vertically, Arla Food's historical and societal roots as a frontrunner within industrialization of dairy production and growth are evoked. Horizontally, the analysis highlights how each comment in the ongoing discussions references and anticipates previous and future comments in and across

80 Trine Susanne Johansen

different blogs. The main contribution lies in producing new insights into consumer counter-narration as part of the continuous, digital construction of organizational identities. Amongst the strategic, managerial implications is the need for organizations to acknowledge that their self-narrations never stand alone. Rather they are embedded in markets characterized by consumer empowerment and cynicism enforced by the ability of social media to connect consumers—and potentially act as a catalyst of counter-narratives. Moreover, organizations need to understand how counter-narratives work by juxtaposing opposites. It is potentially through identifying and recognizing these opposites that organizations can enter into dialogue with consumers and thereby attempt to harness their co-creating abilities.

Notes

1. The voice-over stems from a short video titled *What Is Closer to Nature?* uploaded to arlavideos on YouTube on November 21, 2011. The video is available at https://www.youtube.com/watch?v=lV_CG-WODXY.
2. Farmers are considered organizational insiders as they are the owners of the cooperative. In the analysis, organizational insiders are referenced by their titles instead of by their names in order to ensure a certain level of anonymity. Organizational outsiders are not identified by name with the same purpose in mind.
3. The Cluetrain manifesto consists of 95 theses on how organizations can interact with and engage consumers and markets (see www.cluetrain.com).

References

Alvesson, M., and D. Kärreman. 2007. "Constructing Mystery: Empirical Matters in Theory Development." *Academy of Management Review* 32 (4): 1265–1281. doi: 10.5465/AMR.2007.26586822.

Alvesson, M. and D. Kärreman. 2011. *Qualitative research and theory development: Mystery as method*. Thousand Oaks, CA: Sage.

Andersen, S. E., and T. S. Johansen. 2014. "Cause-Related Marketing 2.0: Connection, Collaboration and Commitment." *Journal of Marketing Communications* (ahead-of-print): 1–20. doi: 10.1080/13527266.2014.938684.

Arnould, E. J., and C. T. Thompson. 2005. "Consumer Culture Theory (CCT): Twenty Years of Research." *Journal of Consumer Research* 31 (4): 868–882. doi: 10.1086/426626.

Bamberg, M. 2004. "Considering Counter-Narratives." In *Considering counter-narratives: Narrating, resisting, making sense*, edited by M. Bamberg and M. Andrews, 351–371. Amsterdam: John Benjamins.

Bamberg, M. and M. Andrews. 2004. *Considering counter-narratives: Narrating, resisting, making sense*. Amsterdam: John Benjamins.

Bazerman, C. 2004. "Intertextuality: How texts rely on other texts." In *What writing does and how it does it: An introduction to analyzing texts and textual practices*, edited by C. Bazerman and P. Prior, 83–96. Mahwah, NJ: Lawrence Erlbaum Associates.

Belk, R., E. Fischer and R. V. Kozinets. 2013. *Qualitative consumer & marketing research*. London: Sage.

Boje, D. M. 1995. "Stories of the Storytelling Organization: A Postmodern Analysis of Disney as 'Tamara-Land'." *Academy of Management Journal* 38 (4): 997–1035. doi: 10.2307/256618.

Boje, D. M. 2001. *Narrative methods for organizational and communication research*. London: Sage.

Brown, A. D. 2006. "A Narrative Approach to Collective Identities." *Journal of Management Studies* 43 (3): 731–753. doi: 10.1111/j.1467-6486.2006.00609.x.

Cheney, G. 1992. "The corporate person (Re)presents itself." In *Rhetorical and critical approaches to public relations*, edited by E. L. Toth and R. L. Heath, 165–183. Hillsdale, NJ: Lawrence Erlbaum Associates.

Coupland, C., and A. D. Brown. 2004. "Constructing Organizational Identities on The Web: A Case Study of Royal Dutch/Shell." *Journal of Management Studies* 41 (8): 1325–1347. doi: 10.1111/j.1467-6486.2004.00477.x.

Cova, B., and S. Pace. 2006. "Brand Community of Convenience Products: New Forms of Customer Empowerment—The Case of 'My Nutella The Community'." *European Journal of Marketing* 40 (9/10): 1087–1105. doi: 10.1108/03090560610681023.

Czarniawska, B. 1997. *Narrating the organization: Dramas of institutional identity*. Chicago and London: University of Chicago Press.

Dailey, S. L., and L. Browning. 2014. "Retelling Stories in Organizations: Understanding the Functions of Narrative Repetition." *Academy of Management Review* 39 (1): 22–43. doi: 10.5465/amr.2011.0329.

Fairclough, N. 1992. "Discourse and Text: Linguistic and Intertextual Analysis within Discourse Analysis." *Discourse & Society* 3 (2): 193–217. doi: 10.1177/0957926592003002004.

Foster, D., and J. Jonker. 2005. "Stakeholder Relationships: The Dialogue of Engagement." *Corporate Governance* 5 (5): 51–57. doi: 10.1108/14720700510630059.

Fournier, S., and J. Avery. 2011. "The Uinvited Brand." *Business Horizons* 54 (3): 193–207. doi: 10.1016/j.bushor.2011.01.001.

Gioia, D. A. and S. Patvardhan. 2012. "Identity as process and flow." In *Constructing identity in and around organizations*, edited by M. Schultz, S. Maguire, A. Langley and H. Tsoukas, 50–60. Oxford: Oxford University Press.

Glynn, M. A. 2008. "Beyond constraint: How institutions enable identities." In *The Sage handbook of organizational institutionalism*, edited by R. Greenwood, C. Oliver, R. Suddaby and K. Sahlin-Andersson, 413–430. London: Sage.

Goffman, E. 1959. *The presentation of self in everyday life*. Garden City, NY: Doubleday.

Handelman, J. M. 2006. "Corporate Identity and the Societal Constituent." *Journal of the Academy of Marketing Science* 34 (2): 107–114. doi: 10.1177/0092070305284970.

Hartmann, P. and V. Apaolaza-Ibáñez. 2009. "Green Advertising Revisited: Conditioning Virtual Nature Experience." *International Journal of Advertising* 28 (4): 715–739. doi: 10.2501/S0265048709200837.

Hatch, M. J., and M. Schultz. 2002. "The Dynamics of Organizational Identity." *Human Relations* 55 (8): 989–1018. doi: 10.1177/0018726702055008181.

Hatch, M. J., and M. Schultz. 2010. "Towards a Theory of Brand Co-Creation with Implications for Brand Governance." *Brand Management* 17 (8): 590–604. doi: 10.1057/bm.2010.14.

Heath, R. L. 1994. *Management of corporate communication: From interpersonal contacts to external affairs*. Mahwah, NJ: Lawrence Erlbaum Associates.

82 Trine Susanne Johansen

Heding, T., C. F. Knudtzen and M. Bjerre. 2009. *Brand management: Research, theory and practice.* Oxon: Routledge.

Holt, D. B. 2002. "Why Do Brands Cause Trouble? A Dialectical Theory of Consumer Culture and Branding." *Journal of Consumer Research* 29 (1): 70–90. doi: 10.1086/339922.

Holt, D. B. 2004. *How brands become icons: The principles of cultural branding.* Boston, MA: Harvard Business School Press.

Humphreys, M., and A. D. Brown. 2008. "An Analysis of Corporate Social Responsibility at Credit Line: A Narrative Approach." *Journal of Business Ethics* 80: 403–408. doi: 10.1007/s10551-007-9426-0.

Ind, N., and N. Coates. 2013. "The Meanings of Co-Creation." *European Business Review* 25 (1): 86–95. doi: 10.1108/09555341131287754.

Johansen, T. S. 2010. Transported Essence or Collaborative Telling? Towards a Narrative Vocabulary of Corporate Identity. Published in the ASB PhD thesis series, Aarhus.

Johansen, T. S. 2012. "The Narrated Organization: Implications of a Narrative Corporate Identity Vocabulary for Strategic Self-Storying." *International Journal of Strategic Communication* 6 (3): 232–245. doi: 10.1080/1553118X.2012.664222.

Johansen, T. S. 2014. "Researching Collective Identity through Stories and Antestories." *Qualitative Research in Organizations and Management: An International Journal* 9 (4): 332–350. doi: 10.1108/QROM-08-2012-1092.

Johansen, T. S., and S. E. Andersen. 2012. "Co-creating ONE: Rethinking Integration within Communication." *Corporate Communications: An International Journal* 17 (3): 272–288. doi: 10.1108/13563281211253520.

Johansen, T. S., and A. E. Nielsen. 2011. "Strategic Stakeholder Dialogues: A Discursive Perspective on Relationship Building." *Corporate Communications: An International Journal* 16 (3): 204–217. doi: 10.1108/13563281111156871.

Kozinetz, R. V., and J. M. Handelman. 2004. "Adversaries of Consumption: Consumer Movements, Activism, and Ideology." *Journal of Consumer Research* 31: 691–704. doi: 10.1086/425104.

Nielsen, A. E., and C. Thomsen. 2009. "Investigating CSR Communication in SMEs: A Case Study among Danish Middle Managers." *Business Ethics: A European Review* 18 (1): 83–93. doi: 10.1111/j.1467-8608.2009.01550.x.

Nyilasy, G., H. Gangadharbatla, and A. Paladino. 2014. "Perceived Greenwashing: The Interactive Effects of Green Advertising and Corporate Environmental Performance on Consumer Relations." *Journal of Business Ethics* 125 (4): 693–707. doi: 10.1007/s10551-013-1944-3.

Odou, P., and P. de Pechpeyrou. 2011. "Consumer Cynicism: From Resistance to Anti-Consumption in a Disenchanted World?" *European Journal of Marketing* 45 (11/12): 1799–1808. doi: 10.1108/03090561111167432.

Prahalad, C. K., and V. Ramaswamy. 2004. "Co-Creation Experiences: The Next Practice in Value Creation." *Journal of Interactive Marketing* 18 (3): 5–14. doi: 10.1002/dir.20015.

Rhodes, C., and A. D. Brown. 2005. "Narrative, Organizations and Research." *International Journal of Management Reviews* 7 (3): 167–188. doi: 10.1111/j.1468-2370.2005.00112.x.

Smith, W., and M. Higgins. 2000. "Cause-Related Marketing: Ethics and the Ecstatic." *Business & Society* 39 (3): 304–322. doi: 10.1177/000765030003900304.

Solin, A. 2004. "Intertextuality as Mediation: On The Analysis of Intertextual Relations in Public Discourse." *Text* 24 (2): 267–296. doi: 10.1515/text.2004.010.

4 "Speaking through the Other"
Countering Counter-Narratives through Stakeholders' Stories

Astrid Jensen, Cindie Aaen Maagaard and Rasmus Kjærgaard Rasmussen

Introduction

Because corporate social responsibility initiatives constitute a kind of promise of moral and ethical accountability for an organization's values and practices, organizations that promulgate their corporate social responsibility (CSR) policy are particularly susceptible to the monitoring of external stakeholders, including the press. "While CSR is generally associated with positive corporate values and reflects an organization's status and activities with respect to its perceived societal obligations, corporate CSR messages have also proven to attract critical attention" (Morsing and Schultz 2006, 323). Especially in a time when transparency is an expressed value and goal, the legitimacy of CSR policy rests on there being a correspondence between stated morals and intentions and actual practice—that is, that the organization "walk the talk." Critique and exposure of practices that violate the promise of CSR therefore threaten the organization's legitimacy, and management can be revealed as being all talk, hypocritical or, even worse, a liar.

In the case that provides the basis of our discussion, a policy titled "Company Karma" reflects the potential duality inherent in any CSR policy between doing business and doing good, between profit and philanthropy (Morsing and Schultz 2006), because its two terms explicitly fuse two seemingly incongruous domains—the commercial as opposed to the moral and spiritual. In order to support the conviction that these two domains are in fact compatible, and that the organization can indeed do good by doing business, management uses narratives as a tool for sense-giving, for unpacking the meanings of policy. Through narratives, the policy is dramatized in structures having temporal progression and a dynamics of purpose and desire that help to demonstrate how the policy involves specific people performing specific actions in specific situations. Although the specifics of the stories told by management vary, they feed into a master narrative about the compatibility of the terms; the point of the narrative is that good deeds for others, motivated and guided by a commitment to karma and the interconnectedness of people, generate a return that is both financially and spiritually rewarding.

This master narrative has come under critique by the sense-making of the press in counter-narratives that thematize the incompatibility between the two

84 Astrid Jensen et al.

terms, portraying the organization as hypocritical and thereby threatening the legitimacy of the CSR policy. This, in turn, has made the need for countering the counter-narrative urgent for management. As a strategy by which to manage the organization's image, other stakeholders, such as employees and a collaborating nongovernmental organization (NGO) have been invited to tell stories that counter potential 'gossip' and critical narratives of the press. Thereby, the management regains control (Boje 2008, 128) of the master narrative.

Our chapter examines the mechanisms of this control of the master narrative through communicative strategies intended to bolster the legitimacy of policy and the credibility of the organization. Our central questions of investigation, therefore, are the following:

- Why and how does management counter the counter-narrative by using stakeholders to coauthor the master narrative through personal stories?
- How does management's exertion of narrative authority influence both the design of employees' stories and the degree to which they actually counter the counter-narratives?

In order to answer these questions, we adopt a dialogic perspective to discuss how the reiterated master narrative is consistently organized as a response to counter-narratives from an anticipated opponent, "the third other" (Linell 2009), in this case, the press. Drawing on examples from the case study of Company Karma, we show how narratives by employees and an NGO become means to form this response by ventriloquizing (Cooren 2010, 2012) the master narrative and thus create evidence that the policy is indeed an integral part of the organization's identity. We analyze verbal and visual components of the narratives to show how the organization asserts the power to control the narratives as a part of organizational image management. Based on our analysis, we argue that management's exertion of power through its narrative authority over stories actually reenforces the counter-narratives' theme that CSR policy is more a communicative ploy by management than a thoroughly implemented aspect of organizational identity.

By considering how stakeholders' personal stories ventriloquize the master narrative of CSR, we contribute to the understanding of counter-narratives in and around organizations by showing how the assertion of authority necessary to counter the critical counter-narratives of external actors may ultimately reiterate the themes of those same narratives. This is particularly true in the case of corporate policies like CSR, which are authoritative texts that become particularly vulnerable to monitoring by external actors.

Corporate Social Responsibility and Stakeholder Communication

The concept of corporate social responsibility has received increasing interest from both businesses and the research community in the past decades. The interest has particularly intensified as a consequence of globalization and expansion, which has stimulated attention to, and concerns about, pollution, climate change and human rights violation (Margolis and Walsh 2003).

CSR can be defined as the adoption by an organization of "the responsibilities for actions which do not have purely financial implications and which are demanded of an organization" (Cornelissen 2006, 63). Through CSR, a company engages in voluntary relationships with its stakeholders. Traditionally, three general approaches, which reflect historical development (Nielsen and Thomsen 2007), are taken to CSR. First, according to the classic approach, social responsibility is considered to be primarily the responsibility of the government, and "the social responsibility of business is to increase its profits" (Friedman 1970). Second, CSR is viewed as a strategic business principle (Freeman 2010), in which stakeholder relationships are understood to form the basis on which companies are founded and critical to strategic management. Finally, CSR is viewed as philanthropy (Carroll and Buchholtz 2006), with the primary aim of being a good "corporate citizen" by engaging in philanthropic activities and contributing to the local community.

As CSR initiatives may be undertaken either for moral reasons or as instrumental to a favorable market position, it may be difficult to determine to what extent business behavior is actually grounded in moral motivation or is based on a reputational strategy, which may explain why corporate CSR messages have proved to attract criticism. Merkelsen (2013) thus argues that CSR shares many of the fundamental challenges from the "double-edged sword of legitimacy" inherent in Public Relations: that a practice that has legitimacy as its object becomes particularly vulnerable to critique. The question then arises: How do corporations gain and maintain legitimacy in and through communication?

According to Morsing and Schultz (2006), CSR reporting is often understood through a one-way model of PR communication (Grunig and Hunt 1984), in which interpenetration between organization and environment is ignored; CSR communication has been seen primarily as a tool for influencing the way in which stakeholders perceive the organization and can be calibrated to fulfill a corporation's strategic goals most effectively. Offering a different perspective, Morsing and Schultz (2006) propose an involvement strategy whereby third parties (like NGOs) are drawn in as "symmetric partners" in the communication. While clearly representing a more processual view of communication and able to account for different forms of stakeholder engagement, their model still operationalizes a traditional view of organizations and communication as separate entities.

Unlike Morsing and Schultz, we employ a CCO (Communication as Constitutive of Organizations) perspective on CSR (see Schoeneborn and Trittin 2013). From the perspective of the "constitutive view on communication" (Ashcraft, Kuhn and Cooren 2009; Cooren 2012), CSR communication can extend the boundaries of the organization, which becomes clear when third parties are invited to co-constitute these communicative boundaries (Schoeneborn and Trittin 2013, 194). CSR communication is not seen only

86 *Astrid Jensen et al.*

as an instrument for achieving strategic goals but also as one of several texts voiced by multiple stakeholders that invoke notions of ethics and responsibility within the entire organization.

In order to understand the role of these many voices, we draw on the principle of dialogism, which is defined as "different voices, styles and ideas expressing a plurality of logics in different ways" (Boje 2008, 55). Linell (2009, 80) emphasizes the concept of "other-orientedness" as a basic point in dialogical theory, as well as the role of third parties in dialogue. Third parties may be concrete third parties who are physically present or may be "remote audiences" (Linell 2009, 101) in communicative activities, for example, future gossipers—or critics. Accordingly, concrete third parties, present or absent, may give rise to "split audience design" (Linell 2009, 101), whereby the primary communication parties orient to how third parties, such as the media, might react. This dialogic perspective explains how third parties (such as NGOs, the media, employees and other stakeholders) jointly contribute to the communicative constitution of organizations, thus co-constituting organizations through their involvement in CSR communication. This approach provides the opportunity to focus on the principle that legitimacy and responsibility are constituted in complex processes of meaning negotiation involving not only the organization itself but also various other actors.

In these communicative processes, CSR policies, in our view, function as "authoritative texts" in and around the organization. According to Kuhn (2008), authoritative texts are abstract representations of a collective that "direct attention and discipline actors by portraying particular phenomena, as well as forms of knowledge and action, as (in)appropriate and (un)desirable" (1236). Authoritative texts can be both figurative (as institutionalized practices) and concrete (in the form of documents). The CCO perspective thus makes it possible to analytically handle the ability of CSR policies to simultaneously direct organizational attention in practice and represent abstracted interests. Specifically, we use authoritative texts as a methodological device that can help us understand organizational texts (and narratives) as sites for struggle over authorship.

Our focus on the struggle over authorship in the organizational narrative links it to the subject of power in organizations (see also Brown and Humphreys 2006). Our position is that narrative constitutes a form of power, and in following Mumby (1987) we contend that a complex relationship exists between power and narratives in organizations: "narratives not only evolve as a product of certain power structures, but also function ideologically to produce, maintain, and reproduce those power structures" (ibid. 113). In the case study we perceive power as a discursive phenomenon, in which actors struggle for control "over the organization as a discursive space" (Brown and Humphreys 2006). In our analysis that follows, we discuss how this discursive struggle takes place through the master narratives of CSR told by management and ventriloquized by stakeholders and through the counter-narratives told by the press.

Master Narratives and Counter-Narratives

In the following we show that the authoritative texts of policy that direct organizational understandings and knowledge generate further interpretations and understandings by external stakeholders. These in turn include forms of narrative. As narratives transform abstract formulations into specifics of character, setting, events, problems and resolutions, policy is given concrete, and dynamic, form. Because such specifics constitute responses that express not only understandings of policy but stances toward it, they reflect stakeholder attitudes and positions that themselves enter into dialogic relations in the negotiation of meaning.

As analytical categories "master" and "counter-"narratives provide a heuristic for characterizing positions and stances toward policy voiced through narratives as well as for the dialogic interaction that takes place between them in social contexts, including those of organizations. The terms themselves are indicative of this interaction. As Bamberg and Andrews (2004) assert in the introduction to their edited volume *Considering Counter-Narratives*, "[c]ounter-narratives only make sense in relation to something else, that which they are countering. The very name identifies it as a positional category, in tension with another category" (Bamberg and Andrews 2004, x). The same can be said of master narratives: their very status as "master" depends on there being implicit variations, alternative ways of interpreting and telling that are to be controlled, suppressed or silenced—*mastered*. Accordingly, each category can only be understood through its dialogue with the other, and it is through the dialogic relation that each carries, and may exhibit, traces of the other. As Bamberg and Andrews (2004) assert, citing the observation of Fine and Harris (2001, 13), counter stories "expose the construction of the dominant story by suggesting how else it could be told."

It is precisely the relational nature of "master" and "counter"-narratives that makes them problematic to define categorically and uniformly, as they evade criteria that apply across contexts and situations. In the context of organizations, and the present case, therefore, we find it helpful to associate the terms *master* and *counter* with practices surrounding sense-giving and sense-making of policy respectively. Sense-making denotes social and cognitive processes by which people "structure the unknown" (Waterman 1990, 41). It is the means by which employees interpret equivocal cues by placing them into meaningful narrative frameworks that enable individuals "to comprehend, understand, explain, attribute, extrapolate, and predict" (Starbuck and Milliken 1988, 51). It has been argued that narrative aids sense-making by reducing "the equivocality (complexity, ambiguity, unpredictability) of organizational life" (Brown and Kreps 1993, 48). Yet in practice, narratives often contribute to that complexity or reveal the plurivocality that exists in understandings, attitudes and relations among members.

The plurivocal sense-*making* by stakeholders is contrasted with managerial sense-*giving*, whereby a manager "seeks to influence and gain support

88   Astrid Jensen et al.

for his or her construct of reality, which itself has been the result of sense-making acts (Wright 2005, 90, cited in Hill and Levenhagen 1995, and Ericson 2001) Sense-*giving* is interpreting and making meaning *for* someone else. It has been compared to the imposition of hegemony (Brown and Humphreys 2006). However, although "[m]anagers are institutionally empowered to direct processes [. . .] that redirect understandings" (Morgan 1997, 263–270), powerful individuals or collectives within an organization, or even outside it can also take on, and even completely usurp, this sense-giving function. Accordingly, Gioia and Chittipeddi (1991) show that sense-making and sense-giving are a reciprocal and sequential cycle of feedback and decision making.

The narratives used for sense-*giving* in an organization frame understandings of policy in particular ways or directions that guide practice. We view them as potential "master" narratives by virtue of the institutional power vested in individuals and potentially dominant in that they may exclude or silence diverging interpretations. As Bamberg and Andrews (2004, 360) point out, master narratives seem to "normalize" and "naturalize" certain events and actions as routines, and thus constrain storytellers by reducing the range of actions and interpretations available to them. In organizations, master narratives may take the form of what has been termed a "core story," "a comprehensive narrative about the whole organization, its origins, its vision, its mission (Larsen 2000) or what Deuten and Rip term institutionalized "grand narratives" or "master stories" (Deuten and Rip 2000).

Yet in the alternative interpretations that are voiced by stakeholders, counterpositions arise, and they can be means to gain voice and empowerment, to insert different experiences, perspectives and interpretive potentials into master narratives and thereby disrupt them, while at the same time displaying explicit or implicit traces of the master narrative with which they engage. These, in turn, can lead to narrative responses in the form of new counter-narratives. Consequently, as we discuss in our analysis, different stances, speaking positions and voices—of management, the NGO, the press and employees—permeate both "master" and "counter"-narratives and can raise questions of authorship and stance, as different narrators "speak through" each other's stories. Drawing on a CCO perspective, we theorize that master stories have effects as "authoritative texts" which can become a site of struggle over authorship, that is, whose interpretations and interests are represented.

Coauthorship and Ventriloquism

To capture the notion of giving voice and "speaking through," Cooren employs the term *ventriloquism* to describe the "ubiquitous phenomenon" (2010, 1) which is "our capacity to make other beings say or do things while we speak, write, or more generally, conduct ourselves" (2012, 4–5). In accordance with this focus on "texts" (both figurative and concrete), Kuhn and

Jackson (2008) conceptualized authorship as the result of intertextuality, and their basic assumption—that narratives are the result of a process with more than one author—is comparable to Cooren's notion of dialogue, on which we elaborate next.

Because Cooren (2010) expands the understanding of dialogue to forms of interaction that take place not only between people, but also ideas and material objects, the agents of interaction can have various ontologies: ideas, "principles, values, norms, etc." (2010, 9) and texts, as well as people. Each kind of participant can potentially be given voice through the communication of another. Thus, according to Cooren, not only people, but ideas, values, norms, rules and laws speak through individual agents, making ventriloquism the very "condition of conduct's meaningfulness. Our actions seem meaningful or accountable because we appear to be (or present ourselves as) moved by specific reasons that authorize, allow, or lead us to do what we do, whether these reasons are institutional, ethical, practical, ideological, or even, as we will see, emotional" (Cooren 2010, 7).

The interactants that are spoken, or given voice, through a particular agent are said to "animate" the ventriloquizing agent.[1] In the words of Cooren, "[p]ositioning oneself or being positioned as speaking, for instance, in the name of say, an organization's interests, a specific idea or even a principle thus amounts to claiming that we are attached to them and that, ceteris paribus, it is also they that animate us and our position, that is, lead us to say or do something" (Cooren 2012, 5). Yet animation itself enters into dialogic interaction: a ventriloquizing agent is animated by another agent, but this agent in turn is animated by the ventriloquizer. Thus, the ventriloquist and the animator perform shifting roles, so that agencies "oscillate" between them (Cooren 2012, 5). Accordingly, this can give cause to "wonder who is the ventriloquist and who is the dummy" (2012, 5). The word *dummy* in the analogy of ventriloquism is not to be taken literally; it does not mean "silent" or "voiceless" or carry the connotation of "unintelligent." Rather, in Cooren's conceptualization, action, such as speech or conduct, requires a form of passivity, of the speaker's being animated by or being led to do something (Cooren 2012, 4) by another agent. Thus, passivity can paradoxically be what empowers a speaker within a communicative situation.

The Case and the Data

We use a case study as a means to exemplify the dialogic interaction between master and counter-narratives and the use of stakeholder narratives to ventriloquize the master narrative. This study is based on a research project investigating the implementation of the Company Karma policy in Thornico A/S, a global conglomerate with headquarters in Odense, Denmark. The Thornico group structure comprises several industries that reflect a high degree of diversity: food and technology, financing, shipping, real estate and sport/fashion, the last of which includes the sports equipment and clothing firm hummel. The use of *Company Karma* as a term for Thornico's approach to business stems from and reflects the personal philosophy of the chief executive officer (CEO), Christian Stadil. In a book coauthored by the Danish businessman and professor of management Steen Hildebrandt, Company Karma is explained as a guiding principle for management and employees that derives from a moral attitude underlying human interactions (Hildebrandt and Stadil 2007).

In addition to the book *Company Karma*, the data for this chapter consist of sources in which the policy has been interpreted in narrative form: the organization's *Company Karma Report* published in 2012 as well as a film titled *Change the World through Sport*, which is one of the projects included in the report. Counter-narrative data stem from press coverage in response to Company Karma, collected from major Danish newspapers from 2009 to 2014. Finally, we include filmed employee narratives from the My Karma project launched in January 2015.

Analysis

In this section we present our analysis of how the CSR policy of Company Karma generates a dialogic of master and counter-narratives. We begin with an introduction of the concept's conceptual domains, then turn to the sense-giving narratives used by management in the book *Company Karma* and the organization's *Company Karma Report*, which create a master narrative with central themes for the organization. Next we discuss how these themes are countered by stories generated by the media and how these counter-narratives in turn are countered by narratives in the employee platform My Karma, which ventriloquize the master narrative themes through the personal narratives of individual, narrating employees.

The Conceptual Domains of Company Karma

The concept of Company Karma can be considered a conceptual blend (Fauconnier and Turner 1999) emerging from the integration of two separate conceptual domains: the corporate domain, which introduces a focus on financial return on investment and value creation for company and society, and the religious, or spiritual, domain of karma, a principle which presumes the interconnectedness of people and according to which actions return to the doer. The concrete meanings of the merger of these abstract domains are not inherent in the concept itself as an equation like "CSR = Company Karma" but, rather, emerge in communicative interaction or dialogue between sense-giving and sense-making practices.

In our analysis, we see narrative functioning as a means by which this dialogue takes place, as stakeholders respond to the abstract and polysemous concept of Company Karma. Narratives unfold the concept through the particulars of specific characters in specific settings living specific events.

These are represented in various degrees of verbal completion, from compacted fragments or snippets of stories, as "antenarratives" (Boje 1991), to expanded verbal and visual texts. These narrative forms can be created in interaction with others, shared and employed as an aid to understanding what the policy of Company Karma means.

The Master Narrative

The Master Narrative Told through Authoritative Texts

The book *Company Karma* and the *Company Karma Report* are authoritative texts through which management engages in sense-giving and wields power to define the CSR policy. The book *Company Karma* is, as previously mentioned, a collaborative work that grew out of conversations between the CEO Christian Stadil and the coauthor, Steen Hildebrandt. The *Company Karma Report* is a CSR report addressed to the organization's internal and external stakeholders. Since 2009, Denmark's largest companies have been legally obliged to identify in their annual report the measures they take to voluntarily improve societal or environmental conditions. Accordingly, the stated aim of the report is to "elaborate on Thornico's approach to CSR called Company Karma" (*Company Karma Report* 2013, 2), and it does so through articles and photographs documenting activities sponsored by the various subsidiaries around the world. It is prefaced with a foreword from the CEO.

In both documents, two key, and closely related, ways of defining and giving sense to Company Karma emerge:

1. Company Karma as a principle of return in which financial and moral return are compatible, and
2. Company Karma as the interconnectedness of human beings.

The principle of karma, as explained by Stadil in the book, is that of consequence: one's actions leave traces in the world, as well as in one's own mind, which are a form of return (Hildebrandt and Stadil 2007, 17; our translation from the Danish here and in all subsequent quotations from the book, the report and newspaper articles). This means that "everything we do, say and think makes a difference. If we change the way we think and relate to the world right now, our future will also change" (Hildebrandt and Stadil 2007, 18).

A prerequisite for karma is the understanding of the interconnectedness and the mutual care and responsibility which creates obligations among people (Hildebrandt and Stadil 2007, 27). Indeed, karma goes beyond CSR in its emphasis on the interconnectedness of people: "CSR stands for being intent on having an environmentally friendly production, and that we don't use child labor, and so on. But the karma part is a more holistic approach,

92   Astrid Jensen et al.

in that it includes both the consumer and the employee" (Hildebrandt and Stadil 2007, 30).

When karma becomes a guiding principle for business practices, it is Company Karma. It demands an awareness of consequences of business practices for human beings and for the environment; consequences are returned in accordance with the principle of karma. Such awareness of karma is itself good karma, according to Stadil: "companies win by being aware of their karma" (Hildebrandt and Stadil 2007, 38). An awareness of karma can lead to increased sales, good PR and positive stories within the company (Hildebrandt and Stadil 2007, 41). Hildebrandt and Stadil see no conflict among the moral philosophy, its principle of interconnectedness, and the financial benefit to companies: "it's perfectly fine that one also profits from it. If business is to be sustainable in the long run, all parties should preferably get something out of it" (Hildebrandt and Stadil 2007, 41).

The two definitions of Company Karma—as interconnectedness and return—are also developed in the *Company Karma Report*, which states that "an essential part of a joint Thornico identity and pivotal to our interconnectedness and transparency[] is our dedication to doing a difference while doing business. We call it Company Karma, and it is a core aspect of our business strategy and integrated into all of our companies" (*Company Karma Report* 2013, 5). The link to return is explicitly given as "the belief that every action Thornico makes has a consequence or impact somewhere that will in one way or another return to Thornico" (*Company Karma Report* 2013, 13).

The theme of interconnectedness is found in antenarratives which stress the organization's needs to "grow even stronger ties to the people we work with" and to "strive to keep a "small company and family feeling by maintaining close relations to all people, partners, employees and customers that are part of our Thornico world" (*Company Karma Report* 2013, 5). Interconnectedness and return are developed throughout the report in articles and photographs telling stories of philanthropic projects: football as a means of reconciliation in war-torn communities, chickens for farmers in Malawi as a means of helping them achieve a sustainable income and beehives on the rooftops of the corporate offices in Amsterdam, as a way to benefit the environment and people (*Company Karma Report* 2013).

The Film as Coauthorship in Support of the Master Narrative

The master narrative theme of interconnectedness told in the antenarrative "grow even stronger ties to the people we work with" (*Company Karma Report* 2013, 5) is expanded in the report into a more detailed narrative about hummel, a subsidiary of Thornico. The narrative begins with a brief account of the sponsorship of the football team of war-torn Sierra Leone, as one of hummel's many projects that use football "as a way to bring people together, create a sense of team spirit and develop the country further" (*Company Karma Report* 2013, 18). The story relates the rise of the team in the FIFA rankings, to become "hummel's best positioned national football team, making hummel very proud" and leads to hummel's decision to develop a partnership with the NGO Play 31: "In order to have a true feeling and contact with the people in Sierra Leone, hummel has also established a partnership with the Danish NGO, Play 31[, which] uses the unifying power of football to bring together people and communities who have been torn apart by armed conflict" (*Company Karma Report* 2013, 18).

For the organization, "joining" with Play 31 is itself an act of "grow[ing] stronger ties" with the people with whom the company works through cooperation in an "important and life improving" cause. This creation of interconnectedness in turn enables activities which, again, enable human beings to connect: "[T]his partnership combines sport and education to nurture friendships and the understanding of teamwork. Using football as a tool enables hummel to bring people together in school activities and community gatherings, which contributes to the development of peaceful societies where children can once again exercise their right to play" (*Company Karma Report* 2013, 18).

This story of interconnectedness through football is in turn ventriloquized through a film on the corporate website presenting the collaboration between hummel and the NGO. The film incorporates footage from the community of Kailahun and the narrative of the founder of Play 31, Jakob Silas Lund, who relates from a personal perspective what he finds meaningful about the use of sports to create opportunities for dialogue and reconciliation. The film constitutes part of the company's overall multimodal CSR statement, demonstrating what the concrete particulars of interconnectedness entail in practice, the efforts they require and the changes they enable in the lives of human beings, including that of the narrator, for whom "return" is "tremendously gratifying" personal insight into processes of reconciliation.

In the film, Jakob Silas Lund narrates:

> Our work in Sierra Leone has given us a great insight into the reuniting power of football. [. . .] Seeing two communities coming together, setting aside grievances and celebrating the beautiful game after having signed a peace accord is tremendously gratifying.
>
> I especially recollect one occasion where I really felt the influence of our work in overcoming individual and communal divides. During a match in Kailahun, a woman saw the man who had raped her during the war. She told her confidants, who contacted the man's community. The two communities agreed to sit down under the village's "peace tree" the next day, where the man told the woman that he was extremely sorry about all he had done in the war. He had been forced into the rebel army as a child and had never wanted to fight. He begged the woman for forgiveness and apologized for the pain she'd been through. The woman ended up granting him forgiveness and the two communities took part in the ensuing healing ceremony.
>
> (*Company Karma Report* 2013, 19)

94 *Astrid Jensen et al.*

Jakob relates the master-narrative themes of interconnectedness and return through a personal story, revealing the experientiality of events and their realized emotional significance (Fludernik 2003), both for the characters in the story and, powerfully, for himself. From his position outside the organization, he ventriloquizes master-narrative themes through his first-person account of particular circumstances, places and characters. Thus, at the same time that the voice of the organization becomes displaced into the first-person voice of an external narrator, the themes and points of the master narrative are carried as traces within it; by incorporating the NGO into the Company Karma Report, management uses the NGO to legitimize the master narrative. Moreover, by placing the narrative on the corporate website, management appropriates this narrative and retains the power of authorship over the master narrative.

Counter-Narratives in News Media

The susceptibility to critique of the master narrative of CSR becomes apparent in the dialogic relation that emerges through the counter-narratives told by media. Attention to the degree to which the actions of the organization correspond with the intentions verbalized in its CSR policy and stories amounts to a form of surveillance of its conduct. Particularly the organization's claims about interconnectedness and return—including the compatibility of the two forms of return, financial and moral—are made to ring hollow in narratives constructed to have a high degree of narrative interest, or tellability (Bruner 1991; Labov 1972, 1997). These narratives invest the master-narrative themes with alternative specifics of actor, setting and events deriving from the conduct of the organization and to a large extent, the CEO himself.

The theme of interconnectivity is challenged in a counter-narrative that offers an alternative version: the "betrayal" of the Tibetan national football team, which Thornico had sponsored with money, equipment and training, by withdrawing its support. As laid out by the tabloid *EkstraBladet* (06.05.2012) this was to avoid compromising the organization's opportunity to do business in China. In this counter-narrative, Tibet is "ditched for China" by the CEO, Stadil.

Similarly, the master-narrative theme of return is countered through reports of weapons transports on the shipping vessels of one of Thornico's subsidiaries. As reported by the press, "[Stadil's] main mantra is 'What you ship out into the world comes back to you again.' Maybe this is what happened this week, when all the missiles Stadil shipped out have returned to the front page of *EkstraBladet*" (*EkstraBladet* 06.05.2012).

Characteristic of the narratives in the press is the focus on the CEO as a metonymic representation of the organization: it is Stadil who "ditches" China, and Stadil, whose mantra of return, is being called into question. Exploiting the newsworthiness of celebrity figures (Galtung and Ruge 1965),

"*Speaking through the Other*" 95

counter-narratives revolve as much around the person as the business and, in critical portraits, exploit a second criterion, that of negativity (Galtung and Ruge 1965). Accordingly, narratives emerge that counter Stadil's own assertion that money and karma are compatible or, indeed, mutually necessary (*Børsen* 28.06.2014), as in the oxymoronic description of Stadil as the "buddha capitalist" (*EkstraBladet* 06.05.2012), which plays creatively with the integration of the two conceptual domains of corporation and religion in Company Karma. Biographical narratives depict the CEO as a "daddy's boy" and show readers that "daddy's boy is stinking rich" and that he values "gold before karma."

Nevertheless, even the discourse of news coverage that produces these counter-narratives is fraught with ambivalence and is animated by the master narrative. For example, stories portray Stadil as a hero *and* a villain or expressly either state the complexity of his personality or show it through his words and actions.

In an article from the Danish *Berlingske Tidende*, a journalist accompanies Stadil to Sierra Leone and invites the reader to "[c]ome along on hummel-owner Christian Stadil's journey to spread good karma and establish football schools in Sierra Leone. A bumpy road full of intrigue, power, and sheer poverty" (*Berlingske* 12.02.2012). In the article, Stadil inserts his perspective, and many of the quotations in the articles are embedded versions of the master narrative, conveying Stadil's experiences as motivations for karma, as in this example:

> I was the ambassador for Save the Child and was looking at some statistics and saw that Sierra Leone was the poorest country in the whole world. The poorest! That made me go into Sierra Leone. We have sponsored their national team since 2008, and now we're going to combine the sponsorship with building football academies in Sierra Leone, so we can give value to the most poor, and combine sports with education. And thus light a candle in the dark for these people.
>
> (*Berlingske* 12.02.2012)

By inviting the journalist on his journey, the values of the master narrative of doing "good around the world" animate the newspaper article through this brief embedded narrative, with the reporting journalist as a ventriloquist.

The result of news media attention to CSR is a structure of voices in which master- and counter-narrative interpretations of the policy interact and animate each other. Opposed to the master narrative maintained by Stadil is the critique voiced by news media which portrays the CEO as not only privileged but hypocritical, and the CSR policy as a hollow statement of intention undermined by actual conduct. Together, these media narratives have the power to challenge the master narrative of the CEO, as well as to threaten not only the legitimacy of the CSR policy but the reputation of the entire organization.

96 *Astrid Jensen et al.*

Countering Counter-Narratives through Employees' Stories

In the strategic communication by management, news media become a constant, if remote, presence. Due to the power struggle over authorship of the organizational narrative, a need arises to counter the counter-narratives told by the media—their critique not only of the themes of interconnectedness and return but also of the very assertion that the CSR policy is in fact a guiding principle. In response, a project that grew out of the need for employees to make sense and take ownership of the policy of Company Karma inside the company becomes a communicative strategy for countering counter-narratives outside it. The employees ventriloquize the master narrative through their personal narratives.

This project, titled "My Karma," is designed to elicit employees' narratives about their own karma practices. Employees are given an Internet platform for short films that show and tell how their participation in charitable activities exemplifies good karma. Addressed to employees, the website is intended as a place to voluntarily "celebrate and share the Karma that exists within each and every Thornico Company and each and every Thornico employee. We thereby encourage you to open up your world of Karma and help us share the many stories about karma existing in Thornico and beyond" (My Karma site). In doing so, My Karma is a means to share and "spread the Karma to every corner of the world" (My Karma site).

The public page of the website includes inspiration for employees' topics: "Are you the voluntary coach for the city's little league players? Do you spend most of your weekend's fund-raising for a good cause? Or were you the one who started the recycling initiative in your neighborhood? No matter how big or small, your actions count and they help spread Karma to your community and beyond." In addition, four model videos by actual employees provide further examples of both what to tell and how to tell it. Thus guided in content and form, employees are told, "Now it's your turn to show everyone what you do. Upload your own MyKarma Project [. . .] explaining what you do and who it benefits" (My Karma site).

The model videos that are publically available are narrative interpretations of karma, with employees narrating in their own voices about their work in projects around the world and why the projects are personally meaningful. Brief summaries of the videos follow.

In the video titled *Denmark's Most Charitable Old Boys' Football Club*, Simon Schiølin, director of international sales for hummel, tells the story of his activities in a football club that travels the world to play matches that raise awareness and money for impoverished children all over the world, from Greenland to Africa, using football as a leverage for change. Results of the project include 11 million crowns in sports equipment donated through the Red Cross and vaccines for children through UNICEF.

The title of a second video, *WAWCAS*, is the acronym for the project narrated by Søren Schriver, the CEO of hummel: Women at Work, Children

"Speaking through the Other" 97

at School. Schriver tells the story of his involvement in a project designed to help "very, very poor women" in Nepal by donating money, instruction and support with the aim of empowering them to start running their own small businesses.

A third video, *Relay Run for Life*, is narrated by Rudy Helbord, an employee of Sanovo. Rudy tells about his work as a volunteer for the Danish non-profit "Fight Cancer," helping to organize and participating in an annual 24-hour walk for cancer awareness and fund-raising.

The title of a fourth video, *Sole Hope*, refers to a project narrated by Michele Noss, an employee with Sanovo Foods USA. Michele relates how a search for God's purpose in her life led her to join a ministry in Uganda. Volunteers provide children foot care, shoes and instruction in order to avoid debilitating sores that arise when children's daily lives include long walks on unpaved roads with poor sanitary conditions.

As the summaries indicate, two of the videos are narrated by managers and two by nonmanagement employees, yet common to all the model videos is the inclusion of what the projects mean to them. As in narratives told by the NGO and Stadil, the narratives evoke the narrators' recognition of the emotional significance of events, which motivates the telling of the story (Fludernik 2003). In the videos, for example, Søren Schriver says that he finds personal inspiration in the fact that women are able to endure difficult social, environmental and personal conditions. Similarly, Simon Schiølin relates the following:

> What do I get out of it? There's no doubt that it gives me a fantastic boost of energy in my everyday life to be able to help kids all over the world. In addition to that, I'm able to help 35 football players, or fiery souls, as I call them, make a difference in their everyday lives. [. . .] I give more both on and off the field because I have this exciting project outside my work at hummel.

Thematically, they reinforce themes of interconnectedness and return that the CEO emphasizes in interpretations of karma. The interconnectedness of human beings manifests itself in the desire to help others, to "make a difference" in the lives of others (Simon Schiølin), to "do something good" for others (Rudy) and, in Michele's story, to be called to, as she puts it, "not to turn away" from others.

Similarly, the concept of return is interpreted by the individual narrators. For Søren Schriver, it is tied to the feeling of obligation: "when you have something, you want to give something [. . .] As Christian [Stadil] would say, 'what goes around comes around,' and I completely agree." For Simon Schiølin, return means that his philanthropic activities outside his work at hummel enlivens him and makes him "able to give more both on and off the field." For Rudy, return comes through friendship and networks, and for Michele, the effort to change the world is something that makes one's "heart sing."

98　*Astrid Jensen et al.*

As they give voice to the themes and values developed in the master narrative of Company Karma, employees' stories are used to ventriloquize management's interpretations through personal narratives. These stories are animated by an understanding of the master narrative of karma that is reinforced by the model videos and instructions that show what qualifies as karma—good works beyond the borders of the workplace—as well as how to tell about it. Therefore, these employee stories are not solely their own, and management to an extent controls their formation. Ventriloquism of the master narrative therefore is an act of asymmetrical co-tellership of these employees' narratives. On one hand, the stories portray real employees and real, lived events, documenting them *as* real through employee names and job titles, photographs and film sequences from activities, as well as the use of narration and voice-over in the voices of employees themselves. On the other hand, the communication is orchestrated and realized through means that lie beyond employees' control: the guidelines for telling, the recording and the editing, including the interspersion of visual images into the story. Because the stories' content and design are constrained and published on the company website to legitimize policy, their possible interpretations become framed by their persuasive function in the immediate context, which gives management the ultimate narrative authority.

Similarly, while employees speak in their own voices, their texts seem to address an unseen other. Simon Schiølin, for example, poses the rhetorical question, "What do I get out of it?" and Søren Schriver prefaces his story of return with a reference to the CEO's version of karma, "As Christian would say . . ." Rudy's narration includes self-corrections that suggest an effort to remember to get information, including the name of the event, just right, and Michele ends her story by saying, "This is my story. I encourage you to write your own," a reference to the purpose of the My Karma project. The dialogic of coauthorship is also documented on the webpage, where each employee name is indicated and each video is given a title that reflects its theme, yet the byline "By Ci Eschel" accompanies each story.

Accordingly, although employees have been encouraged, indeed told, to tell their stories, the personal significance of events for these employees becomes a strategy to counter the counter-narratives. Personal narratives that show individuals' commitment to karma serve as a form of evidence for the policy being implemented and integral to the company.

Discussion and Conclusion

Because the conceptual blend of Company Karma unites two seemingly incongruent domains of "doing business" and "doing good," this chapter's case study of how the policy is interpreted by stakeholders illustrates issues raised by CSR policies more generally: potential conflicts of interest, between profit, on one hand, and moral and ethical concerns, on the other, make organizations that communicate their CSR particularly susceptible to critique.

"Speaking through the Other" 99

Schisms between the two interests open spaces for interpretations that can test the policy's—and the organization's—legitimacy.

As the chapter demonstrates, a CCO approach with a dialogic perspective helps explain how legitimacy and responsibility are constituted in complex processes of meaning negotiation and power struggles for authorship of the corporate story, involving not only the organization itself but also various other actors, such as NGOs, the media, employees and other stakeholders. As discussed in our analysis, it is through the dialogic interaction of master and counter-narratives that the interpretive testing of CSR policy takes place, through the sense-giving of management and the sense-making of stakeholders within and outside the organization. As they reveal understandings of CSR policy, narratives also reveal attitudes toward it. Moreover, and perhaps more important, the narratives reveal the mechanisms of narrative authority and of testing that authority, which is the true measure of the degree to which the domains of business and ethics are compatible.

Management attempts to *give* sense through a master narrative that directs understanding through central narrative themes (here, of interconnectedness and return), and positions stakeholders as ventriloquists of the master narrative. When responses to the master narrative become countered—for example, by news media—these counter-narratives exert an influence on the communicative strategy of management to address an ever-present, critical other. Stakeholders' stories and voices are co-opted to counter these counter-narratives. In the present case, narratives of individuals' experiences, told in the first person, depicting events lived by real people, and employing experientiality, ultimately serve to ventriloquize the master narrative, which in turn is a constant animator of ostensibly personal stories.

As a result, narratives that demonstrate individuals' commitment to CSR policy serve to legitimize it by closing the rupture between "doing business" and "doing good." Narratives demonstrate a commitment that goes beyond the workplace, as if this commitment is an inherent quality of individuals. Nevertheless, the "problem"—and the rupture that remains—is that although employees and management coauthor stories, it is management that has the ultimate narrative authority over them, constraining their content and design and publishing them on the company website to legitimize policy. It is thus as the master narrative exerts its force *as* master that the master narrative ultimately counters itself.

Ultimately, this case helps us understand the implications of the vulnerability of master narratives of policies like CSR, which constitute a promise of ethical behavior, to monitoring and scrutiny by external actors. As authoritative texts, such policies are wide open to counter narrativizing, especially when formulated in catchy abstractions. By focusing on the interaction of master and counter-narratives, we contribute to an understanding of ventriloquism as a narrative activity by which interpretations of abstract policy, including stances toward it, are given more concrete form through temporal structures with specific people performing specific actions.

100 *Astrid Jensen et al.*

Moreover, our dialogic perspective on the interaction of master and counter-narratives contributes to an understanding of how counter-narratives influence the dynamics by which managerial control of the master narrative is maintained. We find that the master narrative is reiterated as an ongoing response to the themes raised in the counter-narratives; in turn, the counter-narrative is a constant, if implicit, presence that can be traced in the master-narrative. Yet, as we demonstrate, management's use of personal narratives from employees and an NGO to ventriloquize the master narrative becomes an assertion of authority which may ultimately function to confirm the very counter-narratives that it is intended to counter.

Note

1. Cooren's use of the term *animate* differs from Goffman's, as Cooren himself points out. "Animator" is one of the three participant roles that Goffman distinguishes in his concept of "footing," which describes how interactants position themselves, or are positioned, in communication. For Goffman (1981) the "animator" is the human agent who speaks or writes a message; the "author" is the agent who designs, or writes, the message, gives it its linguistic realization; the "principal" is the agent whose values, viewpoint and intention inform the message. According to Cooren, Goffman's concepts are limiting because in recognizing only human participants, they exclude what Cooren maintains are the agency and performativeness of texts and ideas. Moreover, Cooren defines animation as the ability to inform utterances and actions with meanings, where for Goffman, the animator provides a "sound box" (Goffman 1981) for the meanings of other interactants and thus is more the puppet being animated than the animator in Cooren's terminology.

References

Ashcraft, Karen Lee, Timothy R. Kuhn, and Francois Cooren. 2009. "Constitutional Amendments: 'Materializing' Organizational Communication." *Academy of Management Annals* 3 (1): 1–64. doi: 10.1080/19416520903047186.

Bamberg, Michael G. W. and Molly Andrews. 2004. *Considering counter-narratives: Narrating, resisting, making sense*. Vol. 4. Amsterdam and Philadelphia: J. Benjamins.

Boje, David M. 1991. "The Storytelling Organization: A Study of Story Performance in an Office-Supply Firm." *Administrative Science Quarterly* 36 (1): 106–126.

Boje, David M. 2008. *Storytelling organizations*. Los Angeles: Sage.

Brown, Andrew D., and Michael Humphreys. 2006. "Organizational Identity and Place: A Discursive Exploration of Hegemony and Resistance." *Journal of Management Studies* 43 (2): 231–257.

Brown, Mary Helen and Gary L. Kreps. 1993. "Narrative analysis and organizational development." In *Qualitative research: Applications in organizational communication*, edited by S. L. Herndon and G. L. Kreps, 47–62. Creskill, NJ: Hampton Press.

Bruner, Jerome. 1991. "The Narrative Construction of Reality." *Critical Inquiry* 18 (1): 1–21.

Carroll, Archie B. and Ann K. Buchholtz. 2006. *Business and society: Ethics and stakeholder management*. Mason, Ohio: South Western.

Cooren, François. 2010. "Figures of Communication and Dialogue: Passion, Ventriloquism and Incarnation." *Intercultural Pragmatics* 7 (1): 131–145. doi: 10.1515/IPRG.2010.006.

Cooren, François. 2012. "Communication Theory at the Center: Ventriloquism and the Communicative Constitution of Reality." *Journal of Communication* 62 (1): 1–20. doi: 10.1111/j.1460-2466.2011.01622.x.

Cornelissen, Joep. 2006. "Metaphor in Organization Theory: Progress and the Past." *The Academy of Management Review* 31 (2): 485–488.

Deuten, J. Jasper, and Arie Rip. 2000. "Narrative Infrastructure in Product Creation Processes." *Organization* 7 (1): 69–93.

Ericson, Thomas. 2001. "Sensemaking in Organisations—Towards a Conceptual Framework for Understanding Strategic Change." *Scandinavian Journal of Management* 17 (1): 109–131.

Fauconnier, Gilles and Mark Turner. 1999. "Metonymy and conceptual integration." In *Metonymy in language and thought*, edited by Klaus-Uwe Panther and Günter Radden, 77–90. Amsterdam: John Benjamins.

Fine, Michelle and Anita Harris. 2001. *Under the covers: Theorising the politics of counter stories*. London: Lawrence & Wishart.

Fludernik, Monika. 2003. "Natural narratology and cognitive parameters." In *Narrative theory and the cognitive sciences*, edited by David Herman, 243–267. Stanford, CA: Center for the Study of Language and Information, CSLI.

Freeman, R. Edward. 2010. *Stakeholder theory: The state of the art*. Cambridge: Cambridge University Press.

Friedman, Milton. 1970. "The Social Responsibility of Business Is to Increase Its Profits." *New York Times Magazine* 13: 32–33.

Galtung, Johan, and Mari Holmboe Ruge. 1965. "The Structure of Foreign News the Presentation of the Congo, Cuba and Cyprus Crises in Four Norwegian Newspapers." *Journal of Peace Research* 2 (1): 64–90.

Gioia, Dennis A., and Kumar Chittipeddi. 1991. "Sensemaking and Sensegiving in Strategic Change Initiation." *Strategic Management Journal* 12 (6): 433–448.

Goffman, Erving. 1981. *Forms of talk*. Philadelphia: University of Pennsylvania Press.

Grunig, James E. and Todd Hunt. 1984. *Managing public relations*. New York: Harcourt Brace Jovanovich College Publishers.

Hildebrandt, Steen and Christian Stadil. 2007. *Company karma*. Kbh: Børsens Forlag.

Hill, Robert C., and Michael Levenhagen. 1995. "Metaphors and Mental Models: Sensemaking and Sensegiving in Innovative and Entrepreneurial Activities." *Journal of Management* 21 (6): 1057–1074.

Kuhn, Timothy. 2008. "A Communicative Theory of the Firm: Developing an Alternative Perspective on Intra-Organizational Power and Stakeholder Relationships." *Organization Studies (01708406)* 29 (8/9): 1227–1254. doi: 10.1177/0170840 608094778.

Kuhn, Timothy, and Michele H. Jackson. 2008. "Accomplishing Knowledge: A Framework for Investigating Knowing in Organizations." *Management Communication Quarterly* 21 (4): 454–485.

Labov, William. 1972. *Language in the inner city: Studies in the Black English vernacular*. Vol. 3. Philadelphia: University of Pennsylvania Press.

Labov, William. 1997. "Some Further Steps in Narrative Analysis." *Journal of Narrative and Life History* 7: 395–415.

Larsen, Mogens Holten. 2000. "Managing the corporate story." In *The expressive organization linking identity, reputation and the corporate brand*, edited by Mary Jo Hatch, Majken Schultz and M. Holten Larsen, 196–207. Oxford: Oxford University Press.

102 *Astrid Jensen et al.*

Linell, Per. 2009. *Rethinking language, mind, and world dialogically: Interactional and contextual theories of human sense-making.* Charlotte, NC: Information Age Pub.

Margolis, Joshua D., and James P. Walsh. 2003. "Misery Loves Companies: Rethinking Social Initiatives by Business." *Administrative Science Quarterly* 48 (2): 268–305.

Merkelsen, Henrik. 2013. "Legitimacy and Reputation in the Institutional Field of Food Safety: A Public Relations Case Study." *Public Relations Inquiry* 2 (2): 243–265.

Morgan, Gareth. 1997. *Images of organization.* Thousand Oaks, CA and London: Sage.

Morsing, Mette, and Majken Schultz. 2006. "Corporate Social Responsibility Communication: Stakeholder Information, Response and Involvement Strategies: 1." *Business Ethics* 15 (4): 323. doi: 10.1111/j.1467-8608.2006.00460.x.

Mumby, Dennis K. 1987. "The political function of narrative in organisations." *Communication Monographs* 54 (2): 113–127.

Nielsen, Anne Ellerup, and Christa Thomsen. 2007. "Reporting CSR—What and How to Say It?" *Corporate Communications: An International Journal* 12 (1): 25–40. doi: 10.1108/13563280710723732.

Schoeneborn, Dennis, and Hannah Trittin. 2013. "Transcending Transmission: Towards a Constitutive Perspective on CSR Communication." *Corporate Communications* 18 (2): 193–211. doi: 10.1108/13563281311319481.

Starbuck, William H. and Frances J. Milliken. 1988. "Executives' perceptual filters: What they notice and how they make sense." In Hambrick, Donald *The executive effect: Concepts and methods for studying top managers*, 35–65. Greenwich, CT: JAI Press

Waterman, Robert H. 1990. *Adhocracy: The power to change.* New York & London: WW Norton & Company.

Wright, Alex. 2005. "The Role of Scenarios as Prospective Sensemaking Devices." *Management Decision* 43 (1): 86–101.

Part II

Counter-Narratives in Changes of Identity and Practices

5 Organizational Identity Negotiations through Dominant and Counter-Narratives

Didde Maria Humle and Sanne Frandsen

Introduction

> The role of the ticket inspector is—and it is still fundamental in my view of the terminology and the soul of the company—to take care of the customers. Furthermore, the concept is, of course, talking to Mr. And Mrs. Smith, when they get on the train [. . . and . . .] to take care of those who do not have their ticket.
>
> (Ticket inspector at E-rail)

E-rail is a European-based public rail service—an organization that is domestically well known—however, not for something good. 'Scandals' are frequently in the news in relation to the organization's financial endeavors and unethical behaviors. In particular, the ticket inspectors have been criticized for being brutal and inhuman, kicking off, fining or verbally insulting the passengers, such as children or handicapped. In this chapter, we focus on how the ticket inspectors manage such identity threats by using counter-narratives in their story work to construct alternative versions of 'who we are' and 'what we do' creating multiple, yet rather stable, understandings of the organizational identity in their own storytelling community.

To arrive at such insights, we first introduce literature on organizational identity formations linking the construction of the organizational identity to the micro-level story work of the organizational members. Subsequently, we introduce our generation of empirical data along with our thematic, structural and performative approach to analyze the counter-narratives found in the case study of E-rail. In the Findings section, we first introduce the dominant narratives of the media and management before we examine the clusters of counter-narratives in depth—both opposing and constructing an alternative version of 'reality' than the dominant narratives.

Organizational Identity as Conversations between Outsiders and Insiders

Within organizational research there has been an increased interest in the dynamic, polyphonic and open-ended nature of organizational identity.

106 *Didde Maria Humle and Sanne Frandsen*

Several scholars argue that organizational identity is not only constituted in the conversations between organizational members but also constructed through conversations between outsiders and insiders. Hatch and Schultz (2002) point to the interplay among external narrative forming the organizational image; management, whose official stories narrate the organizational vision; and the employees' stories rooted in the organizational culture. Coupland and Brown (2004) claim that "organizations are best characterized by having multiple identities, and that these identities are authored in conversations between notional 'insiders,' and between notional 'insiders' and 'outsiders'" (2004, 1325). Similarly, Boje claims that organizations are "existing to tell their collective stories, to live out their collective stories, to be in constant struggle over getting the stories of insiders and outsiders straight. It is a sense-making that is coming into being but not/never finished or concluded in narrative retrospection." (2001, 4).

The interplay among outsiders, management and employees has been studied in contexts of identity threats posed by a poor organizational image (Dutton and Dukerich 1991; Frandsen 2012), as well as within celebrity organizations (Kjærgaard, Morsing and Ravasi 2011). Our ambition for this chapter is to contribute to this line of research by proposing a narrative approach to the study of organizational identity and sense-making processes (Brown 2006; Chreim 2005, 2007; Coupland and Brown 2004; Humphreys and Brown 2002), with a specific focus on the role of 'counter-narratives' (Bamberg and Andrews 2004; Boje 2006; Linde 2001, 2009). Thus, we connect matters of identity construction to the conversations between outsiders and insiders, and in particular, we turn our attention toward the everyday story work and struggles of organizational members as they go about their daily work negotiating "what we do" and "who we are" as individuals, as groups and as an organization.

Organizational Identity as Everyday Storytelling Practices

The growing interest among scholars of organizational identity in polyphonic and dynamic identity formation reflects an increased focus on the intertwined nature of the relationship among individual, collective and organizational identity construction processes (Coupland and Brown 2004; Humphreys and Brown 2002). The complex understanding of identity as something that is constantly in a flux of being negotiated and retold is by now well established (Belova 2010; Chreim 2005). Furthermore, many scholars view individual, collective and organizational self-understandings as intertwined and as something that is continuously reconstructed, negotiated and enacted in daily dialogues and practices in and around pluralistic and polyphonic organizations (Hazen 1993; Humphreys and Brown 2002).

Similar to various other scholars, we focus on narrative aspects of individual and organizational identity construction processes (Chreim 2005,

2007; Coupland and Brown 2004; Driver 2009; Humphreys and Brown 2002; Linde 2001, 2009) and acknowledge storytelling to be central to sense-making and identity construction processes "narratives are the means by which we organize and make sense of our experience and evaluate our actions and intentions" (Cunliffe and Coupland 2012, 66). In addition, we turn our attention to the everyday storytelling practices of organizational members as important in understanding the identity-formation process (Humle 2014; Humphreys and Brown 2002; Linde 2001, 2009).

Paying attention to the everyday storytelling practices of organizational members makes it possible to study the many voices of organizations and the polyphonic nature of organizational storytelling in the construction of organizational identity. Linde (2009) demonstrates how organizational storytelling practices are polyphonic and have stabilizing effects, creating coherence and a sense of continuity among organizational members. The organization can be seen as a storytelling community (Linde 2009), where different understandings of organizational identity are negotiated and passed on to new members through everyday storytelling practices. We adopt Linde's (2009) image of organizations as storytelling communities to conceptualize how organizational contexts create certain storytelling conditions affecting the story work of individual members. We want to draw attention to the media as an important and dominating voice influencing the identity formation processes of organizations.

Studies outside the narrative approach have demonstrated that media attention has a significant influence on organizational identity formation processes (Dutton and Dukerich 1991; Elsbach and Kramer 1996; Kjærgaard et al. 2011). Differing narratives between outsiders and insiders may be conceived as an organizational identity threat and lead organizational members to revisit and reconstruct their sense of organizational identity (Gioia, Schultz and Corley 2000). Consequently, outsiders' perception of the organizational identity may spur organizational change and call for actions among insiders to adjust the divergent identity narratives (Gioia et al. 2000; Elsbach and Kramer 1996; Ravasi and Schulz 2006). Several narrative studies focus on the role and the power of management in authoring the organizational identity (Boje 1995; Chreim 2005; Strangleman 1999). However, they also demonstrate that management's efforts to author a specific organizational identity are rarely incontestably adopted by organizational members (Harrison 2000; Humphreys and Brown 2002). Inspired by these studies, we aim to illustrate how members at the employee level counter, negotiate and rewrite 'who we are' and 'what we do' at the intersection of the media's and the management's dominating narratives. Thus, we contribute to the existing literature of the interplay between outsiders and insiders, who primarily tend to focus on the managements' efforts to counter the media's narrative of the organization (Ravasi and Schultz 2006).

Story Work

Turning the attention toward the work of individuals in constructing identity and making sense of their work-life experiences, we consider storytelling as a central part of how we construct and perform ourselves as individuals, groups and organizations (Cunliffe and Coupland 2012; Driver 2009; Linde 2001, 2009; Mishler 1999). We adopt the term story work (Humle and Pedersen 2015) to emphasize the ongoing and open-ended processes of making sense of our experiences and construct different stories of self, others, the work and the organization, not as finished, consistent or well-structured narratives but as responsive narrative performances (Cunliffe and Coupland 2012) connected to certain storytelling episodes/contexts and intertextually related to other story performances going on across time and space. In this way, story work is perceived to be a relational and dynamic process of negotiating, describing and interpreting what has happened, what is going on at the moment and what we anticipate or desire of the future. In addition, we claim that everyday work stories and the story work involved in constructing such stories are antenarrative and polyphonic (Humle 2014) in the sense that the construction of self, others, work and the organization is never finished. It is an ongoing process of negotiating and handling many potential and sometimes contradictory story lines simultaneously.

Therefore, we use the term *story work* to conceptualize how we navigate and make sense by allowing tensions and contradictions and by constantly introducing parallel stories and handling different story lines simultaneously. As such, the stories and the story work of individuals are constituted in the many conversations going on in and around organizations. It is a process of constantly reconstructing and negotiating—not only the past, present and future but multiple pasts, presents and futures (Jørgensen in Boje 2011). Thus, our interest is not only to explore how stories are fragmented and unfinished but also how some story lines are persistently pursued, and how shared meanings and understandings of, for example, organizational identity and the work done come into existence.

Counter-Narratives

Bamberg and Andrews (2004, x) state that "[c]ounter-narratives only make sense in relation to something else, which they are countering. The very name identifies this as a positional category, in tension with another category" (Bamberg and Andrews 2004, x). This is similar to Linde's (2001, 2009) notion of counter-stories as a form of noisy silences "accounts explicitly oppositional to specific, and usually more official, accounts" (Linde 2001, 2009). Linde has examined the role of counter-stories and claims that it is interesting to explore—not only if they have a life within the organization they criticize but also whether they succeed in creating an ongoing counter-memory. Noisy silences are stories of issues, episodes and organizational histories that may not be spoken of officially but are spoken of or discussed nonetheless; they are "[w]hat is saliently unsaid, hearably unsaid, what could be said but is not" (Linde 2009, 197). They are the unofficial stories of the organization and are often relatively unstructured.

In his study of Disney, Boje (1995, 2006) uses the play of *Tamara* as a metaphor for organizational life to describe how organizational storytelling is always in the making. "*Tamara* is open conversation as a multiplicity of minor narratives; small stories collectively and dynamically constitute, transform, and reform the storytelling organization. Instead of one character acting one story line, there is diversity, multiplicity, and difference." (1995, 1031) The official stories narrated by Walt Disney effects organizational members and "dominate, socialize, and marginalize others' experience" (1995, 1031) and thus affects the story work of organizational members. However, simultaneously opposing counter-stories were being told "in other Disney rooms, and by tellers outside Disney's empire" (2006, 36), and the front-stage image of the organization was contested by "the emergence of the backstage (somewhat gossip) counter-stories" (2006, 36) authored by, for example, journalists.

To advance our theoretical understanding of counter-narratives and their performative role in negotiating organizational identity, we build on the work of Bamberg and Andrews (2004) and Linde and make additions by combining it with Boje's (1995) work on counter-stories and antenarrative organizational storytelling (See e.g. Boje 2001, 2011) to adopt a less narrow definition of counter-narratives. Thus, we are able to focus on stories that are in direct opposition to the official and dominating stories of the media and management but also the parallel stories presenting alternative realities of organizational life without necessarily being in direct opposition to specific dominating narratives. Inspired by the work of Boje (1995, 2001, 2006, 2011), we study narratives and fragments of storytelling as a web of voices constantly constituting and negotiating organizational identity (Humle 2014). In this way, we are able to avoid the static dichotomy between master and counter-narrative and still use the concept of counter-stories (Linde 2001, 2009) as a valuable tool in studying the tensions between official, dominant and discursively powerful voices of, for example, management and the media and the constant struggle of organizational members in making sense of their everyday work life and negotiating individual and collective organizational identity constructions. Combining the work of Linde and Boje, it is of interest to study not only the story work that goes into performing critical counter-stories but also what kind of organizational counter-memories or "realities" they form and facilitate.

Generation of Empirical Data

This chapter is based on a case study of a highly contested organization, E-rail, a European national rail service. In image rankings, E-rail is always found among the five least attractive organizations and has been subject to several

110 *Didde Maria Humle and Sanne Frandsen*

public 'scandals.' In 2000, it purchased new trains, which turned out to be so flawed that they were unable to run. Today, using the worn trains means recurrent delays, and angry customers. Moreover, E-rail's financial conducts have been criticized as the organization has run a deficit from 2007 to 2011. Most notably, E-rail is often portrayed in the media as an illegitimate provider of public transportation due to poor service. (The media's presentation of E-rail is elaborated on at the beginning of the Findings section.)

Ticket inspectors were selected as primary participants of the study, as they can be regarded as the frontline face of the organization vis-à-vis the customers. Ticket inspectors are often the sole representative of their organization in critical situations, where they more or less successful try to uphold a service-oriented spirit in interactions with frustrated, angry and sometimes threatening customers. Besides checking the tickets (this was in fact not first priority) the ticket inspectors' work comprise safety matters, selling food and beverages from a small sales trolley, providing traffic information and cleaning the trains. They often work alone or in teams consisting of two or three colleagues—depending on the size of the train. A union representative described them as "free-range birds" as they worked without direct supervision. The lack of direct supervision also meant that the ticket collectors had the sole responsibility for making the right decision and taking action in critical situations such as acute illness among passengers, violence or vandalism on the trains or in case of accidents, such as a suicidal person jumping in front of the train.

The following analysis is primarily based on interviews with 20 ticket inspectors. The overall case study also comprises observations and recordings of four information meetings, 10 hours of shadowing on the trains and a collection of corporate information material, power points, employee magazines and newsletters from the union. News articles of events leading up to the time of study have been collected as well. The 20 interviews were all tape-recorded and lasted from 49 minutes to 2 hours 41 minutes. In total, the interviews lasted 26 hours 13 minutes, averaging 1 hour 18 minutes each. The interview guide was semistructured and inspired by Critical Incident Technique (Flanagan [1954] in Czarniawska 2004), which is a set of flexible principles designed to direct the conversation toward concrete episodes and situations. The technique assists in producing rich elaborations on sometimes short or generalized answers. It made the ticket inspectors refer to specific experiences on the trains and interactions with customers, management or outsiders. It proved a useful approach to get the respondents to talk about their work and practices in a detailed manner. More details on the case study can be found in Frandsen (2015).

Analysis of the Empirical Material

We adopt a broad and non-restrictive definition of narratives, and we incorporate many different kinds of story performances in our analysis. Some of them are full-blown narratives with a plot, beginning, middle and end

Organizational Identity Negotiations 111

(BME narratives; Boje 2001, 2006). Others are fragmented stories, unfinished pieces of story work related to other conversations and always in the making. Furthermore, we acknowledge all types of statements to have narrative qualities in the sense that they are part of the ongoing story work of organizational members as they go about making sense of their work-life experiences. With this definition, it is possible to work with different kinds of stories, story fragments and story performances that are not necessarily well-structured or fully performed as BME narratives to capture the ongoing and open-ended nature of organizational storytelling.

The analytical process was inspired by Riessman's (2008) narrative approach, focusing on the thematic, structural and performative characteristics of the story work of ticket inspectors as they shared stories of everyday work situations during interviews. The interviews were coded in NVivo by using open codes to label the themes narrated by the participant. The thematic analysis was conducted to explore important counter-narrative themes across the story work of the ticket inspectors as they related their stories of everyday work life in and around the trains to the dominating narratives of the media and management. We found five horizontal (across interviews) clusters of themes organized around the contestation of the notion of 'service': (1) "Countering Media's presentation of service"; (2) "service as naturally occurring,"; (3) "service and time pressure," (4) "service as the future of E-rail,"; and, finally, (5) "service as loss of status,". The clusters of themes were examined in more details with focus on the structural characteristics. Here we used Greimas's actantial model to analyze the material with the specific purpose of understanding the participants' self-positioning and positioning of other central characters.

Greimas's actantial model is based on Propp's analyses of folktales to understand the plot structure underlying fiction. The model, exemplified in Figure 5.1, consists of three axes: the quest axis connecting the subject and the object. The subject aspires toward a goal—the object. The subject has helpers and opponents in achieving this goal; these actants are organized around the conflict axis. The sender and the receiver are organized around the communication axis, illustrating a transportation of the object from the sender to the receiver, with the receiver, in some cases, being the subject.

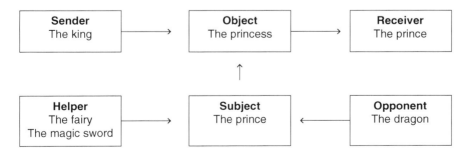

Figure 5.1 Greimas's Actantial Model

112 Didde Maria Humle and Sanne Frandsen

Greimas's actantial model was originally produced to analyze the structure of narratives in fictions. However, other studies have demonstrated its use in analyzing organizational narratives (Czarniawska 2004; Søderberg 2003; Wang and Robert 2005). The actantial model has potential for depicting the characters' narrative positions and linking those positions illustrative of the power relations. Wang and Robert (2005) argue that Greimas's actantial model is valuable in understanding individuals' identity constructions, while Søderberg (2003) demonstrates its usefulness in illuminating similarities and differences in sense-making of the same organizational events. In our case, we use the actantial model to analyze how different voices—the media, the management and employees—position themselves and others when elaborating on the quest of providing E-rail's customers with good customer experiences. Furthermore, the actantial model demonstrates how ticket inspectors in different sets or clusters of counter-narratives adopt, challenge or rewrite their subject positions. The structural analysis is, thus, in this chapter, applied to demonstrate the performative character of the counter-narratives: How the ticket inspectors as members of a storytelling community use counter-narratives in their story work to establish and maintain a sense of identity and legitimacy despite identity threats, ambiguities and contradictions inherent in their role.

Findings

E-rail is a public organization, which has been faced with crisis during the past five years—both financially and regarding an increasing public mistrust. Extensive negative media coverage has portrayed the organization as an illegitimate provider of public transportation due to poor service. The presentation of the results in the following section begins with a brief presentation of the media's and the management's dominating narratives. This is done to contextualize—our primary interest—the ticket inspectors' story work and make it possible to study how these powerful voices interrelate and affect the story work of the ticket inspectors.

The Media's Dominant Narrative of E-rail

Over a period of at least five years, the media consistently position E-rail as a greedy, unfair, unprofessional organization. Stories of overcrowded, delayed or dirty trains often feature in the press and portray E-rail as incapable of delivering a 'proper' service to their customers. In this morass, the ticket inspectors are hailed as E-rail's evil henchmen. One of the major national tabloid newspapers, *T.P.*, in particular, ran a series of articles about the conducts of ticket inspectors. A selection of the headlines illustrates the dominating narrative:

- "E-rail Locked Me Up," about a 12-year-old allegedly locked up while the ticket inspector fined her for not having her ticket ready (*T.P.* August 24, 2010)

Organizational Identity Negotiations 113

- "E-rail Mistake Sent Me to Prison," about a commuter who bought a ticket in a ticket machine, which printed flawed numbers, resulting in the commuter being handed over from the ticket inspectors to the police (*T.P.* 30.08.2010)
- "E-rail's Ticket Inspector Tore Hair from My Head," about a ticket collector who allegedly tried to establish order in the children's section by pulling a six-year-old boy by his hair back to his seat (*T.P.* 2.08. 2010)
- "Brain-Damaged Boy Kicked Off the Train Three Times," about a handicapped boy being asked to leave the train because the ticket inspectors believed him to be older than the 14 years allowed on his child ticket (*T.P.* 28.03.2011)
- "You Are Flippant and a Cheat: Ticket Inspector to a Mentally Retarded Girl," about a mentally handicapped 16-year-old girl who was verbally abused by a ticket inspector (*T.P.* 3.04.2011)

In these articles, the customers are positioned as the active subjects wanting customer service (the object). E-rail is positioned as the potential sender of the customer service to the customer (the potential receiver); however the ticket inspectors, who are positioned as the opponents, obstruct this quest for the customer, who instead receives poor customer service. As a result, the customers are clearly marked as the victims in these stories. The stories were all accompanied by bold headlines and graphic pictures showing, for instance, the (now partly bald) scalp of the six-year-old boy. These stories appear on multiple media platforms along with follow-up stories, background stories and letters from the readers. The media attention is intense and the narratives of the evil ticket inspectors, who are treating their customers poorly, fining everyone and kicking the weakest passengers of the trains, are repeated over and over again.

Management's Dominating (Counter-)Narrative of E-rail

The way management communicates in the media during the smear campaigns is interesting to notice. Their voice is an important and powerful voice of the storytelling community of E-rail and often opposed or referred to by ticket inspectors in their story work. In the story about the 12-year-old girl being locked up, a deputy director explains: "We do a lot to make our customers happy, but sometimes, our employees have a bad day [. . .] I will take it seriously as this is, of course, not a method that we use. Furthermore, we certainly do not instruct our personnel to do such things" (*T.P.*, 24.08.2010). In a follow-up article "Now E-rail Offers Julie Psychological Counselling," the deputy director is quoted again: "That we have a guest, a 12-year-old girl, who feels she has been treated badly, this makes me truly sad, I am sad on behalf of the girl as well as on behalf of the employee, who feels bad about this case and is miserable that Julie has had this experience." He announced that E-rail would make a comprehensive investigation of the case: "We will interview her [the ticket inspector] thoroughly and repeatedly.

Right now it is one person's word against another's, but let us wait and see what happens" (*T.P.* 28.8.2010).

In this article, E-rail is firmly established as the sender of customer service (object) to the customer (receiver), by management positioning itself as the active subject in the quest of providing good customer service. The ticket inspectors are, however, still positioned as opponents obstructing the quest, while the managerial rules and investigations are positioned as helpers. Management emphasizes how ticket inspectors "can have a bad day" and do not follow the (managerially dictated) "rules" and how the particular inspector referred to should be interviewed "thoroughly and repeatedly." Thus, they aim at breaking with the established "truth" in the media's dominating narrative, but they refrain from changing the position of the ticket inspectors as opponents. The management rather position themselves as the active subject saving the day and preventing this from happening again.

The extensive negative media coverage led to new strategic considerations on behalf of management, who decided to launch a new 'service concept' labeled Service A-B-C. The service concept requires a substantial shift in the professional identity of ticket inspectors. A member of the management team explained at the first meeting: "We are going through a shift in our culture and priorities. We are no longer to control tickets but to provide a service instead. . . . Riding the train without a ticket no longer leads to a fine. The most important thing is that everyone has a pleasant journey, including those who do not pay. [. . .] Society around us is changing. Therefore, we must change, too. Our customers expect more. They will no longer tolerate being abandoned on the next station because they do not have a ticket" (Notes from meeting). Here the management uses the inclusive "we" implying that management and ticket inspectors work as united subjects ensuring that a proper service is provided to the customers, who "expect more." Because of this new concept, ticket inspectors are now required to not only check tickets and ensure safety matters on the trains, but also—and this is in fact the first priority—provide service by using the sales trolley. The sales trolley, similar to the food trolleys on airplanes, are according to the management at the core of the new service offerings to the customers on the trains. Service guidelines are described in minute details in a 'service guide' booklet. Meanwhile, substantial cuts are made to the personnel on the trains, and new electronic equipment is subsequently introduced in order for the ticket inspectors to inspect electronic tickets. However, the electronic equipment has, according to the ticket inspectors, the dual function of not only advancing efficiency but also to monitor the ticket inspectors' performance.

The Ticket Inspectors' Counter-Narratives

Turning our attention to the ticket inspectors, we have identified clusters of counter-narratives in the interview texts focusing on (a) countering the media, (b) countering the management and (c) countering the employees

Organizational Identity Negotiations 115

themselves. Each cluster of the counter-narratives comprises story work, which both directly counter the dominating narratives narrated by the media or management, and which proposes alternative worldviews and understandings of the organizational identity of E-rail. Thus, the counter-narratives enable the coexistence of multiple narrations of 'who we are' and 'what we do.' Service is a central matter of concern in all the counter-narratives. However, the analyses conducted by using the actantial model show that the understanding of what service is and who provides it—is far from static or fixed. Instead, there is a constant struggle of defining what service is, who provides the service, who opposes, and who assists. In the following sections, the different types of counter-narratives are presented.

Countering the Media—Opposing the Media Narrative

One type of counter-story often performed by the ticket inspectors opposes the dominating media narrative of the ticket inspector as E-rails evil henchmen treating their customers poorly, fining everyone and kicking off the weakest passengers. These stories specifically oppose the images presented by the media of, for example, the girl who was allegedly locked up by a female ticket inspector:

> There was this case in [name of city . . .] It was one of my really, really good colleagues. [. . .] She locked up this girl. However, she had not. Not at all. [. . .] It ended up on the front page of *T.P.*, and the management of E-rail reacted by hauling her over the coals. They simply hauled her over the coals, so she had to take sick leave. This is management doing this. Moreover, in the end there was nothing to the story. She did not lock anyone up, and she was subjected to grueling examination. It was good front-page material. But oh—[management is] reluctant to deal with *T.P.* and all that, so they do not stand up for their people. They do not.
>
> (Eva)

The story of the girl who was locked up was frequently told in the interviews (without being prompted), also by ticket inspectors who did not know the ticket inspector in question. The narrative refers to what seems to be a significant event, creating a shared frame of reference and understandings of the situation and its implication. Although there are variations of the story, there are three main story lines persistently pursued across storytelling episodes: (a) the ticket inspector was simply doing her job. "Why are we to be hunted down because we are just doing our job? That is probably what was most annoying to me and most painful to the staff" (André); (b) the media are only out to get you: "They went to the press with this story, and then the snowball started rolling. They began to dig out old stories. It was truly

116 *Didde Maria Humle and Sanne Frandsen*

a crusade against E-rail, and of course, also against our colleague" (Maria); and (c) management did not stand up for her in the media: "You would expect that our company would counter the story, but it is apparently company policy that you do not discuss things through the newspaper" (Noah).

Applying Greimas's actantial model to the counter-narratives opposing the media, we see that the protagonist and active subject are narrated as the ticket inspector who simply wants to do her job, which in this case is understood as fining and reprimanding a passenger without a ticket. Implicitly, E-rail remains in the fixed position of the sender and the customer the receiver; however, the ticket inspector is narrated as a person without support in battling—not only customers' misbehavior but also the negative press and management denouncing the ticket inspectors. No one is assigned the position of helper in these narratives; management is narrated as the anticipated helper but one that turns out to be an opponent as they leave the media's accusations against the ticket inspectors unquestioned. In their story work, many of the ticket inspectors mention that the ticket inspector involved in the episode had to be on a sick leave for a long period after the incident.

Countering the Media—Narrating an Alternative Identity of the Service Worker

Another cluster of stories often performed by the ticket inspectors during interviews oppose the dominating narratives of the media portraying the ticket inspectors as providing poor customer service, fining and mistreating the weakest massagers without necessarily referencing to specific episodes or incidents portrayed in the media. In these story performances, the ticket inspectors primarily construct themselves in opposition to this negative image by accentuating their roles as 'service workers' and as dedicated people taking pride in doing the job well and providing a good service to the customers:

> I have had some nice conversations on the train with people. I like to tell people, when I walk through, for example, "[O]h, this is really beautiful, what you are knitting." Then we have a short [moment . . .] I have noticed when I do things like that, when I praise a small child, it spreads. Then others might have listened, so the next people you meet—you have already established a good communication with them. Then somebody can say—this is not real, but for me it is real. For me this is who I am. (Lillian)

> I have even accomplished, when we come home at night, and we have been delayed, if they [customers] have not reached the last bus, I have given old ladies a lift home. I could be completely indifferent . . . [. . .] People who need to go to a funeral, who we get there on time. Yes, we really, really pull many chestnuts out of the fire, which never come to

Organizational Identity Negotiations   117

E-rail's knowledge. I do not expect to get any extra acknowledgment or extra pat on the back, I see it as part of my job, and I consider it as a huge challenge and a mega-advantage of my job, that I can do these things. (Noah)

Providing good service is often narrated as something natural and frequently occurring: "I think, I do it all the time—help with the luggage if it is an old lady, because it doesn't say, that we have to do this. I help with a stroller, we are not expected to do that either. I think that is the little extra thing" (Anna). Furthermore, as in this example, service is often constructed as something extra not expected of the ticket inspectors as part of their formal obligations or job description. In these types of story performances, the service work is described as defining who the service workers are as individuals. "For me this is who I am" and as a group of employees "we really, really pull a lot of chestnuts out of the fire," often *we* signifies 'the ticket inspectors as oppose to E-rail and management—"which never comes to E-rail's knowledge." The ticket inspectors own discretion and ability to bend the rules is narrated as vital helpers in providing good service, "that is the good thing about being here—the level of freedom. We can bend the rules, as we like." (Martin)

Applying Greimas's actantial model to the counter-narratives makes an alternative understanding of 'who we are.' In the story work, positioning themselves as 'service workers,' the ticket inspectors are the main subjects wanting to provide good customer experiences (objects) to the customers (receivers) in the name of E-rail (sender). They highlight their freedom, their own discretion and ability to bend the rules as necessary in providing "the little extra." The customers are given a superior position as people who should be 'pleased' in all situations. In these counter-narratives, there are very few explicit positioning of an opponent and conflicts are toned down to naturalize the alternative narration of *who we are*, by accentuating that this is how it has always been. The counter-narratives of the ticket inspectors as *service workers* stands in stark contrast to the dominating media narratives positioning the ticket inspectors as someone who treats the customers poorly and unethically.

Countering Management—Opposing the Management's Narrative

As illustrated above, the ticket inspectors often oppose the negative image constructed by the media and instead perform themselves as workers dedicated to provide good service. Related to these stories, the ticket inspectors simultaneously counter the dominating narratives of management where management position themselves as heroes who ensure a good customer service by their initiatives of, introducing the sales trolley and a new service manual as well as adjusting the rules of ticket inspection. Counter to this, the empirical material consists of many everyday work stories of ticket inspectors' where management is constructed as the opponents in the quest of providing good

118 *Didde Maria Humle and Sanne Frandsen*

customer experiences. These stories are about how the ticket inspectors, though they do their best, cannot provide superior customer service because management pushes them to become more (time) efficient and makes rules and regulations that do not match the everyday work conditions or ideals of the ticket inspectors:

> I have told some of our managers that I am afraid that we are going to snap at some of the customers out there because we are a little short-tempered. Because we might try to achieve more than we can, and E-rail also says that we must learn to realize that we cannot do it all, even though we have got a nice little book telling us how to prioritize. [. . .] However, I guess I have an idea that I should try to do it all. Then I get a little snippy. I did that last week. Last week, I had one [passenger] who should have a discount. [. . .] There has been a lot [of new types of tickets], and I probably have a little difficulty in remembering the different types, and I could not find the code that I needed. [. . .] I stood there and was about to boil over because I was busy, and I was getting off at [name of city], and this was right before [this city]. Without asking her, I just take her phone and show it to my colleagues in the crew compartment. It is right next-door. Therefore, I will just take it and slip out to ask my colleagues who are out there. What do I do? They also looked at it, and one said she do not get a discount on that, it is only in the metropolitan area. Then I went back to her, and she was all mad at me because I had taken her phone without asking. I did not realize that I had done something wrong by taking it with me. 'It was not satisfactory that I took her phone', she gave me a rant. Then I tell her that I had to ask a colleague for advice, and then I say that I cannot find the ID from the text message. [. . .] Thus, she did not get discount. Moreover, the way I was apologizing to her was probably not as wholeheartedly.
>
> (Maria)

In this piece of story work, the ticket inspector narrates herself as someone who wants to do her job and provide a good customer experience. However, she is prevented from doing this because of the managements' new initiatives, added time pressure and more complicated work tasks in her job on the train, which leave her overworked, stressed and short-tempered. This narrative starts out positioning her discretion to solve the problem as the helper in enabling her to provide service. Though this is not received well by the customer, thus the ticket inspector 'snaps' back and shifts her focus toward management as opponents—holding management responsible for the incident. E-rail is narrated as a synonym with management, and thus exclusive of the ticket inspectors' "we" in this quote. The divide between 'us' as ticket inspectors and 'them' as management is significant in these counter-narratives. Management is often positioned as the opponent of providing good service as they, according to the stories of the ticket inspectors,

Organizational Identity Negotiations 119

ignore the human factor and are only preoccupied with standardization and efficiency. By this conduct they question if E-rail (excluding the ticket inspectors) should be a legitimate provider (sender) of good customer service (object) to the customer (receiver).

The ticket inspectors instead narrate themselves as concerned with helping the passengers and taking their different predispositions and needs as human beings into considerations:

> However, we work with people. Not boxes or things to be painted, which run on the assembly line. It is Mr. And Mrs. Smith, it is little Louise and Peter and Christian with cats and dogs, prams and bicycles. It is like in hospitals. You cannot write that it takes Ms. Smith 10 seconds to climb aboard and multiply by 200. Some people need much help—others do not. [. . .] Some spend all our time.
>
> (Daniel)

The narratives of 'failed' customer service portrays the ticket inspector as the hero, trying to provide good customer service but is prevented from it by the opponent management because of 'their' new rules, service guidelines and added time pressure.

Countering the Management—Narrating an Alternative Identity of E-rail

In the ticket inspectors' story work, they do not only position themselves as 'service workers' but also as heroes saving the future of E-rail. These counter-narratives counter management narration of service as driving the sales trolley and following the guideline. The counter-narratives should also be analyzed in the light of internal talk about outsourcing or downsizing the entire department of service personnel on the trains. While this is an acute threat, it is not very explicit in this cluster of counter-narratives; often the 'us'/'them' conflict is downplayed, and a more inclusive 'we' signifying the entire organizational is used. In these narratives, the ticket inspectors suggest a variety of alternative understandings of what it means to provide service as legitimization of why they are needed on the trains—also in the future:

> The role of the ticket inspector is—and this is still fundamental in my view of the terminology and soul in relation to the company—it is to take care of our customers. In addition, the concept is, of course, having to talk to Mr. And Mrs. Smith, when they get into the train. Give them the appreciation, when you come and ask for their ticket because they have spent time and effort to buy it, and there are many people who consider it as a kind of appreciation, that we are present. The next problem is to take care of those who do not have their ticket, and it is to defend

120 *Didde Maria Humle and Sanne Frandsen*

the interests of the company because if we were not there, people could just travel free, and those who do have a ticket, feel cheated if those who do not have tickets will not be confronted. (Daniel)

I believe that the customers are extremely pleased with us. I often speak to our customers about how the future scenario may look like. We often hear this song, "there is never any service here" or "oh, now you have the time to check my ticket? I have been sitting here for two hours". Then I take the time to talk to people about how the scenario would be [without us . . .] There is certainly no help for the disabled, senior citizens, and those with heavy suitcases. Moreover, when you talk to people, you can see that they become almost wild in their eyes "this must never happen." I have a feeling that people like that we are out there. They want us there. (Brian)

In terms of Greimas's actantial model, the narrative structure of the counter-narratives proposing an alternative understanding of "what we do" and "who we are" follows a similar structure to the other sets of counter-narratives, in which the ticket inspectors position themselves as active subjects working to provide good customer experiences (object) to the customer (receiver) on behalf of E-rail (sender). In narrating an alternative understanding of 'what we do,' the ticket inspectors highlight ticketing as a way of providing service, similar to helping those in need and providing the little extra (as helpers). As such, they argue that they are in fact 'wanted' on the trains and compose the very 'soul' of E-rail. The management as opponent is rather implicit in these narratives, again downplaying the conflict suggesting that this is a more 'natural' or institutionalized way of understanding the role. Implicitly, the counter-narratives do refer to the perceived threat of being laid off from E-rail by downsizing.

Ticket Inspectors Countering their Own Stories

The previously presented counter-narratives appear to be grounded in a certain narrative practice signifying the importance of the storytelling community created among ticket inspectors, where the narratives are told, refined and polished. They seem well rehearsed and 'finished'; everyone follows the same actantial structure and fixed positioning of ticket inspectors, customers and management. These counter-narratives, we propose, have a stabilizing effect and emerge as powerful sense-making narratives successfully coexisting with the media and management's dominating narratives and creating a parallel 'reality' among ticket inspectors. The interviews, however, also reveal a different type of counter-narratives in the ticket inspectors' story work that is more subtle, fragmented and less rehearsed. They follow a different actantial model and position the ticket inspector and customers differently. Furthermore, they are counter-narratives to the ticket inspectors'

Organizational Identity Negotiations 121

collective understandings of 'who we are' and 'what we do.' These stories are about misbehaving or even threatening customers:

> Especially young people who have been at the pub, and then you will inspect their ticket. As a woman, you may well face unpleasant expressions like "dirty whore." (Maria)

> However, it does happen quite often that people spit at us. It is an ugly experience, but I guess it says more about them than it does about us. It is still you who are being attacked, though. (Noah)

> Researcher: "You got slapped in the face?" "Yes, when I was about to exit the train. He hit me with his elbow so that my glasses came off and were destroyed. It evolved a little more than it should have done." (André)

The counter–story lines of misbehaving customers are found in almost all the interviews. However, they are often just hinted at or shortly touched upon. Often, they are fragments of storytelling and not full-blown retrospective narratives like many of the stories presented earlier.

The customers are no longer named customers but rather 'people' or 'society'. Despite the severeness of the situations narrated—pregnant ticket inspectors being kicked, ticket inspectors being threatened with knives or guns, ticket inspectors being physically attacked on the train or the platforms—the frequency is often downplayed "I have been here for 25 years, and I have never had any remotely violent experience." It appears as if it is difficult to find a 'place' for these types of counter-narratives in their own dominating stories of the customers in the position of 'the one to please.'

The ticket inspectors' position as a hero is challenged in these counter-narratives, and the ticket inspectors are portrayed as victims. They argue that their authority as a ticket inspector has been eroded due to the increased demands of providing service:

> Earlier, there was an authority of being a ticket inspector. People listened to you, but it is not like that anymore. On top of that, they [more experienced ticket inspectors] also need to go with a sales trolley and put up with the many pertinent comments from the audience, who think we are stupid. (Eva)

> I have also been spat upon. They shall not do that. They shall not touch me, and they shall not spit on me. That they call me a stupid bitch, I do not care. You can easily shake that off.
> Researcher: Does that happen often?
> Anna: Yes. There was one the other day—because I told him that it was his responsibility to have a proper ticket "but there must be some service on the train, and I had to get my act together and provide service"—"well,

I cannot buy your ticket for you". The man who spat on me, it was very close and right in my face, and then he ended up leaving. He said that he would kill me as he walked out of the train. You think about it for a few days, but then it is over. It is not me—it is the uniform, and you must always remember that. I am just doing my job. (Anna)

In both examples, 'providing service' is evoked as something eroding the authority of ticket inspectors. The passengers are positioned as misbehaving, violent or threatening people, preventing the ticket inspectors from "doing their jobs."

Applying Greimas's actantial model, the narrative structure of the counter-narratives challenging their own dominating narratives is similar to the counter-narratives opposing the media, and they share the victimization of the ticket inspectors and stress that the ticket inspectors are being subject to unfair treatment by the press (in the previous examples) or by the "'people' or 'audience' in the present examples. Again we see, that E-rail is implicitly positioned as the sender of customer service (object) to the customer (receiver). However, here the customers' position as the 'superior' receiver, 'the one to please' is destabilized, as 'passengers' and 'providing service' are described as opponents to the ticket inspectors' quest of doing their jobs. In contrast to the counter-narratives specifically opposing the media, the role of management is conspicuously silent in these types of stories. No one is identified as helpers, and the ticket inspectors are portraying themselves as being 'alone' without any help battling the misbehaving customers. This notion of working alone is constructed notably differently than in the earlier examples, where being independent and autonomous made the job interesting and rewarding while simultaneously allowing the ticket inspectors to do that little extra thing and provide good service to the customers.

Discussion

In this chapter, we see organizations as a storytelling communities (Boje 2001; Linde 2001, 2009) and contribute by highlighting the role of dominant and counter-narratives in organizational identity formation processes as a web of stories (Humle 2013, 2014) performed and negotiated by organizational members and external stakeholders, here exemplified by the voice of the media. The counter-narratives presented in this chapter demonstrate how the ticket inspectors directly draw upon, negotiate and challenge the externally narrated, yet dominating narratives of the organization. In particular, the notion of *customer service* emerges as a contested space. Performing stories directly counter to the dominating narratives of the media and of the management the ticket inspectors are occupied with setting the stories of outsiders and insiders straight (Boje 1995)—negotiating through their everyday story work alternative answers to important questions of, for example,

Organizational Identity Negotiations 123

"Who provide service?" and "Who assists and who obstructs the quest of providing good service?" This is a constant process of negotiating many possible story lines and different actantial positions. The ticket inspectors explicitly draw upon and counter the media's dominating narrative of the organization, yet they also use counter-narratives to construct an alternative 'reality.' While some counter-narratives appear relatively fixed and finished, a set of more subtle and fragmented counter-narratives were also detected. In these more fragmented and antenarrative counter-stories the ticket inspectors were countering themselves by constructing and positioning customers not as the ones to help and positively attend to by providing good service but as rude and violent opponents making everyday work troublesome and difficult to cope with. On the basis of these findings, our case study contributes in several ways to extend the current understanding of counter-narratives and their roles in organizational identity formation and storytelling community dynamics and complexities.

Theoretical Contributions

First, the findings enhance our existing knowledge on counter-narratives by demonstrating that the tension between dominant and counter-narratives are visible in different actantial positioning of organizational actors. In the empirical material there are examples of stories narrated by media, management and the ticket inspectors referring to the same event, as in the example of the episode of the 12-year-old girl being locked up by a ticket inspector; however, the positioning of subjects, helpers and villains shifts and classes. The stories have the same fabula but different syuzhets (see Scheffel [2010] for the distinction between fabula and syuzhets). In this way the actantial model enables us to explore the performative aspects of the story work of organizational members and illustrate how the negotiation of meaning between dominant and counter-narratives is in part about casting heroes, helpers and villains in syuzhets. Thus, the characters of dominant and counter-narratives are often the same (customers, ticket inspectors, management), yet they are appointed variating actantial positions and thus different understandings of possible intensions, motives and possibilities of actions are produced. Utilizing the actantial model in analyzing the relationship between dominant and counter-narratives enable us to see that one important defining feature of counter-narratives is the creative recasting or replacement of actantial positions against the ones prescribed by dominant narratives.

Second, the findings demonstrate how counter-narratives produce parallel, yet rather stable, understandings of the organizational identity. The performance of counter-narratives created for the ticket inspectors shared references and alternative, understandings opposing the dominant identity narratives told by the media and management, resulting in coexisting, parallel understandings of 'who we are.' Simultaneously, a relatively fixed positioning of heroes, villains, opponents and helpers by both organizational members

124 *Didde Maria Humle and Sanne Frandsen*

and external stakeholders (e.g., the media) created rather stable understandings of the organizational identity. Previous studies of organizational image and identity (Dutton and Dukerich 1991; Elsbach and Kramer 1996; Gioia et al. 2000; Ravasi and Schultz 2006) tend to focus on organizational-level changes and efforts to convert the organizational image. Gioia et al. (2000) used the term *adaptive instability* to describe the mutual influencing alignment of self-definition with the environment. However, this study shows no evidence of successful organizational transformation as a result of the dominating, negative media narrative. Instead, the study bears witness of a different set of organizational dynamics rooted in the counter-narratives creating coexisting, multiple (and even conflicting) understandings of organizational identity in ongoing processes of establishing a sense of continuity and stability. As such this study similar to Linde (2009) suggests that the counter-narratives create pluralistic understandings of 'who we are.' Multiple story lines and understandings coexist in an unfolding *Tamara* conversation taking place across time and space, constantly negotiating the identity of the organization, the members' role and work, and central organizational phenomena like 'customer service.'

Third, the findings illuminate the important role of counter-narratives in establishing and maintaining a storytelling community among the organizational members. The sharing of counter-narratives allows the ticket inspectors to collectively make sense of their role, the organization and their everyday work by introducing different measurements of success and understandings of what it means to provide good service in a time when a positive narration of the organizational identity is under pressure. Paradoxically, by constantly referring to the dominant narratives of the media and management the counter-narratives keeps the dominant narratives alive and consolidate their dominant power (for more see Gabriel's chapter in this volume), yet by telling and retelling the counter-narratives the *counter-narratives* gain the authority (Kuhn's chapter, in this volume) to guide the members meaning making and behaviors. The counter-narratives does not only counter but also almost marginalize the dominating narratives of management and the media, thus facilitating the coexistence of multiple story lines of 'who we are.' The sharing of counter-narratives enables the ticket inspectors to successfully form an 'us' against 'them,' protecting the members against accusations and creating a shared sense of community among the ticket inspectors, who largely work independently on the train. The parallel understandings of the 'who we are' and 'what we do' allow the ticket inspectors to gather around more productive and positive notions of their role and everyday work to establish a positive storytelling community. While the media and management predominantly position the ticket inspectors as deviant villains, the ticket inspectors' story work enables them to collectively navigate these dominant narratives and through counter-narratives create positive self-positionings, protecting their self-image and increasing their space of action (Holmer-Nadesan 1996). Future research may, however, seek to more

Organizational Identity Negotiations 125

fully understand how a community solely engaged in counter-narrative story work may experience a negative closure, which leaves little space for narratives positive toward the management and organization as a whole.

Fourth, the study of the ticket inspectors at E-rail illustrates the significant and necessary role of counter-narratives in producing meaning and positive collective identities. As such the counter-stories of our study is different than the 'noisy silences' described by Linde (2009) as they display an ability to not only counter the official stories of the organization but to give voice to alternative understandings, which may not 'win' over the dominant narratives yet still significantly challenge their authoritative status. However, we also encountered more subtle, fragmented, antenarrative counter-stories related to the misbehaving customers and the ticket inspectors as victims of abuse on the trains. These stories were 'noisy silences' often only hinted at or partly told, rarely shared as full-blown BME narratives. The fragile counter-narratives opposing the ticket inspectors' stable and well-rehearsed counter-narratives remained 'silenced,' because they opposed the collectively narrated positive self-positioning of ticket inspectors as heroes. Yet, they were 'noisy' because the painful and disturbing events, though not easy to talk about, continued to be a part of the everyday life of the ticket inspectors and thus difficult to completely disregard. The 'noisy silences' of the ticket inspectors direct our attention to the dynamic, fragmented and polyphonic nature of story work, which at times, particularly when working with interview transcripts, emerge as a form of "cognitive dissonance" (see Czarniawska's chapter in this volume), however, also bearing evidence of the construction of multiple story lines intersecting in ongoing *Tamara* conversations. Other examples are when the ticket inspectors tell counter-narratives about themselves as exclusive of 'E-rail'—'E-rail' signifying management, and simultaneously as central organizational members and saviours of 'E-rail's' future. Or when they narrate themselves as free, independent, autonomous agents and simultaneously as dupes of management's initiatives and increased control. The image of the organization as a Tamara-conversation enables us to see the multiplicity of potential story lines being narrated and performed across time and space some more elaborated or visible and others more fragile and disclosed.

Methodological Contributions

Besides these theoretical contributions our case study also provides methodological insights into the empirical work with counter-narratives. While dominant and counter-narratives in some cases may be easily distinguishable, our case study shows how media, management and the ticket inspectors all engage in dominant and counter storytelling, and thus, the categories of dominant and counter-narratives becomes blurred and more of an analytical distinction than an empirical observation. Even so in our analysis it became clear that the ticket inspectors story work was intertextually related

126 Didde Maria Humle and Sanne Frandsen

to and often constructed in direct opposition or 'response' to the dominant narratives of the media and management. The dominant voices of the media and management served as a backdrop against which the ticket inspectors positioned themselves as organizational members. Furthermore, the dynamics of dominating and counter-narratives were embedded in complex and sometimes reversed processes of everyday storytelling practices. When studying both stabilizing and dynamic aspects of organizational storytelling, this leads to methodological and analytical challenges in deciding when something is dominating or counter. The division between the two, if one is not careful, easily leads to simplified or static portraits of storytelling practices not adequately describing the everyday story work of organizational members as they struggle to make sense of their experiences and negotiate different notions of 'who we are' and 'what we do' as individual, groups and organizations. Taking this into consideration the conceptual framework of dominating and counter-narratives still proved useful in explicating how different voices and notions become dominating in the sense that they construct powerful positioning of organizational members not easily ignored. At the same time the counter-storytelling practices of the ticket inspectors in our case form a strong opposition almost marginalizing the stories of management.

Practical Contributions

Previous research has argued that negative perceptions of outsiders would serve as a mirror for the organizational identity formation and often prompt organizational members to revise the organizational identity in the eyes of both 'outsiders' *and* 'insiders' (Dutton and Dukerich 1991; Gioia et al. 2000; Hatch and Schultz 2002). In this paper, we illustrate that such collective organizational 'soul-searching' and change may not automatically follow a public discredited image. As the dominant and counter-narratives repeatedly maintain a relatively stable, oppositional actantial positioning and syuzhets, the different parties appear to naturalize different, opposing worldviews and conceptions of organizational identities. These different notions do not seem to intersect or blend but instead to coexist in parallel, yet ongoing struggles over meaning. The counter-narrative storytelling practices of ticket inspectors enables them to handle the negative stories of the media and management; however, it does not succeed in challenging the dominant narratives and change the negative conceptions of external stakeholders such as the media and customers. The prospective of E-rail significantly changing the discrediting dominant narratives thus seem small as of now. Taking this into consideration we advise practitioners to pay close attention the story work of organizational members and their positioning of themselves and others— to engage in more productive and collaborative definitions of 'who we are' and 'what we do,' making the battle of a negative external conception of the organization a mutual one.

References

Bamberg, M. and M. Andrews. (eds). 2004. *Considering counter-narratives: Narrating, resisting, making sense*. Amsterdam and Philadelphia: John Benjamins.

Belova, O. 2010. "Polyphony and the Sense of Self in Flexible Organizations." *Scandinavian Journal of Management* 26 (1): 67–76.

Boje, D. M. 1995. "Stories of the Storytelling Organization: A Postmodern Analysis of Disney as 'Tamara-Land'." *Academy of Management Journal* 38 (4): 997–1035.

Boje, D. M. 2001. *Narrative methods for organizational & communication research*. London: Sage.

Boje, D. M. 2006. "Breaking Out of Narrative's Prison: Improper Story in Storytelling Organization." *Story, Self, Society: An Interdisciplinary Journal of Storytelling Studies* 2 (2): 28–49.

Boje, D. M. (ed.). 2011. *Storytelling and the future of organizations: An antenarrative handbook*. New York: Routledge.

Brown, A. D. 2006. "A Narrative Approach to Collective Identities." *Journal of Management Studies* 43 (4): 731–753.

Chreim, S. 2005. "The Continuity–Change Duality in Narrative Texts of Organizational Identity." *Journal of Management Studies* 42 (3): 567–593.

Chreim, S. 2007. "Social and Temporal Influences on Interpretations of Organizational Identity and Acquisition Integration: A Narrative Study." *The Journal of Applied Behavioral Science* 43 (4): 449–480.

Coupland, C., and D. B. Brown. 2004. "Constructing Organizational Identities on the Web: A Case Study of Royal Dutch/Shell." *Journal of Management Studies* 41 (8): 1326–1347.

Cunliffe, A. L., and C. Coupland. 2012. "Narrative Sensemaking: From Hero to Villain to Hero: Making Experience Sensible through Embodied Narrative." *Human Relations* 65 (1): 63–88.

Czarniawska, B. 2004. *Narratives in social science research*. London: Sage.

Driver, M. 2009. "From Loss to Lack: Stories of Organizational Change as Encounters with Failed Fantasies of Self, Work and Organization." *Organization* 16 (3): 353–369.

Dutton, J. E., and M. J. Dukerich. 1991. "Keeping an Eye on the Mirror: Image and Identity in Organizational Adaptation." *Academy of Management Journal* 34 (3): 517–554.

Elsbach, K., and R. M. Kramer. 1996. "Members' Responses to Organizational Identity Threats: Encountering and Countering the Business Week Rankings." *Administrative Science Quarterly* 41 (3): 442–476.

Frandsen, S. 2012. "Organizational Image, Identification, and Cynical Distance: Prestigious Professional in a Low-Prestige Organization." *Management Communication Quarterly* 26 (3): 351–373.

Frandsen, S. 2015. "Doing Ethnography in a Paranoid Organization: An Autoethnographic Account." *Journal of Organizational Ethnography* 4 (2): 162–176.

Gioia, D. A., M. Schultz, and K. G. Corley. 2000. "Organizational Identity, Image and Adaptive Instability." *Academy of Management Review* 25 (1): 63–81.

Harrison, J. D. (2000): "Multiple Imaginings of Institutional Identity: A Case Study of a Large Psychiatric Research Hospital." *The Journal of Applied Behavioral Science* 36 (4): 425–455.

Hatch, M. J., and M. Schultz 2002. "The Dynamics of Organizational Identity." *Human Relations* 55 (8): 989–1018.

128 Didde Maria Humle and Sanne Frandsen

Hazen, M. A. 1993. "Towards Polyphonic Organization." *Journal of Organizational Change Management* 6 (5): 15–26.

Holmer-Nadesan, M. 1996. "Organizational Identity and Space of Action." *Organization Studies* 17 (1): 49–81.

Humle, D. M. 2013. *Fortællinger om arbejde*. Copenhagen: Copenhagen Business School Press.

Humle, D. M. 2014. "Remembering Who WE Are: Memories of Identity through Storytelling." *Tamara Journal for Critical Organization Inquiry* 12 (3): 11–24.

Humle, D. M., and A. R. Pedersen. 2015. "Fragmented Work Stories: Developing an Antenarrative Approach by Discontinuity, Tensions and Editing." *Management Learning* 46 (5): 582–597.

Humphreys, M., and A. D. Brown. 2002. "Narratives of Organizational Identity and Identification: A Case Study of Hegemony and Resistance." *Organization Studies* 23 (3): 421–447.

Kjærgaard A., M. Morsing, and D. Ravasi. 2011. "Mediating Identity: A Study of Media Influence on Organizational Identity Construction in a Celebrity Firm." *Journal of Management Studies* 48 (3): 514–543.

Linde, C. 2001. "The Acquisition of a Speaker by a Story: How History becomes Memory and Identity." *Ethos* 28 (4): 608–632.

Linde, C. 2009. *Working the past, narrative and institutional memory*. Oxford: Oxford University Press.

Mishler, E. G. 1999. *Storylines*. London: Harvard University Press.

Ravasi, D. and M. Schultz. 2006. "Responding to Organizational Identity Threats: Exploring the Role of Organizational Culture." *Academy of Management Journal* 49 (3): 433–458.

Riessman, C. K. 2008. *Narrative methods for the human sciences*. London: Sage.

Scheffel, M. 2010. "Narrative constitution." In *The living handbook of narratology*. Hamburg: Hamburg University Press. http://wikis.sub.uni hamburg.de/lhn/index.php/Narrative_Constitution

Søderberg, A. M. 2003. "Sensegiving and sensemaking in an integration process: A narrative approach to the study of an international acqusition." In *Narratives we organize by*, edited by B. Czarniawska and P. Gagliardi, 3–36. Amsterdam: John Benjamins.

Strangleman, T. 1999. "The Nostalgia of Organisations and the Organisation of Nostalgia: Past and Present in the Contemporary Railway Industry." *Sociology* 33 (4): 725–746.

Wang, Y., and C. W. Roberts. 2005. "Actantial Analysis: Greima's Structural Approach to the Analysis of Self-Narratives." *Narrative Inquiry* 15 (1): 51–74.

6 Fractal Change Management and Counter-Narrative in Cross-Cultural Change

Marita Svane, Erika Gergerich and David M. Boje

Introduction

Fractal change management as originally developed by Henderson and Boje (2015) is an approach to managing organizing processes and cultural dynamics. By looking for and thematically identifying fractals patterns that emerge in storytelling, fractal change management offers a theoretical framework that help managers to understand what fractal patterns are and how they influence organizational change and development processes. The ambition is to develop a methodology for analyzing and working with fractal change processes. The theoretical framework for fractal change management implies working with key concepts such as fractals, narratives, counter-narratives, living story, as well as the antenarrative sociomaterial organizing processes as an approach to understand organizational change and cultural dynamics.

We define *storytelling* as the whole playing field, with three interweaving energies: 'living story webs' in space–time–materiality event-ness, with more abstract 'grand narratives', interconnected by quantum relationships of 'antenarrative.' Simply put, antenarrative is a bridge between living story webs and grand narratives (and counter-narrative) by underlying antenarrative patterns. Two pathways between living story and grand narrative, the linear and cyclic antenarratives, are from the past and are predicted to recur in the future. This is known as retrospective sense-making. The other two pathways, the spiral and the rhizome, move from the future to the past. In this chapter, we relate these two temporal pathways to Heidegger, Bakhtin and Deleuze's material ontologies, by Boje called 'quantum storytelling.' We want to look at the wider sociality of storytelling, at what is called the fractal patterns of its cross-cultural sociality.

There are patterns of interplay at the level of cultural ritual and other sociality behaviors that are fractal. "A fractal is defined here as a recurrence of self-similar and/or instability processes across scales: individual, unit, inter-unit, organization, inter-organization, regional, international, global" (Boje 2015, 10). Our contribution is a fractal analytic theory and method to understand the dynamics of narrative and counter-narratives.

Our purpose is to work out the patterns in cross-cultural storytelling dynamics, at the level of narrative–counter-narrative, living stories and the

130 *Marita Svane et al.*

antenarrative threads of embodied intentionality that tie the storytelling field to its ritual and ceremonial practices. The contribution therefore is to go beyond the text and orality and to get at the ritual practices, the tacit and prereflexive ones. In this way we endeavor to do something beyond retrospective sense-making and get at the subaltern aspects of the spatializing, temporizing and mattering of the storytelling texture.

In the beginning of the chapter, we present a teaser to two case studies on cross-cultural dynamics. Then we proceed to unfold the fractal analytic storytelling theory and methodology for analyzing and understanding this cross-cultural dynamics. Finally, we discuss the cases by applying the theoretical and methodological framework and close the chapter by summarizing our research contributions and pointing out direction for further research.

Teaser: The Cross-Cultural Merger Case

The merger case presents a story about the struggle between cross-cultural counter-narratives and the antenarrative process toward the formation of a new dominating cultural narrative.

In 2008, and voted for with only a marginal majority, two competing agricultural consultancy nonprofit associations (Alpha House and Beta/Delta House) decided to merge and form a new company. Because of the long history of intense competition and inherited hatred, the merger was strongly opposed by especially Alpha House, including a number of managers, employees, customers and owners. The Alpha opponents preferred to merge with another major competitor on the market called Zeta House as they already had some insight knowledge of this company through their network relations. In fact, this was attempted, but as the merger proposal failed, the only rational option left was then to merge with Beta/Delta House.

As a result of a previous merger, Beta/Delta House is composed by the two houses, Beta and Delta, each located in two different cities, and run from the headquarter of Beta House. Alpha House is located in a third city. After the merger, the headquarter continues to be located at Beta House as the biggest of the three houses, measured in numbers of employees and the size of the city. The merged company employs about 200 employees and is owned by its customers.

The strategic and economic advantages of the merger were clear. Due to the merger, the company became the largest consultancy company in its main market area and the fifth largest at the national level. With a presence in the three main cities, it remained close to the local customers at the same time as it reinforced its market position. By merging, it eliminated its strong competition against each other in a very competitive market characterized by intense rivalry.

Also between the merging companies, severe conflicts arose and ended up endangering the survival of the company. In Alpha House, the merger was referred to as marrying their worst enemy; a storytelling that contributed

Fractal Change Management and Counter-Narrative 131

to reproducing and confirming the Us–Them cross-cultural identity construction. Because the headquarters were located in the home city of Beta House and because Beta House was a bigger company as regard the number of employees and branches, Alpha House feared that the merger would be an acquisition in disguise. To reinforce their position in the merger, Alpha maintained that they economically contributed much more to the merger than Beta/Delta that according to Alpha were performing below expectation. However, because the top management omitted to create an opening balance sheet, this dispute was never clarified, and the balance was never settled. Thus, the issue of who contributed the most was an ongoing dispute, inflaming the relationship and further cementing the Us–Them narrative.

Due to the mutual hatred and the Alpha House resistance to the merger, the top management hesitated to attempt any integrating of the merging companies. Thus, the economic and synergetic advantages of the merger were lost, threatening the survival of the company.

In two-and-a-half years, the organization thus experienced four different CEOs and a board of directors who discussed their disagreements in the public media. A drop in customer and employee satisfaction reflected the lack of trust in the company and the management. Not surprisingly, this development resulted in a growing deficit, increasing from about USD 880,000 in 2008 to 1,690,000 at 2009.

This was the situation when the fourth CEO, Steven, was hired in September 2010 to turn around the company. Initiating cost reduction and taking steps toward a strategic and business development of the company, he succeeded in turning the deficit around to a surplus of $226,000 in 2012 and on $528,000 in the end of 2012. However, as the revenue continued to decrease from $21 million in 2010 to $18 million in September 2012, the company still faced major economic challenges, and Steven still needed to prove that the strategic actions initiated to increase sales and to further develop the business would pay off. Meanwhile, resistance in some parts of Alpha House grew and resulted in a chock when a whole Alpha department chose to resign in order to work with Zeta, the other competitor. As the customers started to flee in order to follow the resigned employees, this event, once more, pushed the company toward the precipice.

Teaser: The Homeless Veteran Theater Case

The second case involves homeless veterans in southern New Mexico. This case presents a storytelling between the dominant cultural narrative, in which the homeless are negatively stereotyped and the transformation of this narrative through antenarrative theater performance.

Veterans were identified at two locations in Las Cruces, New Mexico. The first was a Department of Housing and Urban Development (HUD) apartment complex, designed specifically for veterans in transition. The second location was the Mesilla Valley Community of Hope (MVCH). The

132   Marita Svane et al.

Community of Hope offers tent shelters, along with a number of social support services, all located in a single locality (MVCH 2015). There is an over-representation of veterans in the homeless population; therefore, MVCH offers services specific to the veteran population (Perl 2014).

Homeless individuals are often negatively stereotyped by the dominant culture in a number of ways. Knecht and Martinez (2009) suggest that labeling the homeless as alcoholics, drug abusers or mentally ill most likely occurs due to infrequent intergroup contact between those who are homeless and those who are not. Veteran's Theater was developed in an attempt to counteract negative stereotypes of the homeless. Interestingly, this project may have a more unique means of dispelling myths in that this method includes storytelling by homeless veterans to the public rather than the public offering assistance to homeless veterans.

In this chapter, the proposed fractal analytic theory contributes by providing a framework for understanding the cross-cultural storytelling dynamics as it occurs in the interplay between dominant narratives and cross-cultural counter-narratives played out at the level of antenarrative processes in the two cases. To comprehend the dynamics of the two cross-cultural cases, we need to develop the fractal storytelling framework.

Antenarrative Fractal Theory and Methodology

The "quantum storytelling field" theory has been worked out in several books (Boje 2014; Boje and Henderson 2014; Henderson and Boje 2015) and articles (Haley and Boje 2014; Boje, Haley and Saylors 2015; Boje, Rosile, Saylors and Saylors 2015; Svane and Boje 2015) and is the topic of the annual Quantum Storytelling Conference (http://quantumstorytelling.org). The quantum storytelling field is defined here as the relation of grand narratives and living story webs, with antenarrative threads playing important prereflexive transformative relationships in *spacetimemattering*. Spacetimemattering is the inseparability of spatializing, temporalizing, and mattering in the ontological situation. This storytelling ontology is to be unfolded in the following.

The storytelling field consists of three dimensions (see figure 6.1): the interweaving of past-oriented narratives, here-and-now living stories and the antenarrative relation between narratives and living stories.

The dominant narratives and counter-narratives follow the linear storytelling structure from the beginning to the middle (plot) and to the end (BME). Time and space are already defined in the movement from the past (beginning) to the end (the future) through a middle part (the means for change and development). The narrative assumes a coherent pattern according to which the patterns of the past are projected on and repeated in the future. The narratives may branch into several fragmented narratives that may differ from each other or even be contradictory and conflicting. This is further explained in the section on branching narratives. We understand the counter-narrative as those narratives that are arising in opposition to the

Fractal Change Management and Counter-Narrative 133

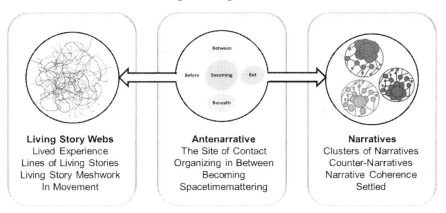

Figure 6.1 Triad Storytelling Model. Designed and developed by David Boje and Marita Svane.

narrative by taking a conflicting position. Both the fragmented narratives and the counter-narratives together form a fragmented cluster of narratives.

As a contrast to the structured and closed (counter-)narrative patterns, the living story web is open-ended and dynamically changing all the time. We understand the living story web as the ongoing development of simultaneous, polyphonic, fragmented story lines. These story lines are constituted from the lived experiences that are exchanged and challenged in open-ended dialogue, not yet collapsed into the narrative coherence but developing from the middle as a rhizome (explained later in the chapter).

The process of developing and organizing the story lines in the living story web is the focus on the antenarrative dimension of the storytelling field. The antenarrative contributes to a theoretical framework for understanding the processes that occur in the meeting between the living stories and the (counter-)narratives.

In the following, these three dimensions of the storytelling field are unfolded.

The main dominating narrative give rise to the production of not necessarily just one counter-narrative as a reaction but to a series, an assemblage of counter-narratives (Henderson and Boje 2015). The main narrative and the surrounding counter-narratives form a narrative cluster characterized by the tensed interplay between the different, competing, centripetal narratives. As the counter-narrative is a counter-reaction to the dominating narrative, they create their own 'fractal narrative' patterns. *Fractal narrative* is defined as "a narrative that finds its best accomplished form in the Web" in hyperlink networks (Boje 2015; Durate 2014, 284). The web need not be the Internet; rather, it can be constituted by a web of communicative praxis in discourse and in ritual relationships.

One way to think of the counter-narrative fractal is that it is a patterning called a 'branching fractal,' splitting into more and more counter-narratives

134 *Marita Svane et al.*

until the founding narrative is morphed into some new directionality and dissolubility of new facets (Heidegger 1962). The veteran case develops primarily as a branching fractal and provides an example of this fractal. The branching fractal may occur in a multidimensional way as illustrated in Figure 6.2.

The branching fractal illustrates an organizational change and development process that occurs through a branching process; that is, a growth that is splitting in more and more directions. For instance, an organization may grow through the development of new branches such as new subunits, new subspecialties and so forth. Some of these branches grow stronger than the others, as they are allocated with a growing number of people and other resources to nourish its further growth.

The branching fractal carries some similarity to the tree metaphor used by Deleuze and Guattari (1987). The tree metaphor illustrates that despite the growth, the development and the changes do not deviate from the linear structure of hierarchical growing. A tree can only grow in a vertical, more or less linear direction as from beginning to end. As such, the branching process follows a fractal narrative pattern of coherency and self-similarity. This is referred to as a narrative fractal pattern. The fractal pattern is repeated over and over again, permeating all the branches in accordance with the narrative

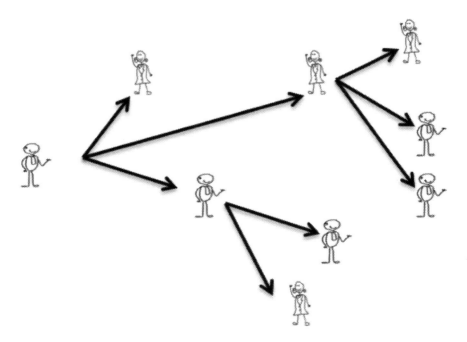

Figure 6.2 The Branching Fractal Narratives
Source: Designed and drawn by David Boje.

Fractal Change Management and Counter-Narrative 135

root. Hence, an assemblage or cluster of fractal narrative self-similar patterns emerges. This is, for instance, the case when the organization keeps on recruiting similar others. As the narratives belong to the same narrative root, there are no counter-narrative positions.

The branching fractal process may be open to diversity as the root fractal splits into a multidimensional number of branches from none at all to any number of branches (Henderson and Boje 2015). This type of branching process leads to diversified or conflicting fractal patterns. In our terminology, we refer to these fractal patterns as counter-narratives.

Another much more dynamical patterning is the rhizome fractal where parts are self-organizing, reterritorializing and deterritorializing lines of flight, generating nonhierarchical fractal patterns of multiplicity (Deleuze and Guattari 1987). As illustrated in Figure 6.3, "rhizome has no beginning or end; it is always in the middle, between things, interbeing, *intermezzo*" (1987, 25).

In a rhizome, the development and changes do not form a linear structure from beginning to end, from point to point, from position to position, but "it grows between," in the middle, along the lines of becoming (Deleuze and Guattari 1987, 19, 21; Ingold 2011). They contrast the narrative by being a short-term memory or even antimemory, as it works by variation, expansion, conquest and offshoots (Deleuze and Guattari 1987, 21). Consequently, the movement is not controlled by the past-oriented sense-making and collective memory of the organization.

In line with the definition of a rhizome, Deleuze and Guattari define an assemblage as the "increase in the dimensions of a multiplicity that necessarily changes in nature as it expands its connections. There are no points

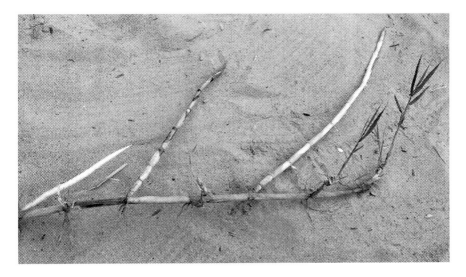

Figure 6.3 The Rhizome

136 *Marita Svane et al.*

or positions in a rhizome, such as those found in a structure, tree, or root. There are only lines" (1987, 8).

The assemblage consists of a multitude of rhizomatic antenarratives that move from present to future-shaping (Boje 2011, 9). Each of them is open and connectable, reversible and susceptible to constant modification and reworking, and still has multiple of entryways and exits, or lines of flight (Deleuze and Guattari 1987, 12, 21).

Applied on organizational change and development processes, the rhizomatic lines of flight illustrate the organizing processes in the political subterranean of the organization. Management may not always be successful in suppressing the voices of resistance, which may instead continue to influence the organizing processes from the shadow. In this chapter, the merger case is an example of such a process. Furthermore, taking a practice oriented perspective on organizing and strategizing processes, the rhizome may also illustrate how organizational development and change may occur in an open-ended process at the micro-practice level of the organization. As such the rhizome is made up from simultaneous, continuously changing and fragmented story lines that differ, overlap, contradict or even conflict with each other. This is what we refer to as fractal stories. When the stories collapse into one story, a rhizomatic narrative emerges. We use the rhizome to illustrate their process of development. The merger case works as an example of this sort of fractal development. In particular, the case clearly illustrates how an unnoticed ghost story line develops in the shadow as a line of flight.

Hence, the fractal branching narrative and counter-narrative patterns are not the complete picture of the storytelling occurring. Dominant cultural narratives and counter-narrative fractal patterns are interactive with the living stories, those individual, lived experiences. These form a different sort of fractality, which Boje (2015, 38) calls the fractal story: "A 'fractal story' is defined here as a web of fluid 'living story' interrelationships between urban-chaos and fractal-cyber-order that is centrifugal, veering away from order, toward anarchism, discontinuity, and the erratic, violent urbanism." The living story, unlike narrative (or counter-narrative), is happening in the middle as a rhizome and does not have the coherence of the narrative, which is always attempting to be monologic, to achieve generality and universality, be exorcising all its living stories. At the contrary, the centrifugal forces of the living story web foster the emergence of Little Wow Moments (LWM) that may lead to new story lines that break/rupture the narrative patterns.

LWM refer to events where we experience a moment of disclosure. The dominant narrative tends to overshadow and mediate our experience and works as a veal or closure, making us repeat its fractal pattern. LWM are thus those moments of greater clarity or insight that set the dominant narrative in relation to living stories and subsequently make the narrative less oppressive and reduces its control over living stories (Boje, Helmuth and Saylors 2013). In the context of this chapter, we understand little wow moments as fractal exceptions to the expectations of the fractal narrative patterns and rules. As such, the fractal story may rupture the fractal patterns (Svane and Boje 2015).

Fractal Change Management and Counter-Narrative 137

The LWM is a concept that contributes to our understanding of cultural dynamics. When organizational members achieve a moment of clarity, an insight into how they are caught by the stereotyping dominant counter-narratives, they may be able to reach beyond this estranging and inauthentic (to be explained later in the chapter) way of relating to each other. Hence, in the meeting between the living stories and the narrative, new rhizomatic directions may occur that rupture the narrative self-repeating pattern.

The process of narrative and counter-narrative relation to living story marginalization is worked out at the level of antenarrative. As visualized in figure 6.1, the before-bet-beneath-between-becoming antenarratives are in the lines *in between* the living story web and the (grand) narrative clusters, which may change through the antenarrative processes of transformation. The narratives morph more slowly, almost imperceptibly so, as compared to the living story webs, which are in the middle in an open-ended process of becoming. The antenarratives are not-yet, and barely if at all perceptible, yet are part of the swirl and flow of the narrative discourses and the living story dialogues, both social and material (sociomaterial). Hence, the overall pattern is the meeting between the narrative fractals and story fractals associated by and through antenarratives.

Storytelling is defined as grand narratives, living story webs, and the processes of their antenarrative connections which all come together in a dynamical storytelling assemblage. The storytelling assemblage, thus defined, has a pattern. It is not just random and is not nothingness. Rather, there are patterns that can be studied and changed. Small eddies of antenarratives produce big effects in living story webs and eventually in grander narratives. This is what the moving space of storytelling is all about.

The ongoing negotiation among the production of grand narratives, the counter-narrative reactivity and the ongoing living story webs occurs at the subtle and prereflexive level of the antenarrative lines. The antenarrative ontology is derived from the work of primarily Heidegger, Bakhtin and Deleuze's rhizome, as well as Merleau-Ponty's embodiment (which we can only review briefly due to space limitations).

Boje (2014), Boje et al. (2015), Boje and Henderson (2014), Haley and Boje (2014), Henderson and Boje (2015), and Svane and Boje (2015) began working out three additional aspects of antenarrative: ante as "beneath" narrative and living story, "between" them and "becoming" of care (and uncare) in the storytelling field itself (Boje, Svane and Gergerich, in press).

The antenarrative 5Bs (Figure 6.4) are worked out in relation to Heideggerian being-in-the-world ontology in his "fore" notions and are entirely interrelated and entangled with one another; however, here they are separate for analytical purpose:

- **Antenarrative-Before** narrative coherence (fore-having); "Any assertion requires a fore-having of whatever has been disclosed; and this is what it points out by way of giving something a definite character" (Heidegger 1962, 157).

138 *Marita Svane et al.*

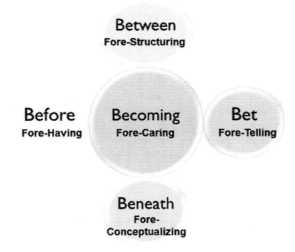

Figure 6.4 The Five B Antenarrative. A further development of the Four B Antenarrative. Svane, M., and D. Boje, 2015.

- **Antenarrative-Beneath** narrative and living story web (fore-conception); "Anything understood which is held in our fore-having and toward which we set our sights 'foresightedly', becomes conceptualizable through the interpretation . . . it is grounded in *something the grasp in advance*—in a *fore-conception*" (Heidegger 1962, #150).
- **Antenarrative-Between** narrative and living story (fore-structure); "All interpretation operates in the fore-structure, which we have already characterized" (Heidegger 1962, #152).
- **Antenarrative-Bets** on the future potentialities that are a multiplicity of paths to choose among (fore-telling); Fore-seeing can be short-sighted (#316) or far-sighted in "the existential meaning of the hermeneutical/situation of a primordial analytic of Dasein" and once again "the authenticity of potentiality-for-Being-one's-Self" and the "*meaning of the Being of care*" Care and Selfhood . . . (#316).
- **Antenarrative-Becoming** of care (and uncare) in the storytelling field itself (fore-care); the care-structure includes the phenomenon of Selfhood as "*the Ontological Meaning of Care*" (#323).

The five antenarrative practices happen in the prereflexive fabric of communicative practices out of which lived story and grander narratives are constructed. The entangled processes of the 5B antenarrative practices are fundamental to quantum storytelling.

Being-in-the-world is a being in a cultural, familiar and known world. Being-in-the-world is thus a container of cultural meaning frames of reference for understanding and interpreting life experiences and events. The

Fractal Change Management and Counter-Narrative   139

container risk turning the spiral of understanding into a "circulus vitiosus" (Heidegger 2008, 194) when it works as the legitimate, predefined understanding that is repeated and repeated as a fractal rule governing retrospective sense-making. Contrary to the closure of the container, fore-caring of the future becoming is an inquiring, sensitive and caring mode of being-in-the-world. Inquiring and caring enables an open and disclosing spiral leading to the emerging of the authentic Self as distinguished from the cultural They Self. (Boje 2012; Svane and Boje 2015). This is referred to as the spiral of selfhood authenticity (Anton 2001). As embodied, emotional and sentient beings at a prereflexive level, we become alert and respond to the vague unnoticed signs of changes, novelty and directions of LWM of exceptions from the expectation of the grander narrative.

The fore-having of beforeness is a way of sociomaterial fore-having the future through performative actions before the narrative coherence of a world-already-in-place. By acting upon our prereflexive alertness, we are sense-shaping and sociomaterializing the future ahead-of-itself, paving the way for the arriving future by enacting its facticity. From possibility, it may turn into potentiality and finally into actuality. The mode of being is a potentiality for Being, a now-ness potentiality. We enact the arriving future in the here and now (Boje 2012; Svane and Boje 2015).

The beneathness reaches into the subtle, prereflexive antenarrative practices that go beyond living story and narrative–counter-narratives as a subterranean level, out of which living stories and narrative–counter-narratives are produced (Boje, 2012). Anything understood in fore-having and seen foresightedly becomes conceptualizable through interpretation (Heidegger 2008, 191). The process of fore-conceptualizing the fore-sighted future is grounded in the embodied, emotional and prereflexive engagement with the world, out of which new real-life meanings emerge as part of an emerging new language practice. Sociomaterial lifeworlds merge through Bakhtinian dialogue, involving the body, feelings, moods and things (Boje, 2015, Svane 2014; Svane and Boje 2015). Through the heteroglossic, transgressing dialogue, different material lifeworlds of languages, cultures and histories merge and emerge, not as the objectified, institutionalized and materialized "world of culture" but as "the world of life" (Bakhtin 2010, 2). (For more on this point, see Boje 2012; Svane 2014; Svane and Boje 2015).

The fore-structure of betweenness refers to the antenarrative as a bridge in between centrifugal living story and centripetal narrative–counter-narrative. As all interpretations operate in the fore-structure, the antenarrative mode is a way of Being-open in Being-with (Heidegger 2008) and is inseparable from the disclosing process of inquiry and care. The antenarrative process continuously connects and transforms the living stories and narratives–counter-narratives. New relations, structures and ways of organizing emerge through the sociomaterial intra-activity as an ongoing, never-ending process. We shift away from the nouns to the verbs of relating, structuring, systematizing, organizing, strategizing, leading, communicating and so forth. (Boje 2012; Svane and Boje 2015).

140 *Marita Svane et al.*

The fore-telling relates to the antenarrative futural mode of being as Being-toward-possibilities. Being-open in an inquiring, caring way may disclose a horizon of endless possibilities of the world-in-its-becoming (Boje 2012; Svane and Boje 2015). Betting on which future to become may be an outcome of a reflexive/reflective choice, but it may also occur as an embodied, sentient, and spontaneous response to signals at a prereflexive level. Through various states of mind, we are already attuned toward the possible futures in different ways. As they are not equally attractive, we may be alerted, turning away, or attracted toward the different, emerging possibilities.

The entangled 5Bs of the antenarrative model bridge the living stories and narrative–counter-narrative and constitute, all together, the quantum storytelling field.

In order to effect change in cross-cultural management, we propose to look at what Henderson and Boje (2015) call "fractal change management." In line with this thinking, the model visualized in the Figure 6.5 has been developed by Svane and Boje (2015).

The model (Figure 6.5) illustrates the 5B antenarrative connection in between fractal narrative and fractal stories; between the sociomaterial fractal patterns of the grand narrative expectations and the sociomaterial fractal ruptures produced by the little wow moments of exceptions that emerge in the living story web. The fractal patterns of self-sameness occur across different

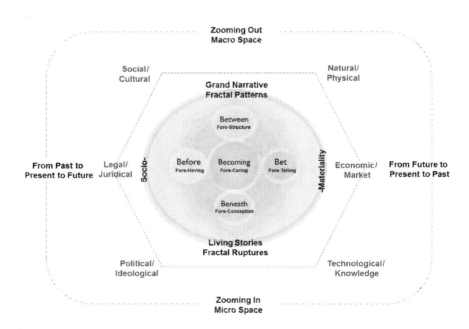

Figure 6.5 Fractal Change Management
Source: Developed by Svane and Boje (2015)

scalabilities ranging from the micro to the macro level; from the local to the global including the six surrounding dimensions of the political/ideological, economic/market, social/cultural, technological/knowledge, natural/physical and legal/juridical (PESTEL). These dimensions are quite similar to the well-known PESTEL dimensions. Subsequently, Fractal Change Management needs the ability to zoom in and out in order to identify the fractal patterns, to notice the fractal ruptures and to manage the tensed interplay out of which transformations occur (Svane and Boje 2015).

Fractal change management looks not only into the spatial scalability of sociomaterial sense-shaping but also into the temporality of past, present, and future. The fractal narrative is conceived to reproduce itself in a temporal movement from past to present to future. In this retrospective reproduction, the little wow moments of ruptures tend to be silenced, ignored or remain unnoticed. This temporal pathway of retrospective, reproductive sense-making is the linear and cyclic antenarratives that reproduce the past by predicting its reoccurrence in the future. Unlike this, the rhizomatic and spiral antenarratives take a different temporal pathway as they move from the future to the present to the past. This temporal pathway is the antenarrative, prospective sense-shaping of the future in an open-ended process of becoming. (Svane and Boje 2015).

In this open-ended process of becoming, fractal change management relates to the prereflexive level of embodied, emotional and sentient beings alert and responding to the vague signs of little wow moments indicating changes, novelty and new directions. Hence, antenarrative fractal change management manages the entangled processes of spatializing across scales, temporizing, and mattering (the sociomateriality; the entangled processes of meaning and matter) in the quantum storytelling field (Svane and Boje 2015). Antenarrative managing is managing spacetimemattering in the ontological situation.

Theoretical Discussion of the Cross-Cultural Merger Case

The merger case story encompasses dominating cross-cultural narratives and counter-narratives that emerge as a resistance throughout the process of merging and integrating the two companies. In the analysis of the case, it turns out that the narratives and counter-narratives are produced, repeated and also transformed at the antenarrative level, as the antenarrative connects the centrifugal living story webs of lived experiences with the dominating centripetal narratives and counter-narratives. The case is adopted from Svane (in press) and Svane and Boje (2014).

In the following analysis of the case, we identify the dominant narratives and counter-narratives. Figure 6.6 provides an overview of the organizational storytelling of the merger. Thereafter, we draw attention to the dialogical process through which the narratives and counter-narratives transform at the antenarrative level in the interplay with the living story web.

142 *Marita Svane et al.*

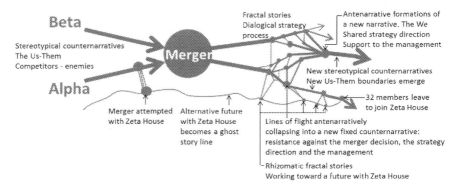

Figure 6.6 The Storytelling of The Merged Company
Source: Developed by Marita Svane

The story of marrying the worst enemy constitutes a dominant fractal narrative that is shared and repeated over and over again among the organizational members and their customers, especially in Alpha House. The fractal narrative is related not only to the fact that the two companies intensively competed against each other but also to an inherited hatred that dates long back in time. When inquired about, nobody seems to be able to remember the events causing the hatred except for an understanding that it was caused by some incidents that once happened at a farmer's market more than a half century ago. Passing on the stories of the hatred to newcomers and continuously maintaining the hatred by repeating the stories of the worst enemy, the narrative turns into a socializing cultural device predefining and stereotyping the relation between the two organizations.

This fractal narrative pattern affects Beta/Delta House, sensing the hostility in all aspects of the intraorganizational communicative practices. Consequently, the Us–Them cultural identity constructions are co-produced and lead to a kind of ritualized fractal relationship patterns in the merged company. These fractal patterns manifest in specific sociomaterial ways of relating to each other that seems to impede intraorganizational collaboration and task accomplishment. For instance, the three houses refused any attempt to advance an integration between their separate but related agricultural disciplines. In the same fractal way, they also fought against job rotation among the three houses, which otherwise might have produced more synergy. In line with the fractal pattern, the management of the merged company decided not to take the necessary steps to rationalize and optimize the operations of the merged company for which reason the obvious economic benefits of the merger were lost. In fact, the managers ceased to act out of fear of producing more resistance.

The fractal narrative reproduces and repeats the predefined sociomaterial structure without any further inquiry. In so doing, it materializes in stereotyped and self-stereotyped relations, detaching and estranging the actors not

Fractal Change Management and Counter-Narrative 143

only from one another but also from oneself. Caught by the monologic closure of the narrative, the possibilities for inquiring into and for arriving at the authentic self is lost and subsequently the cross-cultural meeting is stuck in the past-oriented, generalized abstraction of the stereotyped Us–Them identities.

Conceived as a vicious closed circle of interpretation, the fractal narrative interpretations solely operate as a recycling reproducing fractal pattern. As opposed to this is the open, disclosing spiral of interpretation that operates in the fore-structuring, meaning that the cross-cultural relationships are open for new configurations of similarities and differences and subsequently for the emergences of new ways of relating to each other (Svane and Boje 2014). The antenarrative interplay *between* narratives and living stories is a prerequisite for the disclosing spiral and for the transgression of the counter-narratives boundaries. (Please see Figure 6.1.)

The previously mentioned fractal narrative and the disappointing economic performance of the merger gave rise to the emergence of a new fractal narrative produced by Alpha House. This fractal narrative can be conceived as a counter-narrative opposing the merger decision, the strategy direction, the management and the poor economic performance of Beta/Delta House. According to the counter-narrative, the merger was a managerial mistake that eventually would lead to an economic failure. Therefore, Alpha would have been better off standing alone or merging with Zeta, the other major competitor on the market. As it turned out that the merger actually did not meet the economic expectations during the first two years following the merger, the narrative of a more profitable future with Zeta House was further reinforced and repeated. Gradually, Zeta House gained more and more presence in the narrative, almost as a "ghost" (Morson 1994) of a future that could have been. When Steven became the new CEO, he eventually decided to silence this counter-narrative; a decision making that in the end proved to be fatal. The silenced counter-narrative continued to work in the manner that Morson refers to as a "hidden process of change," where small unnoticed, silenced and erased events haunt from the side shadows (Morson 1994, 161, according to Boje 2010, 239).

As a Deleuzian rhizome, the new counter-narrative kept on working in the subterranean of the merged organization, producing and maintaining resistance to the merger, the strategy, and the management, and in the subtle and unnoticed shadow, it continued to bet on (fore-telling) and sociomaterially path the way for (fore-having, fore-structuring, fore-conceptualizing) the arrival of a future with Zeta House. As such, the counter-narrative developed in opposition to the fractal narrative in support of the new strategy direction. The counter-narrative aims at resistance and is grown and reinforced in the antenarrative meeting with the rhizomatic fractal stories exchanged with Zeta House. Still rooted and stuck in the past-oriented, stereotyped relationships, it is not really dialogical oriented or open for antenarrative inquiry into (fore-caring of) the existing merger. At the contrary, the inquiring fore-caring is solely attuned toward the possible future with Zeta House.

When Steven took over the responsibility for managing the future development of the merged company, he consciously decided that the strategy

144 *Marita Svane et al.*

process should not be constituted as an exclusively managerial task but rather as a social construction bottom-up process with a high degree of employee involvement. The strategy process was divided into two steps. In the first step, all employees and managers, the board of directors, as well as a large number of customers and owners, were asked to participate in formulating the strategy by identifying key strategic themes. The strategy formulation process lasted for about a year and was carried out by cross-cultural groups composed of members from each of the three houses.

In the second step, the employees were invited to participate in the implementation of the strategy and in the further development of the strategic themes. Accordingly, strategic groups were formed in order to work with the various strategic themes. Employees who joined the strategic groups would work partly on the strategy and business development of the company and partly on the operative tasks. Essentially, the strategy group work constituted a sense-making process as the employees tried to develop the meaningfulness of the specific strategic theme by relating the theme to their everyday life experience and local knowledge. Based upon their micro-level experience, knowledge and activities, they generated new ideas for business development and strategy change. In so doing, the strategy emerged at the micro level of practices within the framework of the accepted strategy formulation: "The strategic groups run their own life right now. More or less. Steven is actually not part of our strategy group. Once in a while, he is informed about the things that we work on. And only if he thinks that something is way out, then he interferes" (Jill, Delta House, employee).

To the extent possible, also the strategic groups were cross-culturally composed. The managers participated in steering groups in order to coordinate resources and ensure sufficient capacity for the various strategic and business development initiative as well as for the operative tasks.

Finally, every year the whole company was gathered together for three days in order to evaluate the strategy process, business development and organizational performance; retrospectively by sense-making of the past and prospectively by looking into the future.

Organizing the strategy process as a dialogical living story web, Steven aimed at two purposes. First, and in order to enhance a broad organizational commitment and ownership to the strategy, he aimed at creating a shared understanding of and identification with the future strategy and business development of the merged company. Second, and as a side effect, he also aimed at facilitating the emergence of a more "We" based cultural, identity construction in replacement of the Us–Them narrative. According to the following quotations, these purposes are to some extent achieved by this way of organizing and strategizing:

> "It is properly the greatest success of interconnectedness; that we all take responsibility. We know what is in the strategy. We know what to do to make it work." (Philip, Alpha House, employee)

Fractal Change Management and Counter-Narrative   145

"At that time [before the new CEO], we did not feel that we were one big family. But his way of approaching this made us feel more like being employed in ONE organization. It was a long journey because we had to get used to it but both the social and professional cooperation is much different today." (John, Delta House, employee)

"It has become much better, but to begin with, I think we all were frustrated, because we were used to manage our own little house. And there was a feeling of . . . did we dare share with the others? Or would they play games with us? That has disappeared today." (Jill, Delta House, employee)

As indicated in the earlier-mentioned quotations, the identified narrative and counter-narrative are to some extent transformed into new patterns of relationships as part of the multivoiced process of cross-culturally organizing and strategizing. This strategy process relates to the practice and process oriented approach that closely links together strategizing and organizing as two entangled processes that are hard to separate from each other (Tsoukas and Chia 2002, 567; Whittington 2006, 618). Svane and Boje (2014) argue that cultural dynamics is entangled with the strategizing and organizing process at the micro level. Turning to the micro level of actual happenings, events and new emerging situations implies a shift away from the generalizing, abstract level of the fractal (counter-)narrative and toward the polyphonic living story web as it unfolds in the rhizome, here and now, in the subterranean of the organizational life; that is in the beneath of the narrative. The cultural dynamics of the living story web is driven by the open, centrifugal forces of the dialogue through which living stories of lifeworld experiences are exchanged, inquired into, unfolded, merged and transformed (Boje, Svane and Gergerich, in press). According to Bakhtin (1986), the lifeworlds of lived cultural worlds and communities merge in the ongoing dialogical chain of heteroglossic communication. As part of this process, also identity may transgress as "an individual becomes other than what he was" (Bakhtin 1981, 115) through the process of dialogical transformation.

The cross-cultural strategizing and organizing process can thus be conceived as an antenarrative process of connecting the subterranean living stories (*beneath*) with the narrative (*in-between centrifugal living stories and centripetal narrative*) and of initiating an open inquiry into what is *becoming*. Hence, interpretations can operate in the open-ended spiral and produce new meaning structures. As the quotations indicate, the patterns of similarities and differences are antenarratively transformed into new meaning structures and patterns implying new ways of relating to other in the practice of organizational everyday life. Organizations can thus be conceived to be "a pattern that is constituted, shaped and emerging from change" (Tsoukas and Chia 2002, 567) in the antenarrative connection between the dialogical web of fluid, centrifugal living stories and fractal narratives—counter-narratives.

146　*Marita Svane et al.*

The organizational storytelling pattern that emerges from this change process is a fragmented pattern composed by competing narratives and counter-narratives that split the organizational members into at least two dominant groups, those in favor of and those against the strategy development.

The storytelling of the organization leads to a new performative cut of stereotyped relationships. The Us–Them narrative is now a cut between those who are in favor of and those who are against the strategy direction and the management. As several Alpha employees eventually came to identify with the new strategy during the strategy process, the configuration of relationships changed into new groups. Hence, the antenarrative interplay between living stories and fractal narratives–counter-narratives produced new cuts of cultural, fragmented relationships in Alpha House. Accordingly, the employees of Alpha House became critical toward each other depending on their attitude toward the strategy process: "A lot of people here were getting tired of their [the Alpha department who left to work for Zeta, the competitor] negative attitude towards everything" (Lily, Alpha House, team leader).

When the whole Alpha department collectively resigned and left the company in order to work for Zeta, the competitor, the company was left in shock and surprise. According to several employees and Steven, the CEO, the employees of the department kept silent about the plan, not revealing any single sign that this was the decision they were about to make. "It came as a shock . . . I did not see it coming . . . They said nothing . . . How could they manage, 32 people, to keep it a secret . . ." are frequent expressions uttered in the aftermath of the dramatic event. The hidden process of change resulting in this event is an example of a ghost story living in the shadow finding its way in a rhizomatic manner. The organization was part of discursively suppressing it, so perhaps after all the hidden counter-narrative was not that much of a wonder. The silent voices of the department, as well as the fact that the doors to the department were closed as an exception to the open-door office landscape, were sociomaterial signs that the organization ignored and omitted to act upon. Gradually, the CEO realized, "I did not listen enough."

The key lesson learned in the company is the need to engage in a caring inquiry. Inquiry is part of the 5B antenarrative dimension. The process of caring inquiry stopped, as the organization ceased to care about the 32 employees by gradually silencing and erasing their stories and as the 32 employees ceased to communicate as a counter-reaction and even planned to leave the company and to take with them as many customers as possible. Being-in-the-world in a caring inquiring mode could perhaps have helped the organizational members to become more sensitive and alert to the vague unnoticed signs of what was becoming, and to act to either prevent or advance (fore-having) the arrival of different alternative futures (bets). The signs are a manifestation of a sociomaterial fore-having of arriving futures. If the course of events continues undisturbed, it is a fore-telling that this future might very well arrive. Engaging into an antenarrative inquiry is to

Fractal Change Management and Counter-Narrative 147

fore-care about the becoming of the organization and an antenarrative way of managing that process of becoming.

Hence, being-in-the-world in a caring inquiring mode constitutes an antenarrative mode of being-in-the-world encompassing all 5B antenarrative dimensions. It is a mode of being-in that goes beyond the narrative and counter-narrative level and reaches into the more primordial, anterior and antecedent prereflexive level of embodied, sentient and practical engagement.

This development of the case story illustrates how the antenarrative interplay between rhizomatic living stories and dominating fractal narratives give rise to the production of the new emerging fractal narrative patterns. In this way, centrifugal living stories can be conceived as fractal ruptures; that is, the existing fractal narrative patterns and rules are challenged and broken. However, they carry the potential to create new fractal patterns, either as a rhizomatic fractal development as in this case or as a branching fractal development.

Finally, the case also illustrates how rhizomatic spaces emerge as unmanaged terrain with the organization; "a terrain which is not and cannot be managed, in which people, both individually and in groups, can engage in all kinds of unsupervised, spontaneous activity" (Gabriel 1995, 478). According to Gabriel, this is a kind of organizational dream world of desires, anxieties and emotions. In the merger case, the manager ceases to have access to this dream world when communication and inquiry break down, and the dream world becomes sociomaterialized through the hidden engagement with Zeta House. This dream world worked as an escape from the control-resistance struggle of the managed organization; an unmanaged line of flight. This dream world could have shined through the stories and become accessible to management, if the stories had not been silenced. The prerequisite for this to happen is the hermeneutical antenarrative fore-caring inquiry.

Theoretical Discussion of the Homeless Veteran Theater Case

Similarly to the merger case, also the veteran case illustrates the interplay between cultural stereotyping narratives and counter-narratives as well as the antenarrative process of transforming these narratives and counter-narratives through the dialogical living story web. However, this case goes even deeper into the prereflexive methodology of a hermeneutical antenarrative inquiring process than the merger case.

There is a dominant cultural narrative regarding the homeless as alcoholics, drug abusers or mentally ill (Knecht and Martinez 2009). Camp Hope in Las Cruces, New Mexico, offers a counter-narrative to this dominant perspective on homelessness by offering tent shelters and social support services for long-term residents (MVCH 2015). Other cities that have tried to utilize a similar tent city model have come up against the dominant narrative of homelessness. For instance, in 2009, Sacramento homeless individuals created a tent city with campsites, trash pickup and portable toilets; however, police disbanded

148　*Marita Svane et al.*

the community and threatened arrest for those who stayed (Middleton 2014). As a result, a social movement called "SafeGround Sacramento" is working to decriminalize homelessness and offer social services and transitional housing. As a counter-narrative, the movement is attempting to create a sense of home.

The veteran case is thus composed by several kinds of counter-narratives. First, to the city and social welfare agencies' narrative, that states that Camp Hope (the tent city) is not supposed to be a "home" to the homeless, but rather, it is only temporary day shelter. The homeless, in short, should not make the mistake of treating this as their "home." The counter-narrative is that homeless veterans and homeless are building community, individualizing their tent sites, such as by putting flags and flag poles on them: we are patriotic, and we want to fly our own flags.

There is more to be learned than simply hearing the narrative and counter-narrative regarding homelessness in these cities. A deeper understanding of the lived reality of these individuals may be gleaned through listening to the unique lived experiences of the veterans in Camp Hope. The lived experiences of these homeless veterans are articulated through living stories that meet, challenge and transform the fractal narratives and counter-narratives through antenarrative processes. There is no solid coherence for this antenarrative. It is, instead, a 'prereflexive' process through which a new dominant (counter-)narrative and even living stories of individual homeless may be developed.

In the veteran case, Veteran's Theater is developed and used as an antenarrative methodology that works on the antenarrative transformation of narratives and counter-narratives not only at a reflexive but also at a prereflexive level. The project aims at counteracting the dominant negative stereotypes of the homeless.

Veterans for this project held a theater performance on the New Mexico State University campus in April 2015. The play consisted of five separate acts, each with a theme designed to convey the lived experiences of homeless veterans in the region.

The first act involved a monologue by a retired female 1st sergeant of the US Army. She shared the story of how she and her husband came to be homeless (Boje, Svane and Gergerich, in press).

The second act was held as an unrehearsed meeting involving residents of Camp Hope. These meetings take place at MVCH on a weekly basis, wherein residents discuss concerns and jointly decide upon rules to govern the Camp (Boje, Svane and Gergerich, in press). A topic of regular concern is the distribution of the drug "Spice," outside of the Camp and efforts by the residents to prevent the spread of its use.

The third act illustrates the ability of drug representatives to meet with doctors at will. They work to persuade doctors to prescribe medications from the large pharmaceutical companies for whom they work. During this portion of the play, veterans experience a long wait to be seen at the clinic while the doctor is being wooed by a drug representative with gifts and a complimentary meal.

Fractal Change Management and Counter-Narrative   149

In act four, veterans continue to experience difficulty in being seen in a timely manner by the doctors at the Veteran's Administration (VA). One veteran who is quite sick is turned away, with an appointment to be seen a month later. The actor takes a moment to offer a monologue, letting the audience know that this part of the performance is based upon an actual set of events in which he became deathly ill while waiting for his appointment.

Act five works to highlight the potential for more attentive treatment by the VA staff, toward homeless veterans. In this act, a homeless veteran has had his medication stolen at a shelter and is unable to obtain a refill. The social worker maneuvers around agency policy and administrators in an effort to provide the veteran with the care that he desperately needs.

One of the purposes of the Veteran's Theater methodology is to bring to the surface and into the public the various dominant stereotyping narratives and counter-narratives.

In the first act, the theater play zooms in on the veteran's living stories of lived experiences at the micro level. In the second act, fractal narrative rules to govern the Camp and counteract the fractal sociomaterial pattern of Spice distribution is developed through the living story web. The Spice is a fractal-virus for which there is not much possibility of counter-narrative other than 'don't do drugs'; the pharmaceutical industry has its many medications as another sort of virus that affects/afflicts the homeless veterans— since if they cannot get the pain medications, they self-medicate with Spice, which functions as a drug with severe side effects.

The third act offers a glimpse of the power of pharmaceutical industrial narrative practices at a macro level. The pharmaceutical industrial practices produce a dominant fractal grand narrative at a macro level that works as a contextual frame of references. Acting as agential parts in reproducing the fractal narrative pattern at a micro level, the pharmaceutical company representatives may manipulate the doctor and thereby affecting the lives of homeless veterans.

In act five, the play articulates the addiction to the pharmaceutical medications and the desperation that follows from lacking it or for not being treated at all but left to deal with the mental health care problems alone. There is the fractal of stigma that is against all mental health care seeking, especially by the military, toward which the antistigma campaigns in United States and Europe do not compose an effective counter-narrative.

The stigma fractal is a branching sort, subdividing one group versus another, the populace against the veterans, veterans who are macho and don't seek help against those seeking care and so on. The Spice fractal is a downward spiral, to self-destruction, and the ultimate, death. The Pharmaceutical fractal is like Jeff Noon's Vurt, the Curious Yellow Vurt, a trip into a world of drug addiction, and playing the game of risk to the point that one of the times, maybe even the first time user's first toke, and there is a one-way passage to death.

The multifractal pattern leads to the downward spiral of 22 suicides a day, just within the US veterans community (including one who never got treatment for his or her war trauma). The point of the Veterans Theater is

150   *Marita Svane et al.*

to confront the stigma and to speak back to power of illicit institutions like Spice trade and against the power of pharmaceutical company practice that have been shown in too many cases to be unethical.

We often make sense of the world by following the dominant cultural narrative without even being aware of this socializing and sense-making mechanism. Through inquiring about the reality of being in and in-between various narratives, however, we are led to a richer narrative. This is what the Veteran's Theater brings to the surface. The play offers a new understanding of homeless veterans' experiences and challenges dominant narrative beliefs about this group. The following quotes were offered by audience members after attending the play:

> Awareness . . . men and women who serve in our military to keep our freedom . . . our greatest gift . . . need to be taken care of with love and respect regardless of their mental and physical condition. The plan entitled "Dead While Waiting for my VA Appointment" depicts the way veterans are treated within the Veteran Administraton (VA) system. Their individual situations get lost in the system's bureaucracy with untimely appointments, improper diagnoses and medications.

> This project is a very innovative and effective way of enhancing the lives of the participating veterans in the community, but at the same time, it raises public awareness of the issues veterans face as they try to (re) adjust to their old-new home-lives. The play is bound to be entertaining, heartfelt and cathartic all at the same time.

> The vignette of the play "Dead While Waiting for my VA Appointment" was a powerful recounting of the lived experiences of its performers— women and men who served honorably and with distinction in the U.S. armed forces. The play shines light on the challenges they and countless other veterans have faced while trying to obtain medical care and services from the Veterans Administration. Especially notable is the play's depiction of the uneven care offered to different classes of vets (for example homeless vets vs. middle-class ones, or those with physical vs. mental health issues), as well as the potential over reliance on prescription medication as a primary means of treatment.

The Veteran's Theater is an example of a quantum antenarrative methodology. It is a dynamical living entanglement of the living stories of veteran actors, their families, the researchers and the audience who all share and exchange and make sense of, reflectively and reflexively, the lived experiences and the dominant cultural (counter-)narratives. This antenarrative process does not only occur at a reflective and reflexive level, but it reached deeply into the pre-reflexive level as it invokes feelings and emotions as spontaneous immediate embodied responses. By being in the world through this bodily engagement, we find "events happening to us and within us—as a movement of feeling

Fractal Change Management and Counter-Narrative 151

that comes [. . .]—that we ourselves have not initiated" (Shotter 2011, 4). The movement of feelings arises as part of what Shotter expresses as "our outgoing exploratory activities and their incoming results" (Shotter 2011, 10). This embodied engagement in the word is about an embodied attunement with a world of events as Being-attuned (Heidegger 2008, 172). We are in the world by moods prior to cognition, and we are attending to the world from this inner state-of-mind (Svane, Boje 2014). As an antenarrative methodology, the Veteran's Theater is furthermore a sociomaterial entanglement as the theater, the stage and its materiality are parts of the methodological package as well as not only the verbal but also the embodied nonverbal communication, such as conscious and unconscious actions, gestures, tone of voice and facial expressions. Hence, the antenarrative methodology applied in the case constitutes an embodied and emotional sociomaterial fractal storytelling approach that provides access to the veteran's lifeworld and give rise to new counter-narratives opposing the dominant stereotyping narratives of homeless veterans.

In sum, the Veteran's Theater, puts on plays to communicate counter-narratives of what it means to be homeless. We want to understand and interpret what is *home* in all its *spacetimemattering*, but by not using an odometer or a stopwatch but, rather, in attunements. Home seems to be something we can "individualize" in "its ownmost potentiality-for-Being" in a freedom of choice of taking hold of itself, this thing called home (Heidegger 1962, 188). For Heidegger home is "*Being-free.*" It is about being anxious Being-in-the-world, authentically, and moving away from Being-there inauthentically. It is about individualizing and building communities where they feel at home as a contrast to "*solus ipse*" (*Means alone Self*) "*innocuous emptiness of a worldless occurring*" (Heidegger 1962, 188).

There is a "tranquilizing" that is "at the same time *alienating*" (Heidegger 1962, 178). Homelessness is a "groundlessness and nullity" (Heidegger 1962, 178) (literally means, without-home). There is a struggle in the world of homeless veterans, in all of homelessness, and in all the world of Being-veteran, Being-homeless. It is the struggle of being always defined as the "they" that Idle Talk knows all about, being thrown into homelessness world, yet has never spent 24 hours sleeping in a shelter-dorm or the temporary shelter of a tent city. How different Tent City Solutions would be if the mayor and the city council of Albuquerque spent 24 hours in their own shelters.

This is quantum storytelling through the telling of living stories with antenarrative threads, leading to transformed relationships between homeless veterans and residents of the community. The Veteran's Theater is an example of a methodology that works on this transformation. Consideration for only the narrative and counter-narrative ignores the richer reality of these individuals that is fluid and may be responsible for future transformation of the dominant narrative.

Research Contributions and Concluding Remarks

In this chapter, we develop a conceptual and methodological storytelling framework that contributes to analyzing and understanding the cross-cultural

152 *Marita Svane et al.*

storytelling dynamics occurring in the interplay between the cultural narrative–counter-narratives, the living story web, and the sociomaterial, antenarrative connections. The framework helps to identify the cross-cultural interaction and dynamics between cultural fractal narratives—counter-narratives and fractal stories that occur in cross-cultural situations. Our contribution lies in developing an understanding of the subterranean 'fractal' patterns between antenarratives out of which new narratives and counter-narratives are produced and living stories are affected.

We presented two case studies to explore the ways fractals operate in relation to counter-narrative in order to accomplish cross-cultural change. In the two cases, we identify the following learning points:

- How a quantum storytelling framework provides a theoretical and analytical framework for analyzing and understanding the cultural dynamic of changing and managing sociomaterial fractals in spacetimemattering. This two cases illustrates both branching and rhizomatic fractal (counter-)narratives and their transformation
- How the cross-cultural narrative–counter-narrative transforms and change when connected with the living story fractals associated by the antenarrative process, and give rise to the emergence of new cross-cultural narrative–counter-narratives. Hence, it is our contention that the interplay between a dominant cultural narrative and the many less-known counter-narratives is played out at the level of the antenarrative pattern.
- How there is a process of escalation and contraction of the counter-narrative fractal, how it moves and assembles and disassembles and reassembles over time as part of the cultural dynamics. Hence, over time, series of counter-narratives develop and can be conceived as a dynamic assemblage of interweaving counter-narratives.
- How the silenced voices in both cases (the ghost story line and the veterans) still operates in spacetimemattering and brings about sociomaterial consequences—as a breakdown of fractal organizational everydayness or as a rhizomatic line of flight as shown in the merger case—or as a downward spiral leading to self-destruction due to suicide or abuse. Silencing and ignoring voices do not eliminate their sociomaterial consequences in world making.
- Furthermore, both cases illustrate how the cross-cultural stereotyping communications and ritual relationships may continue to further the process of alienation, estrangement and self-forgetfulness as a consequence of the fractal virtuous circle.
- How the hermeneutical antenarrative fore-caring inquiry gives voice to the silenced and create a cultural dynamics that may change the course of the virtuous cycle, rupture the fractal patterns and create new paths of development. This process of inquiry works on not only the reflective and reflexive level but also on the embodied, prereflexive and emotional level of being-in-the-world. The prereflexive threads of antenarrative makeup an underlying becoming, beneath and between.

Fractal Change Management and Counter-Narrative 153

Once we know the patterning of the fractal in spacetimemattering, we have some possibility to intervene in the process of patterning in spacetime and sociomateriality (the entanglement of matter and meaning). Hence, we suggest further research into antenarrative fractal change management as this is about identifying the development of fractal patterns by getting at the subaltern and prereflexive aspects of the spatializing, temporizing and mattering of the quantum storytelling field.

References

Anton, C. 2001. *Selfhood and authenticity*. Albany: State University of New York Press.
Bakhtin, M. M. 1981. *The dialogic imagination: Four essays*. Austin: University of Texas Press.
Bakhtin, M. M. 1986. *Speech genres and other late essays*, Third paperback printing, 1990 edn. Austin: University of Texas Press.
Bakhtin, M. M. 2010. *Toward a philosophy of the act*. Austin: University of Texas Press.
Barad, K. 2003. "Posthumanist Performativity: Toward an Understanding of How Matter Comes to Matter." *Signs* 28 (3): 801–831.
Barad, K. 2007. *Meeting the universe halfway: Quantum physics and the entanglement of matter and meaning*. Durham and London: Duke University Press.
Boje, D. M. 2008. *Storytelling organizations*. London: Sage.
Boje, D. M. 2010. "Side Shadowing Appreciative Inquiry: One Storyteller's Commentary." *Journal of Management Inquiry* 19 (3): 238–241.
Boje, D. M. 2011. "Quantum Physics Implications of Storytelling for Socioeconomic Research Methods: Experiences in Small Business Consulting Research form New Mexico State University." International Meeting of Research Methods Division of the Academy of Management, Lyon, France.
Boje, D. M. 2012. "Reflections: What Does Quantum Physics of Storytelling Mean for Change Management?" *Journal of Change Management* 12 (3): 253–271.
Boje, D, Helmuth, C. A., Saylors, R. "Cameo: spinning authentic leadership living stories of the self." in Ladkin, D., & Spiller, C. (Eds.). (2013). *Authentic leadership: Clashes, convergences and coalescences*, 271–279. Gloucestershire, UK & Northampton, MA: Edward Elgar Publishing.
Boje, D. M. 2014. *Storytelling organizational practices: Managing in the quantum age*. London and New York: Routledge.
Boje, D. M. 2015. "Change solutions to the chaos of standards and norms overwhelming organizations: Four wings of tetranormalizing" in *Organizational Change and Global Standardization: Solutions to Standards and Norms Overwelming Organization*, 1–29. London and New York: Routledge.
Boje, D. M., U. C. V. Haley, and R. Saylors. 2015. Antenarratives of Organizational Change: The Microstoria of Burger King's Storytelling in Space, Time and Strategic Context. *Journal of Human Relations* 1–28. doi: 10.1177/0018726715 585812
Boje, D. M. and T. Henderson. 2014. *Being quantum: Ontological storytelling in the age of antenarrative*. Newcastle upon Tyne, UK: Cambridge Scholars Publishing
Boje, D. M., G. A. Rosile, J. Saylors, and R. Saylors. 2015. Using Storytelling Theatrics for Leadership Training. *Advances in Developing Human Resources* 17 (3): 348–362.

154 Marita Svane et al.

Boje, D. M., M. Svane, and E. Gergerich. In press. "Counternarrative and Antenarrative Inquiry in Two Cross-Cultural Contexts." *European Journal of Cross-Cultural Competences and Management.*

Deleuze, G. and F. Guattari. 1987 (org. 1980). *A thousand plateaus* (B. Massumi, Trans.). Minneapolis: University of Minnesota Press.

Durate, G. A. 2014. *Fractal narrative: About the relationship between geometries and technology and its impact on narrative spaces.* Vol. 12. Transcript Verlag.

Gabriel, Y. 1995. "The Unmanaged Organization: Stories, Fantasies and Subjectivity." *Organization Studies* 16 (3): 477–501.

Haley, U. C., and D. M. Boje. 2014. "Storytelling the Internationalization of the Multinational Enterprise." *Journal of International Business Studies* 45 (9): 1115–1132. http://davidboje.com/vita/paper_pdfs/JIBS_Haley_Boje_2014.pdf

Heidegger, M. 1962. *Being and time* (John Macquarrie, Trans.). Edward Robinson in 1962 from the 1929 German, with 2008 introduction by Taylor Carmon. New York: Harper Row.

Heidegger, M. 2008. *Being and time.* New York: HarperCollins.

Henderson, T. and D. Boje. 2015. *Organizational development and change theory: Managing fractal organizing processes.* London and New York: Routledge.

Ingold, T. 2011. *Being alive: Essays on movement, knowledge and description.* New York: Taylor & Francis.

Knecht, T., and L. M. Martinez. 2009. "Humanizing the Homeless: Does Contact Erode Stereotypes?" *Social Science Research* 38: 521–534.

Mesilla Valley Community of Hope 2015: http://www.mvcommunityofhope.org/

Middleton, M. K. 2014. "'SafeGround Sacramento' and Rhetorics of Substantive Citizenship." *Western Journal of Communication* 78 (2): 119–133.

Morson, G. S. 1994. *Narrative and freedom: The shadows of time.* New Haven and London: Yale University Press.

Noon, J. 1993. *Vurt.* New York: Crown Publishers, Inc.

Perl, L. 2014. "Veterans and Homelessness." Congressional Research Service Report. No. 7–5700, RL34024. https://www.fas.org/sgp/crs/misc/RL34024.pdf

Shotter, J. 2011. "Reflections on Sociomateriality and Dialogicality in Organization Studies: From 'Inter-' to 'Intra-Thinking' in Performing Practices." http://www.johnshotter.com/mypapers/Intra-thinking.pdf [April, 2014].

Svane, M. in press. "Multi-cultural strategizing and organizing in pluralistic context." In *Perspectives on international business—Theories and practice*, edited by J. Kuada and S. T. Marinova, 329–365, London: Adonis & Abbey.

Svane, M. 2014. "Quantum Organizational World-Making—Through Material Embodied Storytelling Practices." Quantum Storytelling Conference.

Svane, M., and D. Boje. 2014. "Merger Strategy, Cross-Cultural Involvement and Polyphony." Between Cultures and Paradigms, IACCM 2014 Conference.

Svane, M., and D. Boje. 2015. "Tamara Land Fractal Change Management—In Between Managerialist Narrative and Polyphonic Living Stories." Sc'Moi, Standing Conference for Management and Organizational Inquiry.

Tsoukas, H., and R. Chia. 2002. "On Organizational Becoming: Rethinking Organizational Change." *Organization Science* 13 (5): 567–582.

Whittington, R. 2006. "Completing the Practice Turn in Strategy Research." *Organization Studies* 27 (5): 613–634.

7 Designer or Entrepreneur? Counter-Narratives in the Professions

Birgitte Norlyk

"Sales? Sales man? *Hell, no!*" was the spontaneous reaction from an exasperated designer voluntarily participating in a course on business understanding and entrepreneurship. The course was designed to enable part-time or unemployed professional designers to set up their own businesses or become part of a greater business or organizational framework.

A total of 25 professional designers participated on a voluntary basis in a business course on entrepreneurship and business skills funded by local government and the European Union in order to facilitate their career opportunities in a business context and potentially generate a stable income. Intellectually, the designers agreed on the need to develop business skills and entrepreneurial understanding to improve their financial situation and enhance their career opportunities. Emotionally, as illustrated in the findings, the course on entrepreneurship was experienced as a power struggle of identities dominated by the master narrative of business and enterprise which designers intuitively opposed. The result was the emergence of a counter-narrative of artistic integrity and design as a reaction to the dominating master story of business and enterprise, which constituted the framework of the course.

Why Professional Counter-Narratives?

Acknowledging the somewhat ambiguous nature of the term *professional* (Cheney and Ashcraft 2007), the present chapter explores the interdependent and dynamic relationship among counter-narratives, professional discourse and professional identity. Taking a professional rather than organizational setting as its starting point, the chapter adds to our existing understanding of counter-narratives by explicating the insights gained from linking critical discourse analysis and studies of professional identity to the study of counter-narratives in the professions.

Counter-narratives are concerned with countering other, dominant narratives. They are often related to organizational, societal or political contexts, where they give voice to alternative representations of reality or experiences of organizational strategy and change applying a tactic of "narrative

156   Birgitte Norlyk

inversion" (Acevedo, Ordner and Thompson 2010) to counter and reframe the dominant narrative. Counter-narratives challenge established powers and the inherent hegemonic structures of societal or organizational master narratives related to the upholding of societal norms or the implementation of organizational strategy and change processes (Bamberg and Andrews 2004; Küpers, Mantere and Statler 2013; Nelson 2001). In a professional context, counter-narratives appear when professional values and norms are being questioned or threatened by powers outside of the professional community as in the present case of redefining professional designers as entrepreneurs in a business context.

Theoretical Framework

An interdisciplinary framework of studies on narrative, discourse and identity is applied in order to examine the counter-narratives of a group of professional designers experiencing an eight weeks course on entrepreneurship and business. Based on a thematic approach to narratives (Riessman 2008), the focus of the present analysis is primarily concerned with the content communicated in participants' discourse and their accounts of events rather than with aspects of narrative structure and style. Consequently, attention is primarily given to the 'told' as related in designers' accounts of experiences rather than to structural issues concerning the actual 'telling' such as plot, narrator, actants, points of view and so on. Following Riessman's observation (2008, 74) that "the thematic approach is suited to a wide range of narrative texts" the chapter explicates four dominant themes which in combination constitute the counter-narrative of the present case.

As both discourse studies and narrative studies are used in interdisciplinary contexts, the borderline between them may be blurred as reflected in van Dijk's inclusion of storytelling as discourse in his statement that critical and ideological discourse consists of "special lexical items or metaphors, [. . .] arguments (and fallacies), storytelling and so on" (2008, 5). In the present study, discourse analysis provides the framework for the micro-level analysis of the designers' lexical choices, framing devices and metaphors presented in the four dominant themes explicated. From a macro-level perspective, the combination of these four dominant themes constitutes a narrative that counters the master narrative of business and enterprise.

Part one of the theoretical framework refers to the study of discourse. First, the analysis bases its understanding of discourse and context on scholarship related to critical discourse analysis as exemplified by especially Fairclough and van Dijk in their studies of discursive choices, framing devices and preferred metaphors in societal and organizational discourse (Fairclough 1989, 1993, 1997; van Dijk 1997, 2008). Second, critical studies of organizational discourse serve to illustrate how organizational expressions of power and preferred systems of meaning are realized discursively (Deetz and Mumby 1990; Kunda 1992; Mumby and Stohl 1991).

Designer or Entrepreneur? Counter-Narratives in the Professions 157

Realized through critical discourses of resistance, counter-narratives oppose approved versions of reality and dominating systems of meaning. In societal settings, critical discourse analysis has demonstrated how public discourse is characterized by manipulations of meaning through promotional strategies and an increased marketization of discourse which promotes certain realities over others (Fairclough 1989, 1993; van Dijk 1997, 2008). In organizational settings, counter-narratives have emerged to challenge patterns of preferred meaning and control realized through dominant discourses and the power of these discourses to define reality and constitute approved norms of behavior (Deetz and Mumby 1990; Mumby and Clair 1997; Mumby and Stohl 1991). In both societal and organizational settings counter-narratives are realized through a set of discourses that navigates between what is perceived as being real or fake (Tracy and Trethewey 2005).

In professional settings, critical discourse and counter-narratives explicate how attempts by outsiders to redefine and restructure professional practices and values meet with opposition and protest. Studies on the professions demonstrate how professional discourse establishes power structures and defines what constitutes reality and professionalism as illustrated in a study of the health care sector in which local government's attempt to create a more business-orientated public sector backfired because the dominant discourse of professional business administrators and management challenged the discourse of the medical profession by framing clinical issues in the language of the market (Doolin 2002).

The present chapter draws on a series of studies of professional discourse in health care (Apker and Eggly 2004; Doolin 2002; Fitzgerald and Ferlie 2000), education and career management (Hanchey and Berkelaar 2015) and engineering (Kunda 1992; Winsor 1993), as well as studies of the discourse of transition processes as illustrated in research on junior professionals in the fields of corporate law and of consultancy (Ibarra 1999; Kuhn 2009). Part two of the theoretical framework is constituted by research on professional identity in different settings. Studies of professional identity in, for example, health care, engineering, management and consulting provide the theoretical conceptualization of how identity is perceived and executed in a variety of professional settings (Apker and Eggly 2004; Ashcraft 2007; Doolin 2002; Fitzgerald and Ferlie 2000; Fournier 1999). Across professions, these studies illustrate how self and professional identity suffer in societal or organizational contexts in which professional identities are being redefined or challenged by new systems of meaning imposed by management or other representatives of power.

Case and Background

The present case concerns a group of professional designers voluntarily enrolled in an eight-week course on entrepreneurship and business skills funded by local government and the European Union in order to facilitate

158 *Birgitte Norlyk*

designers' career opportunities and improve their financial situation. The course aimed at facilitating a transition process from professional designer to design entrepreneur or, alternatively, motivating designers to work in an organizational context in which their designs were defined by management and market.

The course was conceptualized and taught by representatives of local authorities, established entrepreneurs and professors of design, marketing, and entrepreneurship from colleges and universities. To be accepted for the course, participants were to forward a motivated application and an explication of their design concept. Although the course was subsidized by the European Union and local government, participants were still required to pay a modest fee. In all 25 professional designers participated in the course ranging from jewelry designers, fashion designers, arts and craft designers, installation artists to graphic designers of different backgrounds. Due to differences in age, specific designer background, gender, previous business experience and so on, the group did not constitute a homogenous whole.

There was no formal exam after the completion of the course. However, participants were required to develop a professional business plan to enable them to set up as entrepreneurs and to develop sales and business skills. This business plan was eventually evaluated and critically commented on by a group of specialists and representatives of the business and entrepreneurial environment.

Method and Data

Phenomenology was chosen as the research method for the gathering and subsequent interpretation of data as the study was concerned with explicating designers' experience of the course in business and entrepreneurship.

Phenomenology requires the researcher to bridle all preunderstanding and preconceived opinions in order to let the data speak (Dahlberg, Dahlberg and Nyström 2008). Because of its focus on illuminating personal experience of a given phenomenon, phenomenology is increasingly applied in studies of societal, professional and organizational arenas. In studies of health care (Norlyk and Harder 2010), studies of the vocational professions (Conklin 2012), and studies of strategic management, phenomenology provides researchers with a "methodology that remains rigorously open to emergent change, while rendering explicit and visible the biases and power dynamics that are suppressed in the stories we tell about ourselves" (Küpers et al. 2013, 96).

Structured or semistructured interviews were avoided in order not to influence designers' account of their experience of the course on business and entrepreneurship. Interviews were based solely on participating designers' descriptions, and care was taken on the researcher's part to avoid leading questions or preferred themes. The interviews centered on open, nonleading questions such as "How did you experience the course?" "Can you describe

Designer or Entrepreneur? Counter-Narratives in the Professions 159

your thoughts?" "What did you think in that particular situation?" and "How do you feel after the course?"

Data were gathered from 12 phenomenological interviews lasting between 30 and 45 minutes. These interviews were supplemented by the researcher's observations of dominant and contending discourses and preferred metaphors during the eight weeks of the course. These interviews and the researcher's observations of the designers' discourse were subsequently grouped into units of meaning. These meaning units were then condensed and structured into four dominant themes presented in detail in the following.

Findings—Four Dominant Themes

Overall the designers experienced the business and entrepreneurial framework as a severe threat to their professional identity. Intellectually, the designers agreed on the need to develop business skills and entrepreneurial understanding in order to improve their financial situation and enhance their career opportunities. Emotionally, however, designers experienced feelings of being overpowered by the master narrative of business and entrepreneurship. "It's a challenge to accept that you have to choose between professional values and business values" and "I realize the problem but I don't want to embrace a business identity." Generally, the discourse of entrepreneurship and business was experienced as alien and unappealing: "Value Added Tax, business plans, contribution margins, fixed costs, tax allowances, tax reductions . . . it's absolutely mind blowing."

The findings explicate four dominant themes in the designers' experiences of the course on business skills and entrepreneurship: experiences of violence and force, experiences of conflicts of professional identity, experiences of the enemy and experiences of entrapment and confinement of space. In combination, these four themes constitute participating designers' counter-narrative of business and the business world as experienced during the course.

Theme 1: Experiences of Violence and Force

The designers' experience of the course on business and entrepreneurship reflected a shared theme of violence and force. However, the designers acknowledged that an element of force was necessary in order to initiate movement and dynamics if they were to take on the role of design entrepreneur and perform in a business context.

The analysis of the data revealed discursive choices of a physical and aggressive nature indicating movements from safe places (i.e., the designers' workshop) to places of an unknown and potentially dangerous nature (i.e., the business world): "I need to be kicked out of my workshop"; "Somebody has to force me"; "I need to have my backside kicked"; "We need to throw ourselves into this [entrepreneurial and business related context]"; "I realize the problem but I don't want to embrace a business identity."

160 *Birgitte Norlyk*

Complementing the negative images of force and violence, however, a set of positive sports metaphors indicated the designers' recognition of the advantages of being a team player and transcending a purely individual framework: "I need to be part of the team"; "At present I play in my own court yard"; "I've got to play ball."

Concrete experiences of force and violence especially referred to practical, hands-on selling exercises in which designers were forced to call potential business partners or customers after having been given 30 minutes to prepare for the call. Many designers considered these exercises incompatible with their personal and professional identity as designers, and tension was running high during the hands-on sales exercises. Some spontaneously walked out on the training too infuriated to speak, while others refused point blank to take part. Some suddenly had to attend to sick children or excused themselves explaining that their cell phones had unexpectedly gone flat.

The instructor, however, insisted that participants go through with the exercises applying what he later described as a form of constructive force. Much to their surprise, several of the designers who reluctantly took on the challenge of the sales exercises later reported that "[i]t was actually easy," "[h]e [the business contact] was quite friendly and asked me to call back," and "I'm not afraid anymore." Still, although "none of us has had mega-negative experiences [in the contact with the business world or potential business partners] fear still dominates everything."

In retrospect, in spite of initial experiences of external force, a number of designers described the hands-on sales training as a positive experience of breaking new ground and of transcending boundaries at an individual level: "Now, we are finally rolling." Others experienced the sales training in a different light: "Something has provoked me . . . the sales training especially demonstrated no understanding for the designer."

Theme 2: Experiences of Conflicts of Professional Identity

The data illustrate that the question of professional identity was central for the designers. Being a professional designer constituted a central part of their understanding of self as personal and professional identities converged.

Designers took great effort to tackle the question of competing identities. Could they stay true to their designer identity while incorporating a business identity? Was it possible for conflicting identities to coexist? Intellectually, the designers acknowledged the need to compromise on personal and professional values to succeed in a business context. Emotionally, however, the designers experienced the business and entrepreneurial identity as a direct attack on their personal and professional integrity as designers: "We need to do things our way"; "You need to be true to yourself and to keep your integrity"; "We must stand by our values"; "It's hard to find focus"; "I don't want to accept multiple identities"; "It's a challenge to accept that you have

Designer or Entrepreneur? Counter-Narratives in the Professions   161

to choose between professional values and business values"; "When I'm exhibiting my designs in a gallery I'm an artist."

According to the designers in the course, their professional identity is based on immaterial values of an aesthetic and intellectual nature reflecting "purity, authenticity, and minimalism." Some participants described designer identity and core design values in a quasi-religious discourse characterized by terms of a biblical nature such as "holy calling" and "sacred creative powers." Other descriptions of designer identity were characterized by discursive choices relating to immaterial qualities such as imagination, poetry, reflection, innovation, play and the designer's obligation to surprise and think differently: "As a designer you create things that don't yet exist"; "I want to please the eye and to create 'eye pleasure.' "

Designers' conflicts of identity and their experiences of being caught between creative obligations and hard-core business considerations were reflected in their descriptions of having to juggle and balance both identities. At an intellectual level, designers acknowledged the importance of being able to operate successfully in a business context. Key business values such as a basic understanding of production, finance, logistics and marketing and sales, among others, did not, however, have the emotional appeal of the core designer values described earlier. "By nature I tend to forget the stuff that doesn't interest me . . . Budgets, cash flow, business plans . . . not particularly interesting. On the other hand [knowing about it] might save me trouble later on."

Another designer pointed out that designer identity did not necessarily justify an ignorance of financial matters and business realities. "I attended a two days' workshop on entrepreneurship and financing arranged by Deutsche Bank because I wanted to know what it takes [to set up a business]. I don't want to be considered a naive designer . . . I want to be in control."

Theme 3: Experiences of the Enemy

The discourse and metaphors found in the data revealed a set of deeply rooted stereotypes in relation to both business and design. Designers' discourse demonstrated a set of negative stereotypes and counterproductive metaphors in the framing of the business world. Practical sales activities and the image of the sales man provoked strong reactions. The caricature of the sales man was interpreted as the number one enemy as he represented the antithesis of artistic appreciation and demonstrated no concern for design: "Sales? Sales man? *Hell no!*"

The strong emotional reactions to sales activities and the negative image of the sales man were particularly characteristic of designers' discourse and choices of metaphors during the first part of the course. At this point in time, sales representatives were described in a shared cognitive framework casting them as ultimate representations of the enemy. Sales representatives were described as being unreliable, superficial and hyper-materialistic

162 *Birgitte Norlyk*

with no understanding of immaterial values and no sense of aesthetics and design. In classroom discussions and during breaks, designers spontaneously referred to sales representatives as "smarmy, secondhand car dealers" and "sleek, big-city guys." Similar examples of professional stereotypes and negative framing were found in designers' descriptions of financial advisors and accountants as "spread sheets in suits," "hard-core business guys" and "converted versions of Excel."

Over time, references to business-related stereotypes and images of the enemy became less frequent in the designers' discourse. However, the experienced incongruence between the designer identity and the business identity was still a dominant theme in the designers' experience of the course. At an intellectual level, the designers demonstrated an increased understanding of the importance of the business aspect. However, at an emotional level, they still found it hard to integrate the intellectual understanding of business values in their professional identity as designers: "My designs . . . It *is* business . . . After all, I'm making *money*."

The experienced tension between the contrasting value systems of business and design was explicated in the following statement from a designer towards the end of the course. The statement reflects designers' experience of oscillating between different professional identities: "Sometimes I really do see myself as being a part of the business world . . . I think I can learn the ropes . . . But then, later, when they [instructors] talk about different types of costs and budgeting . . . hard-core business . . . Then I feel disheartened . . . Am I a part of this? Can I do it? After all, you need to stay true to your core values."

Theme 4: Experiences of Entrapment and Confinement of Space

The last theme in the data concerns designers' experience of loss of freedom and feelings of being trapped in the potential transformation process from designer to entrepreneur. The free spirit of the designer was confronted with the structured framework of business which participants experienced as rigid and alien: "I'm afraid of being stuck into a box."

To a certain extent and over time, the discourse of some designers reflected a growing awareness and acceptance of the necessity of being able to navigate in business waters. For some designers, the initial experience of being caught in a sea of restrictive systems and inflexible boxes gradually gave way to a more balanced view in which both worlds might coexist in an uneasy symbiosis characterized by sudden flashes of existential fear and self-doubt.

On one hand, designers feared they might lose their identity as designers if they incorporated entrepreneurial thinking and business values into their understanding of their professional self. On the other hand, refusing to accept business and entrepreneurial thinking might lead to a life of non-recognition, waste of talent and a constant struggle to survive financially. Discursive choices revealed that, for the main part of designers, the driving

Designer or Entrepreneur? Counter-Narratives in the Professions   163

Theme 1: Experiences of violence and force

Theme 2: Experiences of conflicts of professional identity

Theme 3: Experiences of the enemy

Theme 4: Experiences of entrapment and confinement of space

Figure 7.1 Resume of findings

force did not concern the maximization of potential profit. Instead, the driving force was rooted in a personal and professional ambition to achieve professional recognition. Motivation was related to name and fame rather than fame and fortune: "I just want to be able to make a living"; "My dream is not to become a millionaire"; "What I really want is for my *name* to be recognized."

Designers' fear of losing their professional identity in the restrictive framework of business models, production plans, taxation rules, and logistic systems were reflected in the following statements: "I'm afraid of being stuck into a box" and "Those boxes full of business models . . . that was some roller coaster ride." However, designers' discourse occasionally reflected a partial acceptance of the usefulness of being able to think in terms of boxes and systems as reflected in the following statements: "I might just make round boxes instead of square ones"; "Sometimes it is hard to see yourself as a person in boxes . . . Still, maybe you can make your own box and change it a little."

An overview of the four themes of the findings is presented in Figure 7.1.

Discussion

In the following, the chapter discusses the findings in two interrelated theoretical frameworks. First, the findings are related to a framework of critical discourse analysis that explicates the use of negative framing, metaphors, and stereotypes as a basis for professional counter-narratives. Second, the findings are discussed within a framework of professional identity and the emergence of hybrid identities in the professions.

Framing, Metaphors and Stereotypes in Professional Counter-Narratives

Framing, metaphors and stereotypes enable individuals to articulate different versions of perceived reality and to express feelings of cognitive and emotive dissonance. Positive or negative framing determines how a situation is perceived and establishes rights of definition and interpretation (Ancona

164 Birgitte Norlyk

2012; Entman 1993; Fairhurst 2011). At several levels, individual, professional and organizational, the framing of a specific situation, problem or act subsequently determines positive or negative categorization.

Counter-narratives are based on negative framing of dominant power structures and approved patterns of meaning. In the counter-narrative of the design professionals, the discursive and metaphorical choices reflected in the findings exemplify designers' use of negative framing in their experience of the course. The discursive choices serve to uphold the designers' professional identity and to distance them from the dominating discourse of enterprise and business. Metaphors of ridicule and stereotypical framing of accountants and financial advisors as "spreadsheets in suits" and "converted versions of Excel" and sales representatives as "smarmy secondhand car dealers" and "hard-core business guys" helped the designers to establish a negative interpretation of the business world and its categories through their applied framing devices (Fairhurst 2011; Holmgreen 2012; Lakoff and Johnson 1980).

To complement the negative metaphors of sales and hardcore business guys, the data revealed a set of positive metaphors related to sport and action. The sports framework was frequently referred to by the specialists who taught the course, and in spite of a certain degree of skepticism in some participants, the sports metaphors and the sports framework struck a chord in many designers and partially counteracted the negative framing of business and enterprise in the designers' counter-narrative.

The appealing and positive framework of sport, teams and collective effort influenced designers' perception of the course and promoted a higher degree of acceptance and positive connotations in some participants. The data reveal their recognition of the advantages of being a team player and of transcending a purely individual framework: "I need to be part of the team"; "At present I play in my own court yard"; "I've got to play ball."

Metaphors and frames of a competing nature appear in the data reflecting the discrepancy between individual and collective values, representations of friends or enemies and, ultimately, of right and wrong. Several statements frame the designer as a representative of the creative elite bound by a sacred moral duty to uphold artistic integrity as in "we must stand by our values." This idealistic frame and its discourse oppose the discourse of enterprise and business, which advocates a framework of return on investment, profit, efficiency, increased productivity and standardization as exemplified by "the hard-core business guys."

The framing of a specific situation or act determines positive or negative categorization inside and outside of the professions. In the present case, metaphors of opposition and dominant frames of negativity affected how business and entrepreneurship were perceived by the designers. The course demonstrates how established patterns of framing may prevent competing interpretations of a given situation or context as "frames can become so taken for granted that it is hard for people "to 'see' or 'do' differently" (Whittle, Housley, Gilcrist, Mueller and Lenney 2015, 378).

Designer or Entrepreneur? Counter-Narratives in the Professions 165

In both professional and organizational settings, metaphors and framing devices constitute a way to express distancing exemplified in counter-narratives of competing and alternative realities. The metaphors we live by and the metaphors we lead by equally contribute to the framing of what is perceived as reality and leadership (Alvesson 2011; Lakoff 2003; Lakoff and Johnson 1980).

The opposing realities articulated in counter-narratives reflect the use of framing as a basis for patterns of inversion that position and reposition conflicting professional values. The inversion mechanisms realized through negative framing and critical discourse facilitate a counter-narrative that reconfigures the dominant master narrative by the strategy of "narrative inversion" (Acevedo, Ordner and Thompson 2010). In the present case, the master narrative of business and enterprise was countered by an opposing narrative of commitment to design and idealism.

Counter-Narratives and the Negotiation of Professional Identity

As illustrated in the present case, professional identity is negotiated and renegotiated in contexts involving professional, organizational or societal change (Apker and Eggly 2004; Ashcraft 2007; Doolin 2002; Fournier 1999). In spite of the difference in professional settings, established professional identities may be pressured by competing systems of meaning typically imposed by organizational management, government or other representatives of power.

As exemplified in their discourse, designers are deeply concerned with the vocational aspect of the design profession and the moral obligation to stay true to one's artistic integrity or calling. The four themes constitute a counter-narrative articulated through a discourse that underlines the element of vocation or calling reflected in the use of biblical terms or references to "holy calling," "sacred creative powers," "holy patterns" and "secret meanings." Furthermore, the findings explicate discursive choices relating to immaterial qualities such as imagination, poetry, reflection, innovation, play and the designer's obligation to think differently: "As a designer you create things that don't yet exist."

The moral self-definition in the counter-narrative of design manifests itself in discursive practices in which certain words or phrases take on an element of 'holiness' and become the property of 'enlightened' individuals who hold the power to challenge or 'de-sacralize' the dominant master story (Küpers et al. 2013). In contrast to the master narrative of business, which places at center stage the material wealth, the counter-narrative of the designers reflects a preference for name and fame over fame and fortune. The concept of name is central to designers' identity. Name is linked to an ambition concerning professional recognition rather than aspirations of financial gain as in the master narrative of business.

166 *Birgitte Norlyk*

The designers' counter-narrative of artistic integrity and immaterial values challenged the approved master narrative of the business course. During the course the designers' counter-narrative functions as identity repair and validates Nelson's observation that "counter stories, which root out the master narrative in the tissue of stories that constitute an oppressed identity and replace them with stories that depict the person as morally worthy, supply the necessary means of resistance" (Nelson 2001, 150).

Depending on context and time, designers oscillated between the master narrative of business and entrepreneurship and their counter-narrative of design and artistic integrity. Toward the end of the course about one-third of the designers acknowledged the master story of business and enterprise as a condition for practicing their design and for making a living. Others continued to oscillate between master and counter-narrative and continuously experienced ongoing conflicts of identity.

The experience of professional identity under pressure is reflected in professionals' articulation of experiences of emotive dissonance (Ibarra 1999). Experiences of threat to one's professional identity constitute a shared basis for counter-narratives in professional settings. Resistance becomes manifest when professionals perceive changes or reforms as "extending central control or challenging the existing professional culture and valued practices" (Doolin 2002, 381). Dependent on context, some professionals may develop a hybrid identity which enables them to take on the double role of, for example, manager and professional or of designer and businessperson. Others experience ongoing conflicts of front-stage and back-stage realities as they perceive themselves as actors in professional performances (Fitzgerald and Ferlie 2000; Hodgson 2005).

The findings illustrate the ongoing negotiation of identities reflected through discourses of difference (Ashcraft 2007). Designers' experiences of being caught between the conflicting identities of the creative professions and the business world are manifest. Their counter-narrative and their discourse reveal a constant negotiation of identities involving a polyphony of multiple and self-contradicting voices: "I realize the problem but I don't want to embrace a business identity"; "Am I a part of this?"; "After all you need to stay true to your values."

Toward the end of the course, a smaller group of designers articulated a budding acceptance of the advantages of incorporating a business and entrepreneurial identity. Statements in the data suggest that these designers found themselves in the process of developing a hybrid identity that incorporated elements of the conflicting professional identities of business and of design: "My designs . . . It *is* business . . . After all, I'm making *money*." Although "I *am* my designs' . . . 'I don't want to be considered a naive designer"; "I want to be in control."

The potential hybridization of the conflicting identities of designers and business representatives does not imply the domination of one over the other. Rather, in the present case, a hybrid identity enables the designers to

Designer or Entrepreneur? Counter-Narratives in the Professions 167

negotiate across a wide set of barriers of a professional, discursive or cultural nature reflecting a social context that necessitates a (re)negotiation of professional roles (Smith 2008).

The development of hybrid identities exemplified in the statements of this smaller group of designers illustrates the dynamic nature of master and counter-narratives. Following Nelson's observation that "optimally successful counter stories *must* be master narratives, since success consists precisely in the counter story's becoming widely circulated and socially shared" (2001, 157) master and counter-narratives may change position dependent on context, time, and perceived identity. In a complex environment involving the emergence of hybrid identities, counter-narratives help constitute a framework that enables individuals to balance conflicting value systems.

An interview with Neil, a graphic arts designer in his late thirties and successfully established in business, illustrates the dynamic relationship between negotiations of identity in a real-life context, which may require the ability to develop and master a hybrid identity as pointed out in Smith's observation that due to increasing modernization and new structures in the labor market "being a hybrid is now a benefit" (Smith 2008, 4).

Acknowledging that he does not belong to the target group of the course as he is already established in business, Neil explains that he intends to sell his company and start a new business based on concerns for design and artistic integrity rather than profit and market shares. Neil's case demonstrates the development of a hybrid identity, which can handle the reciprocal nature of master and counter-narratives. Participating in the course and socializing with young designers has caused Neil to reflect on his personal and professional identity. Who is he? And who does he want to be? Is he today's successful businessman, or is he the enthusiastic designer of ten years ago who had "crazy dreams" and "wild ideas"? His account of his personal experiences during the course indicates that he has developed a functioning hybrid identity of conflicting yet coexisting identities: "I get lots of energy and inspiration from the young designers here . . . I recognize the creative and impulsive Neil. This course is very intense and you need to contribute 100% . . . Some of the young designers would benefit from real experiences of life in business. But then, on the other hand, business might quench their creative spirit . . . That's a bloody hard question . . . What I fear the most is the loss of creativity . . . Don't stay in your comfort zone forever."

The ability to navigate between professional identities and to develop functioning hybrid identities that embrace the reciprocal relationship between master and counter-narratives is illustrated in research on hybrid identities in the professions. Analyzing the attempt of a neoliberal government to introduce a business approach to the public health care sector and to redefine clinicians as "income generators," a study concludes that opposing professional identities may in some cases coexist as the balance between them will change over time and contexts (Doolin 2002). Some clinicians rejected the redefinition of health care framed as business and refused to

168 *Birgitte Norlyk*

redefine established professional identity: "I don't see this as a business and I never would . . . I've got a social conscience." Others, however, integrated the counter-narrative of business and developed a hybrid identity: "I'm a sort of socio-capitalist. I guess I'm an amalgam of the two. In private practice what I'm interested in is dollars. In here [hospital] I'm interested in patient care" (Doolin 2002, 383–384).

Conclusion

The present study has illustrated how professional counter-narratives are constituted through discourses of opposition and (re)negotiations of professional identity. Data consisted of observations of discourse during an eight-week course on business and entrepreneurship funded by the European Union and local government targeting professional designers with no regular income.

A total of 25 designers of different professional backgrounds voluntarily participated in the course, which was taught by specialists from colleges and universities and representatives of the business world. The observations of discourse were supplemented by a series of phenomenological interviews towards the end of the course.

The findings revealed four dominant themes which constitute the designers' counter-narrative: experiences of violence and force, experiences of conflicts of professional identity, experiences of the enemy and experiences of entrapment and confinement of space. As exemplified in the discussion, the interrelatedness of professional discourse and professional identity constitutes an important part in the formulation of counter-narratives in which professional values and norms are being threatened or pressured by powers outside the professional community.

The study concludes that increased knowledge of the interrelated role of critical discourse and counter-narratives in the professions serves to illuminate experiences of professional identities under pressure. The study contributes to existing research on professional counter-narratives by explicating the complex and reciprocal nature of master narratives and counter-narratives in organizational or societal contexts which involve imposed change and forced redefinitions of professional roles and values.

References

Alvesson, Mats. 2011. "Leaders as Saints: Leadership through moral peak performance." In *Metaphors we lead by*, edited by Mats Alvesson and André Spicer, 51–74. Abingdon: Routledge.

Ancona, Deborah. 2012. "Framing and acting in the unknown." In *The handbook of teaching leadership: Knowing, doing and being*, edited by Scott Snook, Nitin Nohria and Rakesh Khurana, 3–19. London: Sage.

Apker, Julie, and Susan Eggly. 2004. "Communicating Professional Identity in Medical Socialization: Considering the Ideological Discourse of Morning Report." *Qualitative Health Research* 14 (3): 411–429.

Designer or Entrepreneur? Counter-Narratives in the Professions 169

Ashcraft, Karen Lee. 2007. "Appreciating the 'Work' of Discourse: Occupational Identity and Difference as Organizing Mechanisms in the Case of Commercial Airline Pilots." *Discourse and Communication* 1 (1): 9–36.

Bamberg, Michael and Molly Andrews. (eds.). 2004. *Considering counter-narratives*. Amsterdam: John Benjamins.

Cheney, George, and Karen Ashcraft. 2007. "Considering 'The Professional' in Communication Studies: Implications for Theory and Research Within and Beyond the Boundaries of Organizational Communication." *Communication Theory* 17: 146–175.

Conklin, Thomas A. 2012. "Work Worth Doing: A Phenomenological Study of the Experience of Discovering and Following One's Calling." *Journal of Management Inquiry* 21 (3): 298–317.

Dahlberg, Karin, Helena Dahlberg and Maria Nyström. 2008. *Reflective lifeworld research*. Lund, Sweden: Studentlitteratur.

Deetz, Stan, and Dennis Mumby. 1990. "Power, Discourse, and the Workplace: Reclaiming the Critical Tradition." *Communication Yearbook* 13: 18–48.

Doolin, Bill. 2002. "Enterprise Discourse, Professional Identity and the Organizational Control of Hospital Clinicians." *Organization Studies* 23 (3): 369–390.

Entman, Robert M. 1993. "Framing: Towards a Clarification of a Fractured Paradigm." *Journal of Communication* 43 (4): 6–25.

Fairclough, Norman. 1989. *Language and power*. London: Longman.

Fairclough, Norman. 1993. Critical Discourse Analysis and the Marketization of Public Discourse: The Universities. *Discourse and Society* 4 (2): 133–168.

Fairclough, Norman. 1997 (org. 1995). *Critical discourse analysis—The critical study of language*. London: Longman.

Fairhurst, Gail T. 2011. *The power of framing: Creating the language of leadership*. San Francisco: Jossey-Bass.

Fournier, Valérie. 1999. "The Appeal to 'Professionalism' as a Disciplinary Mechanism." *The Sociological Review* 47: 280–308.

Fitzgerald, Louise, and Ewan Ferlie. 2000. "Professionals: Back to the Future?" *Human Relations* 53 (5): 713–739.

Hanchey, Jenna N., and Brenda L. Berkelaar. 2015. "Context Matters: Examining Discourses of Career Success in Tanzania." *Management Communication Quarterly* 29 (3): 411–439.

Hodgson, Damian. 2005. "'Putting on a Professional Performance': Performativity, Subversion and Project Management." *Organization* 12 (1): 51–68.

Holmgreen, Lise-Lotte. 2012. "Framing a bank: Reputation management during financial crises." In *Metaphor and mills: Figurative language in business and economics*, edited by Honesto Herrera-Solar and Michael White, 243–264. Berlin: Mouton de Gruyter.

Ibarra, Herminia. 1999. "Provisional Selves: Experimenting with Image and Identity in Professional Adaptation." *Administrative Science Quarterly* 44: 764–791.

Kuhn, Timothy. 2009. "Positioning Lawyers: Discursive Resources, Professional Ethics and Identification." *Organization* 16 (5): 681–704.

Kunda, Gideon. 1992. *Engenering culture—Control and commitment in a high-tech corporation*. Philadelphia: Temple University Press.

Küpers, Wendelin, Saku Mantere, and Matt Statler. 2013. "Strategy as Storytelling: A Phenomenological Collaboration." *Journal of Management Inquiry* 22 (1): 83–100.

170 *Birgitte Norlyk*

Lakoff, George. 2003. "Framing the Issues: UC Berkeley Professor George Lakoff Tells How Conservatives Used Language to Dominate Politics." *UC Berkeley News*, October 23. http://berkeley.edu./news/media/releases/2003/10/27_lakoff. shtml. Retrieved 2015.

Lakoff, Georg and Mark Johnson. 1980. *Metaphors we live by*. Chicago: The University of Chicago Press.

Mumby, Dennis and Robin P. Clair. 1997. "Organizational discourse." In *Discourse as social interaction*, edited by T. van Dijk, 181–205. London: Sage.

Mumby, Dennis, and Cynthia Stohl. 1991. "Power and Discourse in Organization Studies: Absence and the Dialectic of Control." *Discourse and Society* 2 (3): 313–332.

Nelson, Hilde Lindemann. 2001. *Damaged identities, narrative repair*. Ithaca: Cornell University Press.

Norlyk, Annelise, and Harder, Ingegerd. 2010. "What Makes a Phenomenological Study Phenomenological? An Analysis of Peer-Reviewed Empirical Nursing Studies." *Qualitative Health Research* 20 (3): 420–431.

Riessman, Catherine Kohler. 2008. *Narrative methods for the human sciences*. Los Angeles: Sage.

Smith, Keri E. Iyall. 2008. "Hybrid identities: Theoretical examinations." In *Hybrid identities: Theoretical and empirical examinations*, edited by Keri E. Iyall Smith and Patricia Leavy, 3–13. Bosten and Leide: Brill Academic Publishers.

Tracy, Sarah J., and Angela Trethewey. 2005. "Fracturing the Real-Self Fake-Self Dichotomy: Moving Toward 'Crystallized' Organizational Discourses and Identities." *Communication Theory* 15 (2): 168–195.

van Dijk, Teun A. 1997. "Discourse as interaction in society." In *Discourse as social interaction*, edited by T. van Dijk, 1–38. London: Sage.

van Dijk, Teun A. 2008. *Discourse and power*. Basingstoke: Palgrave Macmillan.

Whittle, Andrea, William Housley, Alan Gilgrist, Frank Mueller, and Peter Lenney. 2015. "Category Predication Work, Discursive Leadership and Strategic Sensemaking." *Human Relations* 68 (3): 377–407.

Winsor, Dorothy. 1993. "Owning Corporate Texts." *Journal of Business Communication* 7 (2): 179–195.

8   Rethinking Counter-Narratives in Studies of Organizational Texts and Practices

Rasmus Kjærgaard Rasmussen[1]

Introduction

Narrative studies of organizational practices have traditionally focused on the function of the dominant managerial story and opposing employee stories in the overall culture of the organization. One conceptualization of this relationship is that of dominant narratives and counter-narratives developed by Andrews (2004) and Bamberg (2004). In this chapter I discuss the value of counter-narrative as both a theoretical concept and an analytical device in empirical studies of organizations.

I argue that while the original analytical framework advanced by Bamberg and Andrews (2004) has obvious strengths, it also has some crucial shortcomings that need to be addressed when employing it in empirical organizational analysis. One of these shortcomings is the concept's core ontology that prescribes the *a priori* existence of a fixed dichotomy between a master and a counter-narrative. This is visible in their central claim that counter-narratives "only make sense in relation to that which they are countering" (x). Apart from being at odds with the aims of more inductive ethnographic and narrative approaches to organizational analysis, this dichotomy tends to exclude complex power struggles in and around organizations, which may exhibit more messy empirical configurations than the dichotomy allows for. For instance, power struggles between two master narratives.

I base my critique partly on observations and empirical findings from a case study where there appeared to be two competing 'master narratives'— or institutionalized practices (Fenton and Langley 2011)—rather than a single master narrative opposed by a counter-narrative, such as Bamberg and Andrews's (2004) framework stipulates. Furthermore, because these two master narratives affect organizational practice the case study also illustrates the encounter between two competing narratives, which goes beyond simply describing a static normative relationship (dichotomy). Finally, the original framework does not take into consideration the empirical and practical modalities of counter- and master narratives in the form of texts and documents and the performative role of these texts. Thus, I suggest that the framework needs a *textual* dimension, which embraces the key role played

172 *Rasmus Kjærgaard Rasmussen*

by documents of strategy, policy and so on in modern organizations' exercise of power. Indeed, in this chapter I want to promote a more textual concept of power as struggles over discursive dominance.

The aim of the chapter is thus to critically investigate Bamberg and Andrews's original framework of counter-narrative and, in turn, to retheorize it within an organization-focused analytical framework. I contend that such a move can help reclaim its considerable potential and value in narrative organizational analysis and at the same time contribute to the understanding of organizational practice as the outcome of discursive struggles in the present case study.

Aim and Research Questions

In this chapter, I thus attempt to rethink and bring forth the potential of counter-narrative as an analytical device in organizational analysis. The two main questions that I try answer in the chapter are

> How can the concept of 'authoritative texts' help retheorize both counter- and master narratives as both organizational phenomena and analytical devices?

> How can the organizational power struggles in the case study be conceptualized as a discursive struggle between two master narratives *as* authoritative texts?

Structure of the Chapter

The chapter is constructed in five main sections: the brief first section introduces the case study in order to ground the argument. In the second section I outline what I consider to be the most important shortcomings of the master–counter-narrative framework. This is followed by the third section, which moves on to a stepwise reconceptualizing of counter- and master narratives as both existing organizational phenomena and analytical devices. As a first step in my attempt to remedy these shortcomings I introduce some key approaches within organization theory that seems to address similar issues as the master–counter-narrative framework. Here I privilege the notion of authoritative texts and proceed to reconceptualize master narratives *as* authoritative texts. The second step ties this to notions of institutionalized organizational practices and power. The third and final step integrates the resulting framework into a constitutive approach that allows special attention to the performativity of organizational narratives in the material form of documents. In the fourth section I illustrate the value of this reconceptualization by tying it to the findings of the case study. I conclude the chapter in a fifth section, where I reflect on the theoretical and methodological benefits of master narratives-as-authoritative texts Despite my critical point of departure, I try to show how counter-narrative, when properly amended and reconceptualized, may offer a contribution to

Rethinking Counter-Narratives in Studies   173

central debates in narrative organization studies including the debate of the constitutive role of communication in organizing—or CCO (see Ashcraft, Kuhn and Cooren 2009)—where it offers an empirical contribution to the discussion of *how* organizations are communicatively constituted.

Introducing the Case Study: Struggling Master Narratives

In order to illustrate the concrete implications of the shortcomings of the counter-narrative framework, I depart from an empirical study that was, initially, an explicit attempt to use this framework to uncover narrative practices within the Danish central government administration (see Rasmussen 2014). I use this study to illustrate how the aforementioned reservations are directly relevant for empirical case studies where there may be no clear candidate for the counter- or master narrative as well as cases with no counter-narration at all.

The argument builds on a case study of a Danish ministry's use of the nation branding-recipe (e.g., Anholt 2007) in the wake of the so-called cartoon crisis (see Rasmussen and Merkelsen [2014] for a detailed account). Through participant observation, interviews and document analysis I investigated the interplay between the civil servants, institutionalized organizing practices and the policy documents (texts) in and around the ministry. Importantly, the strategy of nation branding was adopted at policy level via a key government strategy document known as the *Action Plan for the Global Marketing of Denmark* (Danish Government 2007).

I was specifically interested in the relationship between the civil servants and the institutionalized organizing practices they used—or translated—in their local practices (cf. Latour 1986).

The central analytical observation in the case study was that the considerable tensions (Stohl and Cheney 2001) in the daily operations of the ministry were an instantiation of an encounter between two master narratives, that is, branding and bureaucracy. These tensions could be traced both on the level of practice and circulated documents. Furthermore, it could be traced to both micro and macro levels of organization. The tension could be observed in the practitioner's micro-level narratives of practice as a difference between practices based on a case-file logic or on a project logic (see Thornton and Ocasio 2008). At the macro level, it was visible as an ongoing struggle between two institutionalized overall set of practices: a dominant narrative of 'proper' bureaucracy as administration and a competing narrative of nation branding as a 'new' form of governance. Finally, for the civil servant practitioners the encounter also created a tension between two roles visible in their narratives of professional identity. In my conclusion I return to this issue and outline how this can be seen as the result of the struggle between the organizational discourse on bureaucracy and branding in the ministry.

I use the case to substantiate two central claims: the concept of master and counter-narratives (if not properly amended) fails to elucidate alternative

174 *Rasmus Kjærgaard Rasmussen*

configurations of power struggles such as the one prevalent in the case at hand. Here, no clear dichotomy between a master and a counter-narrative presented itself. Instead, the analysis yielded two master narratives that were fundamental to the ongoing competition and struggle over the authority in the organization. In addition, the original framework does not take into consideration the empirical and practical modalities of counter- and master narratives in the form of texts and documents and the performative role of these texts. Here the case, however, illustrates how a specific organizational document became a central *actant* in the power struggle.

A Critique of the Counter-Narrative Framework

Bamberg and Andrews's original framework is aimed at disclosing power struggles between social groups by looking at their narrative productions. According to Andrews, counter-narratives are defined as "the stories which people tell and live which offer resistance to, either implicitly or explicitly, to dominant cultural narratives" (Andrews 2004, 1). The core ontological assumption is that counter-narrative is a relational (or positional) phenomenon that "only make sense in relation to [. . .] that which they are countering. The very name identifies it as a positional category, in tension with another category" (Bamberg and Andrews 2004, x).

The concept of 'counter-narratives' originates from a critical tradition within humanities concerned with societal and discursive phenomena as part of an emancipating agenda. Within critical anthropology and ethnography, counter-narrative phenomena are often—if not always—examined from a minority viewpoint (see, e.g., Jackson 2002; Nelson 2001). The contributions to the original 2002 special issue of *Narrative Inquiry* (collected in the *Considering Counter-Narratives* from 2004), for instance, examined individual counter-narratives toward normality and other hegemonic discourses (see, e.g., Andrews 2004; Thorsby 2004). As Bamberg (2004) notes the practical application of counter-narrative "opens up the possibility of using narrative research in the service of liberating and emancipating agenda" (351).

Theoretically, the main problem is the core ontological assumptions of an inherent dichotomy between master and counter-narrative, where the counter exists as a causal effect of the master. When translated into a research design this results in a methodology with a strong deductive disposition. This leads me to a second theoretical problem with the framework: its normative bias. By placing the *a priori* dichotomy at the center of the framework, the authors implicitly come to suggest a relationship of negative hegemonic power and positive oppositional emancipation. Because of the original framework's foundations within the emancipatory tradition and its empirical application in a critical analysis, Andrews and Bamberg and other proponents of the theory appear to assume that the counter-narrative, simply by virtue of its relational position to the hegemonic master, exhibits an emancipatory potential. In the words of Bamberg (2004), unfolding this

Rethinking Counter-Narratives in Studies 175

potential entails "outlining in fine-grained detail the processes of how master narratives are invoked so that counter narratives can come to existence, that is, *to describe these processes as they invoke potentially liberating and emancipating agenda*" (361, my emphasis).

First, I would argue that this claim of an automatic emancipatory potential is largely empirically unwarranted: although it might turn out to be correct in certain cases, it currently lacks evidence in contemporary organization studies of 'counter-narrative' sense-making that it will always be so. For instance the contributions in this volume by Frandsen and Humle and by Jensen, Maagaard and Rasmussen document how counter-narrating is not automatically part of an 'emancipating agenda' for organizational members. Instead, it sometimes seems to be exploited to further the management's agenda. Second, and more pertinent, such emancipatory claims seem hard to reconcile with current empirical constitutive approaches within organizational studies (many of them ethnographical), which share allegiance to inductive methodological position. This position assumes that organizational practices and narratives do not have a preconfigured structure and, as a direct result, that the job of organization analysis is not to look for a prefixed pattern of values. Finally, the normative bias has the further methodological consequence that it "locks" the set of potentially relevant actors: the focus on counter-narrative implies a fixed analytical vantage point allied with the disenfranchised in this relation.

To be clear, my critique is primarily aimed at naïve, uncritical or biased applications of counter-narratives to organization studies—one might see this chapter as a confessional tale from the field: the main lesson I learned, and I find it important enough to elaborate on it here, is that there is a real risk of taking over the core ontological assumptions from the counter-narrative framework. This can then overshadow or even obfuscate the empirical specificity of individual cases. The danger is that the too simple nature of the concept, that is, its constituent dichotomy, blurs the complex relationship between power, practice, discourse and narratives found in the messy realities of organizational life (see Kuhn and Corman 2003; Stark 2011).

Despite the current problems with the original counter-narrative framework, counter-narratives can, I contend, be integrated as part of a narrative approach to organizational studies: the critical perspective on language and society ties in well with the narrative studies in organization theory over the last two decades (see, e.g., Boje 2001; Cooren 2001; Czarniawska 2000, 2004, 2008—see also the Introduction to this volume).

This link is not surprising as both nonofficial organizational narratives and organizational counterculture have been key subjects in organizational studies since the mid-1980s (see, e.g., Czarniawska 1998; Martin and Siehl 1983; Mumby 1987; Schein 1985). Within this approach to narratives in organizational studies one finds studies of resistance to organizational change (Czarniawska and Sevón 1996; Zorn, Page and Cheney 2000), power relations (Boje 1991; Mumby 1988) and employee narratives on professional

176 Rasmus Kjærgaard Rasmussen

identity (Alvesson 1993; Sveningsson and Alvesson 2003). In the broader field of organizational culture studies the phenomena of 'counter-narratives' ties in well with studies of subcultural sense-making (Martin and Siehl 1983).

In the following I, on the contrary, want to outline the particular connections to organization studies by privileging the other category of "that which they are countering," that is, the *master* narrative. According to Bamberg (2004) master narratives as the dominant cultural narrative has the function that they "'normalize' and 'naturalize'" (360) events and actions as routines, whereby actors' attention is directed toward a reduced range of actions and interpretations. The notion of a dominant or primary narrative that expresses and directs the organization is certainly not foreign to organizational communication studies: for example, Deuten and Rip's (2000) idea of institutionalized 'grand narratives' or 'master stories.'

My argument is that this emphasis on power and struggles, as well as the role of narrative in identity formation, makes the counter-narrative framework especially apt for being integrated with a critical strain of narrative organizational analysis that has investigated power and the political function of narratives (e.g., Mumby 1987, 1988).[2] Like Bamberg's argument for the master narrative's propensity to "normalize and naturalize," Mumby stipulates that that official *organizational* narratives serve as "legitimating devices" that naturalize "the order of things" within the organization

In order to rethink Bamberg and Andrews's original concept of counter-narratives I therefore demonstrate how it is possible to reconceptualize master narratives as authoritative texts in the sense described by Kuhn (2008, 2012). The advantage of this move is that it both privileges a more neutral conceptualization of master narratives and has the potential to account for ambiguities in complex constellations of organizational narratives and texts.

Reconceptualizing Master Narratives as 'Authoritative Texts'

As already mentioned, one of the primary aims of this chapter is to enable empirical studies of organizational practices. In this context, it becomes crucial to enable the observer to unearth how abstract concepts such as narratives may play a role in everyday practices. I would contend that Kuhn's concept of *authoritative text* offers a particularly useful answer to how dominant organizational ideas and documents manage to 'do' something in practice. This is because authoritative texts

> represent the abstracted intentions of the interactants whose conversations create, and previously created, them [. . .] In so doing, they mediate cooriented conversations while they simultaneously coordinate and facilitate practice. Moreover, texts direct attention and discipline actors by portraying particular phenomena, as well as forms of knowledge and action, as (in)appropriate and (un)desirable [. . .]
>
> (Kuhn 2008, 1236)

Rethinking Counter-Narratives in Studies 177

Moreover, authoritative texts are manifest in two forms: as 'concrete' and 'figurative' texts. The former type as "sign and symbols that are inscribed in some [. . .] permanent form" (ibid.), a modality that coincides with the commonsensical idea of organizational texts as policy documents, memoranda and e-mails (as well as products and rules). The latter type, on the other hand, is defined as the "abstract representations of practice sites, communities and firms" (Kuhn 2008, 1235), which encompasses institutionalized practices, abstract managerial ideas and so on. Kuhn stresses the managerial role of such texts with an example from General Motors: "the need to construct and maintain an authoritative text that represented the whole, directed managers' attention, disciplined them, and linked their practices together" (2008, 1237).

Authoritative texts are a thus both a concept and a methodological device that can help identify connections in organizational practice. The definition emphasizes on the practical function in coordinating and facilitating *and* the more abstract function of disciplining actors—for example, the role of concrete documents in institutionalizing practices. This is important in the case study's presence of both nation branding texts and communication practices. Here the authoritative text as an analytical device is able to account for the specific connection between the concrete text (in the form of the *Action Plan*) and the institutionalized practice of nation branding (as a recipe or idea).

Generalizing from this example, Kuhn's concept offers insight to the often-overlooked relation between concrete steering documents and dominant managerial practices in organizations by arguing that authoritative texts become a site of struggle over authorship (2012, 557). Now, Kuhn's dual perspective on both the performativity (i.e., 'disciplining' and 'directing' actors) and on the textual modalities ('concrete' or 'figurative') allows for operationalization within empirical studies. Additionally, this methodological approach can solve some of the analytical shortcomings inherent in Bamberg and Andrews's original concept and the advantage of reconceptualizing master and counter-narratives is twofold.

First, this move levels the normative and relational bias in the original conceptualization of master and counter-narratives considerably as the analytical attention is now directed to any specific organizational narrative phenomena regardless of this is part of a relational dichotomy or not. This makes it possible to home in on various configurations of narratives implicated in struggles of becoming authoritative texts. Second, the authoritative texts and the focus of performativity makes it possible to go beyond merely disclosing representations of binary power struggles in organizations and instead give due analytical attention to how these various normative narratives affect the organization—creating action and in turn new narratives. By conceptualizing master narratives as authoritative texts, emphasis can thus be given to larger panoply of functions and forms over content.

178 *Rasmus Kjærgaard Rasmussen*

Authoritative Texts: Organizational Practices and Power

I argue that this more general conceptualization enables connections to other approaches within organizational analysis, in particular two perspectives, which I will outline in the following.

The first is Fenton and Langley's (2011) notion of *institutional organizational practices*. They define these as "routines, procedures techniques and types of discourse at organizational and extra-organizational levels" (1173). They further argue that such practices are manifest in what they call "institutionalized grand narratives" (1175). This proposition makes it further possible to argue that authoritative texts methodologically can encompass institutionalized practices in the form of dominant managerial ideas (Sahlin-Andersson and Engwall 2002) and organizational recipes (Byrkjeflot 2011) such as nation branding, risk management or corporate social responsibility (CSR). In addition this definition, of course, also encompass other more general types of institutionalized organizing practices such as bureaucracy.

Second, authoritative texts have a clear connection to notions of organizational power. Using authoritative texts as analytical device makes it possible to conceive power struggles as a form of textual, discursive struggle over meaning and legitimacy (see, e.g., Clegg, Courpasson and Phillips 2006). Specifically, I follow the notion by Kuhn (this volume) that the authoritative text "should be understood as a site of struggles over *meaning*" (22, my emphasis) to promote a conceptualization of organizational power struggles as *textual and discursive struggles*. This conception, then, can afford an understanding of power, which I'll promote in this chapter *as the ability of one or the other authoritative text to author, define or shape the other* (see Phillips, Lawrence and Hardy [2004] for a general discussion of the institutionalization of texts). I further operationalize this definition of textual power struggles over discursive dominance as the analytical approach to the case in the next section.

To summarize the argument so far: empirically, authoritative texts provide an *institutionalized discursive organizational resource through which members can align their practices*. Analytically, authoritative texts enable alternative conceptualizations of organizational power struggles as *textual struggles over discursive dominance*. The final step in the present reconceptualization involves connecting this notion of master-narrative-as-authoritative text to the use of narratives and documents in organizational practice.

Narrative Performativity and Discursive Power Struggles

But how do master narratives and documents attain organizational performativity? According to a communicative constitutive approach to organizing (or CCO) both policy and strategy practices in organizations rely heavily on the use of texts and documents (Cooren 2004; Fenton and Langley 2011;

Rethinking Counter-Narratives in Studies 179

Kuhn 2008; Spee and Jarzabkowski 2011).[3] Any investigation of policy or strategy practice must therefore acknowledge documents as a key element in these processes. In answering how counter-narratives-as-authoritative text can have performativity I align myself with CCO studies and their explanation of the role of documents in organizing processes.

These approaches draw on the idea of a "text-conversation dialectic" (Kuhn 2008; Taylor and Van Every 2000) to elucidate how the production of organizational narratives is inseparable from the consumption of organizational texts (e.g., Spee and Jarzabkowski 2011; Yates and Orlikowski 2007). Spee and Jarzabkowsky thus contends that a university action plan gained organizational performativity by a iterative process: "talk and text became more interpenetrated, with talk confirming text and text supporting talk, over successive cycles as the plan was considered to reflect agreed terminology" (2011, 1236). Fenton and Langley (2011) additionally suggest that we focus analytically on the persuasiveness and rhetorical form of strategy documents and their narratives (see also Barry and Elmes 1997).

Drawing on these insights from CCO we can conclude that narratives and documents do more than simply represent the organization: they gain performativity in iterative sense-making processes where they are produced and continually consumed by the organization. Some texts gain enough importance and legitimacy to become authoritative texts. And when they attain this status a struggle over meaning and legitimacy has typically preceded.

Based on this CCO model of textual performativity and Kuhn's notion of authoritative texts as struggles over meaning it is possible to promote the notion of organizational power struggles as a *textual, discursive struggles* over organizational authorship (see also Kuhn, in the this volume). This entails looking at organizational power, as the ability of one or the other authoritative text to author, define or shape the other. This conceptualization of organizational power and practice has ramifications for incorporating the counter-narrative framework in organizational analysis. Where the original counter-narrative framework would focus on power as a static dichotomy ("which narrative is the dominant and which is the counter?") the conceptualization of power as textual struggles over meaning contrary entails a more processual focus. Incorporating the CCO view on power and practice, hence means focusing analytically on *how* a master-narrative-as-authoritative text is *translated* into the other and how this translation (text, narrative) travels in practice afterward (see Cooren 2001; Czarniawska 2008; Czarniawska and Joerges 1996).

Employing the idea of master narratives-as-authoritative texts analytically thus entails focusing on the struggle between the master narratives in the case in both concrete texts and in practice. Specifically, this means examining the main document in case (the *Action Plan*) as a site for the discursive struggle between the master narratives-as-authoritative texts of nation branding and bureaucracy and determining in what ways this struggle created a new local practice. Thereby investigating if this, in turn, could function as competing, new, authoritative text within the ministry as organization.

180 Rasmus Kjærgaard Rasmussen

Revisiting the Case: Narrative Struggles over Authority

The following demonstration of the value of master-narratives-as-authoritative texts builds on a comprehensive study of the organizational implementation of nation branding and its translation into practice via the central document of the *Action Plan* (see Rasmussen [2014] for a detailed account). This was based on a documentary study (and intertextual analysis) of a large corpora of strategy and policy texts and on four-month-long[4] ethnographic fieldwork during 2009 within a Danish ministerial department in a special unit, the so-called Branding Denmark Project Office (henceforth, the Project Office).[5] I draw on this study but focus particularly on the examples of *textual* power struggles and their effects on organizational practice. I do so by, first, exploring how the bureaucratic organization activated the two master-narratives-as-authoritative texts and authored the *Action Plan* and, second, by examining what happened when it was fed into the organization[6] again (cf. Spee and Jarzabkowski 2011). Here I demonstrate how the struggle resulted in a hybridization of the two master narratives and in an emerging, new practice in the ministry.

Producing the Action Plan: The Struggle between Branding and Bureaucracy

The *Action Plan* was the result of the political effort to "rebrand" Denmark after the so-called Cartoon Crisis. It was devised as a bill titled *The Action Plan for Global Marketing of Denmark* that was passed in 2007 by the Danish parliament and founded with some US$77.5 million. The declared objective was that by 2015, Denmark should be ranked among the top ten of all Organisation for Economic Co-operation and Development countries on the Anholt-GMI Nation Brand Index—a ranking of national reputations provided by British consultant Simon Anholt (Danish Government 2007, 4).

This political aim of enhancing the national reputation is clearly authored by the master narrative of nation branding and alludes to core texts of consultancy and practitioner literature on which this analytical plot is based.[7] The plot of nation branding is that globalization has placed all countries in a competition in which the ability to attract resources is linked to a favorable reputation. Countries are the protagonist subject in this tale and they are engaged in struggle (competition) with the antagonist of globalization or other countries. As an institutionalized practice and managerial recipe nation branding is inspired by tourism and destination marketing, but its conceptualization of these practices is clearly marked by an inspiration from corporate branding (see Kavaratzis and Hatch 2013), and it is from this field that it draws on the idea of the valuable and manageable (national) reputation.

The core practice associated with nation branding is planning and execution of "big events" and auditing and ranking of the "nation brand." In some

Rethinking Counter-Narratives in Studies 181

of Simon Anholt's articulations of nation branding, coordination of governments' strategic communication activities is additionally deemed vital. In the *Action Plan* these practices are present at content level when the plan calls for more "attention-grabbing events of world-class caliber events" (Danish Government 2007, 4) and evaluation (i.e., ranking) of the Danish national brand. In this the master narrative of nation branding is effectively enrolled albeit in a bureaucratic fashion.

Detecting the presence of the master narrative-as-authoritative text of bureaucracy in the *Action Plan*, on the other hand seems like a "no brainer"; the plan is after all a policy document published by a government department. However, stipulating *how* bureaucracy manifests itself both intertextually and rhetorically can tell us more about how this institutional practice gains performativity in the case. At the *Action Plan*'s semantic level, bureaucracy manifest itself by employment of the *rhetoric of policy*—a style that, according to Shore and Wright (1997), presents itself as a neutral instrument for promoting efficiency and effectiveness. This occurs when the plan emphasizes improvement of coordination between government agencies as an important goal: "to ensure a more effective and coordinated marketing" (Danish Government 2007, 5).

Furthermore, the authoritative text of bureaucracy also activates a specific linguistic repository related to *action*: a quantitative content analysis of the document disclosed that words like *organizing, coordinating, implementing* or *establishing* were prevalent. Appropriately, the *Action Plan* is rife with tables and figures dedicated to budget and task allocation. In this respect the plan has a crucial proto-performative aspect, as a *model for* concrete actions to be taken by specific organizational actors (see Geertz 1973).

Again, this points to a bureaucratic-administrative plot in which the key component is the idea of coordination *as* administration, a story that also dominated the civil servants' narratives of practice. This plot refers directly to the materiality of the bureaucratic practice as the use of specific and highly institutionalized organizational genres (Orlikowski and Yates 1994) related to handling and controlling cases—for example, the case file, the memoranda and the briefing.

The master narrative-as-authoritative text of bureaucracy thus manifests itself as a specific administrative plotline of control and coordination that stipulates that the call of government bureaucracy is to organize and coordinate (see also Crowston 1997; Kogut and Zander 1996). In addition, another version of the core bureaucratic narrative was found in the practitioners narratives in which bureaucracy was seen a prerequisite for democratic governance. This democratic plot echoes Max Weber's ideal of the rational-legal bureaucracy (Weber 2004) and is an integrated part of the civil servants' identity work—an issue to which I return in the next section.

My initial conclusion is that the *Action Plan* is a hybrid between branding and bureaucracy narratives and that this is visible both semantically and thematically. However, the hybrid can in turn be understood as the

182 *Rasmus Kjærgaard Rasmussen*

bureaucracy's *translation* of nation branding. This is, for example, seen in the plan's call for "events" and "brand ranking," where the authoritative text of nation branding is effectively enrolled although in a bureaucratic manner. Also, this is paralleled in the way that "globalization"—the main culprit of the nation branding narrative—is enrolled in the bureaucratic story of the *Action Plan* as the root cause of the entire political initiative.

Let's turn back to the struggle between the two authoritative texts that I have described as a struggle over discursive dominance. That is, a question of which text was ultimately able to translate the other within its rhetoric and its practices. Drawing on Yates and Orlikowski (2007) one can see the way the PowerPoint genre has been able to appropriate the genre of the business presentation as an exemplum of such a process (see also Schoeneborn 2013). We can conclude that something similarly has taken place in the case: the prose and rhetoric of the plan is shaped more by a bureaucratic discourse than by branding terminology. This is clearly evidenced in the way strategic communication efforts in the *Action Plan* are continually reduced to questions of *form*: how to control and coordinate rather than what content to communicate. Additionally, even the title avoids the word *branding* and uses the more neutral, and possibly more manageable, idea of the global *marketing* of Denmark.

The merit of the applied method, then, is its sensibility to the complexity and situatedness of organizational power struggles. If we had used the counter-narrative framework unamended we would only have been able to examine the authoritative text that dominates in this bureaucratic hybrid—that is, automatically labeling the other text as the dominated "counter." Furthermore, had we used more traditional notions of power we would be limited to simply claiming that the bureaucratic organizing logic and practice 'won' the struggle (see, e.g., Pache and Santos 2010).

Conversely, the CCO approach allows for the ambiguity and messiness of organizational practice. The advantage of 'authoritative text' as device is, hence, that it preserves the analytical multiplicity by making it possible to see the *Action Plan* as a dynamic actant that carries with it the trajectory of both the struggle *and* the branding moniker. As Kuhn (this volume) stipulates, no authoritative text is ever either monolithic or complete but will often incorporate conflicting and ambiguous stories of practice. Moreover, this perspective makes it possible to see that the struggle can be reanimated when the document is fed into the organization after its publication.

Consuming the Action Plan: The Encounter between Branding and Bureaucracy

The pivotal question here is, of course, "In what did way the *Action Plan*'s discursive struggle, as well as its bureaucratic hybrid translation of branding, affected the practice of the civil servants?" That is, how do the civil servants account for their new practice related to implementing nation branding type

Rethinking Counter-Narratives in Studies   183

activities in the bureaucratic setting of the ministry? In answering this, I examine what informed this new practice when the civil servants talk about it: how did they use the *Action Plan*'s hybrid translation and to what extend did they reanimate the discursive struggle between branding and bureaucracy in their accounts?

To get a better understanding of how the *Action Plan*'s translations informed the bureaucrats' organizational practice I investigate three particular illuminating accounts of the nation branding practice in the ministry as a political-bureaucratic organization. Thematically, the accounts, from different viewpoints, revolve around the issue of doing nation branding in a bureaucratic organization. The central motif is that the civil servants attempt to define their 'nation-branding' practice by talking about how it differs from bureaucracy, on one hand, and other types of strategic communication, on the other. Analytically I focus on which of the 'authoritative texts' are mobilized in the accounts and how this is done. Finally, I discuss how the new practice is being established to overcome the tension between the two master practices of bureaucracy and branding not only at the organizational level but also at the level of professional identity.

The first account originates from an interview with the Project Office's communication officer. The narrator of this worked with external communications, and I asked her how she defined the Project Office's practice:

> [W]hat is it we're supposed to do? For me it is branding. Even though Simon Anholt says "You cannot brand a country" what we do in my eyes is more branding than marketing. That's why I think it's so funny that there are so many concepts surrounding what we do.

The Anholt quote referred to by her originated from a conference that the ministry had held in the autumn of 2008. By evoking "Anholt," "branding" and "marketing," she is mobilizing the master narrative of nation branding as an authoritative text that directs practice. However, in this mobilization there is tension between marketing and branding, a point that is further emphasized when I asked her how she would then define the government's intention of branding Denmark:

> [I]t is more branding than marketing because marketing is one-way communication where you try to sell something whereas branding is a holistic approach where we have an image, an identity and a common denominator (pause) it is not a one-way communication but a dialogue where we cannot necessarily control everything.

This account, then, is part of a larger and more complex story of a local practice caught between the impossible ("you cannot brand a country") and the practical ("what we do is more branding than marketing"). A tension prompted by the professional need to deliver on the policy goal in the *Action*

Plan and give the political leadership "branding." The discursive authority of branding is evident as she goes at great lengths to solve the paradox ("you cannot brand a country") by affirming the possibility of nation branding as a bureaucratic practice (i.e., "what we do").

This objective is precisely the topic of the second account albeit from the point of view of bureaucracy. This example originates from an interview with another civil servant and is very illustrative for elucidating the practice of branding in the ministry and the attempt to protect his professional identity as a bureaucrat against being labeled as a communications specialist. The narrator had an MSc in political science, and he had on several occasions reflected candidly on what he perceived as the encounter of the alien element of branding within the institutionalized practice of bureaucracy in the ministry. In the example, his point of departure is the Project Office's practice connected to the implementation of the *Action Plan* and its initiatives and programs. He stresses that this is an altogether different practice due to the organizational setting in the ministry as a political organization:

> *The way they [i.e., the political leadership] have chosen in the* Action Plan *to say: it's not branding in a commercial way—understood as corporate branding—because there are simply other premises for branding a nation. And one has to say, additionally, that many of us are bureaucrats who have a lot to do with the political level of the government.*

In this example, both master-narratives-as-authoritative texts are present, and branding and bureaucracy are enrolled in conjunction with the concrete text of the *Action Plan*. However, only the institutionalized practice of bureaucracy—present by reference to the ministry's bureaucrats—and the *Action Plan* is given the authority as 'master narrative.' Nation branding, on the other hand, is swiftly translated into the bureaucratic practice by questioning its corporate and commercial elements. The account establishes that branding the nation is essentially a bureaucratic, political job because it is carried out by bureaucrats. Although the account reiterates both the *Action Plan*'s struggle between branding and bureaucracy and its mediation, the quote thus represents an even more bureaucratic translation of nation branding because nation branding is quite simply tantamount to what the Project Office's bureaucrats do.

The interesting point is how this tension between the two authoritative texts is overcome. This is achieved by enrolling the *Action Plan* and its bureaucratic translation of nation branding as a discursive resource. This naturalizes the proposition that "branding a nation" is done by "bureaucrats." By virtue of its authority, a new, supplementing narrative is to be authored where nation branding is not a commercial form of branding but a political and bureaucratic practice. In this way the "text-conversation" dialectic facilitates a reiteration of the textual struggle in the *Action Plan*.

Rethinking Counter-Narratives in Studies   185

A way of mediating the struggle between the two institutionalized practices is thus to emphasize their professional identity as bureaucrats: that they despite being subjected to working with branding logics stress that they are *not* in the business of marketing or communication consultancy. Another way of mediating the tension is by claiming that the ministry's practice regarding bureaucratically situated nation branding constitutes an entire special or unique practice. In other words, the bureaucrats have a special way of doing nation branding. This is the topic of the third and final example based on observations in the ministry from an internal seminar for the Project Office. Here the Project Office's members discussed the nature of branding a nation, and their work with it, and to sum up the discussion, a senior member of the Project Office concludes,

> *The difficult part about our job is that the object we are supposed to communicate something about is highly contested. It is constantly subjected to discussions and despite of this we must construct it for a target group out there in the world. Perhaps one of the most diverse and difficult target groups at all. It is not about logos and pay-offs—but what is nation branding?*
>
> *He looks searchingly out on the other members none of whom seem encouraged to pick up that gauntlet when another senior member spontaneously bursts out: "It is feelings." The first senior member continues: "Very fast there arises a discrepancy between logo and perceptions. A gap. This is what is fundamentally different with nation branding compared to other communication activities. Branding requires consistency in the work, and that is a huge challenge. So the conclusion must be that it is a complex task to brand a nation."*

The example rehearses the new narrative about their practice: the complexity. The reason it is complex is, of course, also due to the bureaucratic institution in which this practice is assigned. However, this account also represents a successful attempt at mediating practices. This is achieved by the bureaucrat's repeatedly references to branding terminology: "target group" and "logo," as well as the core marketing idea of "consistency," are integrated into his account of their practice. The political-bureaucratic practice ("to brand a nation") simply becomes conceptualized via the authoritative text of branding to mediate the two.

In these accounts it is a central motif that the civil servants attempt to define their local nation branding practice by talking about how it differs from other types of communicative practices. Nation branding in a political bureaucracy is described as "complex" contrary to consultancy-based nation branding, which is deemed a "simple" and "naïve" extraction. The aim is hence also to differentiate the ministry's communication practice from other practices by demarcating the civil servants' profession as bureaucrats from communications professionals and consultants.

186 *Rasmus Kjærgaard Rasmussen*

However, when they define their practice positively they stress the indeterminacy of their work: they state that it is a "special" and "complex" task to brand a country. An assignment they describe as "huge" and "difficult" because it is "political." In conclusion, this new and local practice of nation branding is, on one hand, deemed more authentic because it is political but is, on the other hand, seen as different from the branding recipe precisely because it pertains to the domain of policy and government bureaucracy.

The central question is what *positional* value and function this new, local narrative of the 'unique' and 'special' practice of the Project Office has. Is it authored in opposition to the institutionalized practice of nation branding or bureaucracy—or to both? Indeed, this question ties in with my initial considerations about the value of using counter-narratives in organizational analysis.

Making Sense of the Case—Revisiting Counter-Narratives as Interpretation

So far, I have identified the local narratives as stemming from the encounter between the two master-narratives-as-authoritative texts—most notably, the narrative of branding in the bureaucratic ministry as a unique and special practice. I have not explicitly reflected on the 'positional value' of this power struggle's resultant *narrativization*. The final part of my argument therefore consists of returning to the counter-narrative framework to discuss the interpretation it can offer of this narrativization and how this can be integrated in my constitutive analysis of authoritative texts in the case.

According to the original counter-narrative framework, the narratives (and translations) found in the case can be interpreted as counternarratives. The interpretation of, for example, the narrative of the Project Office's 'unique practice' is then that it can be perceived as a counternarrative to both institutionalized practices in the case: of course, primarily to the managerial nation-branding concept and, only to a lesser extent, to the practice of bureaucracy that this narrative seems to affirm more than counter. But departing from the original framework it is perfectly valid to argue that the practice narratives can be opposed to both branding and bureaucracy. Again departing from the original framework it is thus logical to argue that the resulting narrativization of the practice struggle possesses countering elements by virtue of its positional value. Such interpretation would be evidenced by the civil servants' local practice narratives' explicit opposition to the professions of corporate branding and strategic communication.

However, as I have argued before, using only the *counter-narrative* lens limits the perspective on the case considerably. Departing from Kuhn's notion of authoritative texts conversely makes it possible to go further and interpret this narrative of the 'unique practice' as an attempt to create a new

Rethinking Counter-Narratives in Studies   187

master narrative in the Project Office. As we saw, it is a hybrid between the two master narratives and in this represents a new local practice. However, it is not yet an institutionalized practice in the ministry as organization or concept able to travel to other organizations. I would therefore argue that these local organizational narratives (and translations) aims at further organizational institutionalization and could in fact, departing from Kuhn's constitutive framework, be interpreted as *proto*-authoritative texts.

Kuhn (in this volume) argues that authoritative texts narrate the collective 'we' of the organization. By creating this new local narrative of the 'unique practice' of the members of the Project Office thus attempt to resolve a struggle between two professional identities by bringing about a new understanding of the collective 'we' in the organization. Furthermore, these countering accounts can be seen as a way of the collective bureaucratic 'we' of the Project Office to position itself within the bureaucracy of the ministry. With their new understanding of the 'we,' these stories are then a part of the practitioners' identity as they make it possible to both work with branding in the ministry and be a 'real' bureaucrat.

This interpretation acknowledge that the resultant narratives of the meeting between branding and bureaucracy can be valorized as local counternarratives while at the same time elucidating that these narratives *in turn* aim at becoming a master narrative *as* authoritative text within the ministry and beyond, whereby this new practice can be further institutionalized. This further points to empirical cases where initial counter-narratives strong enough to attain broad organizational legitimacy could gain status as authoritative texts.

Concluding Remarks

In this chapter I have advanced the counter-narrative framework, by illuminating the struggle of two master-narratives-as-authoritative text over discursive dominance, resulting in the emergence of a new, local organizational practice. This insight contributes to our existing knowledge on counternarratives and organizational practice in two different ways.

First, the counter-narrative framework when conceptualized through the notion of authoritative text can draw attention the role of power struggles in the evolution of new organizational practices. This is due to the concept's analytical features, which makes it possible to identify encounters between different types of institutionalized organizational practices as struggles between master narratives. Here the concept of counter-narratives could further theorize such power struggles as textual and discursive struggles. Second, my retheorizing of counter-narratives contributes to our understanding of the organizing effect of narratives and documents. The combination of the counter-narrative approach with 'authoritative texts' as analytical device provided an increased understanding of how narratives both as concrete and figurative texts gain performativity in the organization.

188 *Rasmus Kjærgaard Rasmussen*

Notes

1. The author wishes to thank Andreas Lindegaard Gregersen for his generous comments and help with the manuscript and Nico Mouton for many valuably discussions on organizational culture that helped sharpen the idea of this chapter. A special thanks also goes to Sanne Frandsen for her inspiring and patient editing.
2. It must be noted that this idea is shared by functionalist and cultural approaches. Schein (1985; cf. Meyerson and Martin 2001), thus, perceives the function of culture as a control mechanism very much like the more specific function of narrative that Mumby argues.
3. For a general account of documents as ethnographic, methodological and historical objects, see also Atkinson and Coffey (2004), Hull (2012), and Riles (2008).
4. However, one might claim that I really never left the field insofar as I continued to collect data in network of actors surrounding the branding project until 2012 when it was officially terminated.
5. Here empirical data consisted of observations of meetings and strategy workshops, interviews with the civil servants aimed at eliciting narratives (cf. Czarniawska 2004) of the their encounters with nation branding and document material in the form of policy documents of various kinds as well as internal background briefs and memoranda. Names of organizational units have been slightly altered.
6. In this move, I assume that the entire central government administration despite its departmental structure in certain respects can be perceived as a single organizational entity. This complex nature of government as an organisation has been discussed from various perspectives within political and administrative science (see, e.g., Rhodes 2005). However, given my point of departure from a constitutive view I contend that an organizing process can consist of many organizations (see Cooren 2001) and that boundaries between organizations are permeable (see Schoeneborn and Trittin 2013).
7. Using Kaneva's (2011) comprehensive review of nation-branding practitioner literature, I identified Keith Dinnie (2008), Simon Anholt (1998, 2000, 2007) and Wally Olins (1999, 2000, 2002, 2005) as core consultancy references. In the original analysis I used intertextuality to identify nation-branding source texts in the *Action Plan*; among these were Simon Anholt Nation Brands Index special report on "Denmark's international image," which is alluded to a the consultancy report on how to brand Denmark and a policy paper strategy paper on Denmark's reputation (Danish Government 2006).

References

Alvesson, M. 1993. "Organizations as Rhetoric: Knowledge-Intensive Firms and the Struggle with Ambiguity." *Journal of Management Studies* 30 (6): 997–1015. doi: 10.1111/j.1467-6486.1993.tb00476.x.
Andrews, M. 2004. "Counter-narratives and the power to oppose." In *Considering counter-narratives: Narrating, resisting, making sense*, edited by M. Bamberg and M. Andrews, 1–6. Amsterdam: J. Benjamins.
Anholt, S. 1998. "Nation Brands of the Twenty-First Century." *Journal of Brand Management* 5 (6): 395–406.
Anholt, S. 2000. *Another one bites the grass: Making sense of international advertising*. New York: Wiley.
Anholt, S. 2007. *Competitive identity: The new brand management for nations, cities and regions*. Basingstoke England and New York: Palgrave Macmillan.

Rethinking Counter-Narratives in Studies 189

Ashcraft, K. L., T. R. Kuhn, and F. Cooren. 2009. "Constitutional Amendments: 'Materializing' Organizational Communication." *Academy of Management Annals* 3 (1): 1–64. doi: 10.1080/19416520903047186.

Atkinson, P. and A. Coffey. 2004. "Analysing documentary realities." In *Qualitative research: Theory, method and practice*, edited by D. Silverman, 56–75. London and Thousand Oaks, CA: Sage.

Bamberg, M. 2004. "Considering counter-narratives." In *Considering counter-narratives: Narrating, resisting, making sense*, edited by M. Bamberg and M. Andrews, 351–371. Amsterdam: John Benjamins.

Bamberg, M. and M. Andrews. 2004. "Introduction." In *Considering counter-narratives: Narrating, resisting, making sense*, edited by M. Bamber and M. Andrews, ix–x. Amsterdam: John Benjamins.

Barry, D., and M. Elmes. 1997. "Strategy Retold: Toward a Narrative View of Strategic Discourse." *Academy of Management Review* 2: 429–452.

Boje, D. M. 1991. "The Storytelling Organization: A Study of Story Performance in an Office-Supply Firm." *Administrative Science Quarterly* 36 (1): 106–126.

Boje, D. M. 2001. *Narrative methods for organizational and communication research.* London: Sage.

Byrkjeflot, H. 2011. "Et kritisk blikk på omdømmeblikket." In *Substans og framtreden. Omdømmehåndtering i offentlig sektor*, edited by A. Wæraas, H. Byrkjeflot and S. I. Angell, 51–70. Oslo: Universitetsforlaget.

Clegg, S., D. Courpasson and N. Phillips. 2006. *Power and organizations, foundations for organizational science.* London: Sage.

Cooren, F. 2001. "Translation and Articulation in the Organization of Coalitions: The Great Whale River Case." *Communication Theory* 11 (2): 178–200.

Cooren, F. 2004. "Textual Agency: How Texts Do Things in Organizational Settings." *Organization* 11 (3): 373–393. doi: 10.1177/1350508404041998.

Crowston, K. 1997. "A Coordination Theory Approach to Organizational Process Design." *Organization Science* 8 (2): 157–175. doi: 10.1287/orsc.8.2.157.

Czarniawska, B. 1998. *A narrative approach to organization studies.* Thousand Oaks and London: Sage.

Czarniawska, B. 2000. *The uses of narrative in organisation research.* Göteborg: Gothenburg Research Institute.

Czarniawska, B. 2004. "Narratives in an Interview Situation." In *Narratives in social science research: Introducing qualitative methods*, 47–59. London and Thousand Oaks, CA: Sage.

Czarniawska, B. 2008. *A theory of organizing.* Cheltenham: Edward Elgar Publishing.

Czarniawska, B. and B. Joerges. 1996. "Travels of ideas." In *Translating organizational change*, edited by B. Czarniawska and G. Sevón, 13–48. Berlin and New York: Walter de Gruyter.

Czarniawska, B. and G. Sevón. 1996. "Introduction." In *Translating organizational change*, edited by B. Czarniawska and G. Sevón, 1–12. Berlin and New York: Walter de Gruyter.

Danish Government. 2006. *Debatoplæg: Danmarks omdømme [Discussion paper: Denmark's reputation]*. Copenhagen: Ministry for Economic and Business Affairs.

Danish Government. 2007. *Action plan for the global marketing of Denmark.* Copenhagen: Ministry for Economic and Business Affairs.

Deuten, J. J., and A. Rip. 2000. "Narrative Infrastructure in Product Creation Processes." *Organization* 7 (1): 69–93.

190   *Rasmus Kjærgaard Rasmussen*

Dinnie, K. 2008. *Nation branding: Concepts, issues, practice.* Oxford and Burlington, MA: Butterworth-Heinemann.

Fenton, C., and Langley, A. 2011. "Strategy as Practice and the Narrative Turn." *Organization Studies*, 32 (9), 1171–1196. doi:10.1177/0170840611410838.

Geertz, C. 1973. "Religion as a cultural system." In *The interpretation of cultures: Selected essays*, 87–125. London: Fontana Press.

Hull, M. S. 2012. "Documents and Bureaucracy." *Annual Review of Anthropology* 41: 251–267.

Jackson, M. 2002. *The politics of storytelling: Violence, transgression, and intersubjectivity.* Copenhagen Denmark: Museum Tusculanum Press.

Kaneva, N. 2011. "Nation Branding: Toward an Agenda for Critical Research." *International Journal of Communication* 5: 117–141. doi: 1932-8036/20110117.

Kavaratzis, M., and M. J. Hatch. 2013. "The Dynamics of Place Brands: An Identity-Based Approach to Place Branding Theory." *Marketing Theory* 13 (1): 69–86. doi: 10.1177/1470593112467268.

Kogut, B., and U. Zander. 1996. "What Firms Do? Coordination, Identity, and Learning." *Organization Science* 7: 502–518.

Kuhn, T. 2008. "A Communicative Theory of the Firm: Developing an Alternative Perspective on Intra-Organizational Power and Stakeholder Relationships." *Organization Studies* 29 (8/9): 1227–1254. doi: 10.1177/0170840608094778.

Kuhn, T. 2012, November. "Negotiating the Micro-Macro Divide: Thought Leadership from Organizational Communication for Theorizing." *Organization Management Communication Quarterly* 26 (4): 543–584. doi: 10.1177/08933189 12462004.

Kuhn, T., and S. R. Corman. 2003. "The Emergence of Homogeneity and Heterogeneity in Knowledge Structures During a Planned Organizational Change." *Communication Monographs* 70: 198–229.

Martin, J., and C. Siehl. 1983. "Organizational Culture and Counterculture: An Uneasy Symbiosis." *Organizational Dynamics* 12 (2): 52–64.

Meyerson, D. and J. Martin. 2001. "Cultural change: An integration of three different views." In *Organizational studies: Critical perspectives on business and management*, 321–345. edited by Warwick Organizational Behavior Staff, London: Routledge.

Mumby, D. K. 1987. "The Political Function of Narrative in Organisations." *Communication Monographs* 54 (2): 113–127.

Mumby, D. K. 1988. *Communication and power in organizations: Discourse, ideology, and domination.* Norwood, NJ: Ablex Pub. Corp.

Nelson, H. L. 2001. *Damaged identities, narrative repair.* Ithaca: Cornell University Press.

Olins, W. 1999. *Trading identities: Why countries and companies are becoming more alike.* London: The Foreign Police Centre.

Olins, W. 2000. "Why Companies and Countries Are Taking on Each Other's Roles." *Corporate Reputation Review* 3 (3): 254–265.

Olins, W. 2002. "Branding the Nation—The Historical Context." *Brand Management* 9 (4–5): 241–248.

Olins, W. 2005. "Making a national brand." In *The new public diplomacy: Soft power in international relations*, edited by J. Melissen, 169–179. New York: Palgrave Macmillan.

Orlikowski, W. J., and J. Yates. 1994. "Genre Repertoire: The Structuring of Communicative Practices in Organizations." *Administrative Science Quarterly* 39: 541–574.

Rethinking Counter-Narratives in Studies 191

Pache, A. C., and F. Santos. 2010. "When Worlds Collide: The Internal Dynamics of Organizational Responses to Conflicting Institutional Demands." *Academy of Mangement Review* 35 (3): 455–476.

Phillips, N., T. B. Lawrence, and C. Hardy. 2004. "Discourse and Institutions." *Academy of Management Review* 29 (4): 635–652.

Rasmussen, R. K. 2014. "Nation Branding in Practice: An Analysis of the Danish Government Administration's Interpretation and Organization of the 'Action Plan for the Global Marketing of Denmark 2007–2010' ". Department of Language and Communication, PhD Thesis, University of Southern Denmark.

Rasmussen, R. K., and H. Merkelsen. 2014. "The Risks of Nation Branding as Crisis Response: A Case Study of How the Danish Government Turned the Cartoon Crisis into a Struggle with Globalization." *Place Branding and Public Diplomacy* 10 (3): 230–248.

Rhodes, R. A. W. 2005. "Everyday Life in a Ministry: Public Administration as Anthropology." *The American Review of Public Administration* 35 (1): 3–25. doi: 10.1177/0275074004271716.

Riles, A. 2006. "Introduction: In response." In *Documents: Artifacts of modern knowledge*, edited by A. Riles, 1–38. Ann Arbor: University of Michigan Press.

Sahlin-Andersson, K. and L. Engwall. 2002. *The expansion of management knowledge: Carriers, flows, and sources*. Stanford, CA: Stanford Business Books.

Schein, E. 1985. *Organizational culture and leadership: A dynamic view*. California: Jossey-Bass Inc.

Schoeneborn, D. 2013. "The Pervasive Power of PowerPoint: How a Genre of Professional Communication Permeates Organizational Communication." *Organization Studies*, 34(12), 1777–1801.

Schoeneborn, D., and H. Trittin. 2013. "Transcending Transmission: Towards a Constitutive Perspective on CSR Communication." *Corporate Communications* 18 (2): 193–211. doi: 10.1108/13563281311319481.

Shore, C. and S. Wright. 1997. "Policy: A new field of anthropology." In *Anthropology of policy: Critical perspectives on governance and power*, 3–30. edited by C. Shore and S. Wright, London: Routledge.

Spee, A. P., and P. Jarzabkowski. 2011. "Strategic Planning as Communicative Process." *Organization Studies* 32 (9): 1217–1245. doi: 10.1177/0170840611411387.

Stark, D. 2011. *The sense of dissonance: Accounts of worth in economic life*. Princeton, NJ: Princeton University Press.

Stohl, C., and G. Cheney. 2001. "Participatory Processes/Paradoxical Practices: Communication and the Dilemmas of Organizational Democracy." *Management Communication Quarterly* 14: 349–407.

Sveningsson, S., and M. Alvesson. 2003. "Managing Managerial Identities: Organizational Fragmentation, Discourse and Identity Struggle." *Human Relations* 56: 1163–1193.

Taylor, J. R. and E. J. Van Every. 2000. *The emergent organization: Communication as its site and surface*. Mahwah, NJ: Lawrence Erlbaum Associates.

Thorsby, Karen. 2004. "Negotiating "normality" when IVF fails." In Considering counter-narratives: Narrating, resisting, making sense, edited by M. Bamber and M. Andrews, 61–82. Amsterdam: John Benjamins.

Thornton, P. and W. Ocasio. 2008. "Institutional logics." In *Handbook of organizational institutionalism*, 99–129. edited by R. Greenwood, C. Oliver, K. Sahlin and R. Suddaby. Thousand Oaks, CA: Sage.

192 *Rasmus Kjærgaard Rasmussen*

Weber, M. 2004 (org. 1919). "Politics as a vocation." In *The vocation lectures*, edited by D. Owen and T. B. Strong, 32–94. Indianapolis and Cambridge: Hackett Publishing Company.

Yates, J. and W. Orlikowski. 2007. "The PowerPoint presentation and its corollaries: How genres shape communicative action in organizations." In *Communicative practices in workplaces and the professions: Cultural perspectives on the regulation of discourse and organizations*, 69–91. edited by M. Zachry and C. Thralls, Amityville, New York: Baywood Publishing Company.

Zorn, T. E., D. J. Page, and G. Cheney. 2000. "Nuts about Change: Multiple Perspectives on Change-Oriented Communication in a Public Sector Organisation." *Management Communication Quarterly* 13: 515–566.

Part III

Counter-Narratives and Narrative Ecologies of Organizations

9 The Fate of Counter-Narratives
In Fiction and in Actual Organizations

Barbara Czarniawska

The Narrative Turn in Organization Studies: A Brief Remainder

The narrative has always been of interest in literary theory and, to certain extent, in the humanities, in general. It began to trickle down into the social sciences toward the end of the 1970s. One pivotal event was the publication of US historian Hayden White's book, *Metahistory* (1973), in which he claimed that the discipline of history could be properly understood and practiced only as historiography. After all, historians "emplot" (White's neologism, to avoid the ambiguous "plot") the events into histories, rather than finding them ready-made. If even historians emplot their narratives, don't social scientists do the same? US sociologist Richard Harvey Brown appealed for "a poetics for sociology" (1977)—a postulate formulated much earlier by Russian Formalist Mikhail Bakhtin (1928/1985). By the end of the 1970s, the trickle became a stream. Walter R. Fisher (1984) claimed that narratives played the central role in politics and should therefore be accorded a central place in political sciences. Jerome Bruner (1986) and Donald E. Polkinghorne (1987) made the identical claim for psychology, Laurel Richardson (1990) for sociology and Deirdre McCloskey (1990) for economics, to name but a few.

This narrative turn became clearly visible in organization theory toward the end of the 1990s, but from the outset it existed in several variations. Joanne Martin (1982) had been inspired earlier by the French poststructuralists, but her follower David M. Boje (1991, 2001) was primarily inspired by the way in which ethnomethodologists tackled narratives in conversation analysis.[1] Yiannis Gabriel (1991, 2000) transferred many insights from folklore studies to organization studies, and I borrowed primarily from narratology (Czarniawska 1997, 2004).

The first studies of stories told in organizations were already making it obvious that at least one other narrative was always in the offing, especially if it concerned important events. The researcher could choose among various options, selecting a story that offers the best or the most convincing explanation, without challenging the truth or falsity of the story's elements. On the other hand, the researcher could quote all or most of the critical

196 Barbara Czarniawska

options, in order to illustrate what I have called "the wars of emplotment" (for examples, see Czarniawska 2002). These wars are common occurrences that provide an abundance of material to the media: here is the version of top management, and here are the unions' versions. Yet the notion of "counter-narratives" suggests much more than that. It suggests that some narrative has been chosen (or enforced) as the official one, or the legitimate one, or the correct one; but that there are others that defy and contradict it (similarly, Yiannis Gabriel suggests in this volume that there would be no master narratives if there were no counter-narratives).

Yet it is practically impossible to undertake a field study that would specifically focus on *creation and further treatment* of organizational counter-narratives, though it is practically certain that such counter-narratives—already made—will be discovered in the process of conducting any study. Counter-narratives are purposefully offered mostly by investigative journalists and/or organizational whistleblowers. But not all of them need be dramatic or dangerous to the narrators. The existence of counter-narratives, their role, and their fate are, or should be, of great interest for organization scholars, as this volume clearly demonstrates. One way to overcome the difficulty of studying the emergence and further destiny of counter-narratives was, therefore, tracing the fate of organizational counter-narratives in the works of fiction.

Why Fiction?

As I have often pointed out (see, e.g., Czarniawska 2014a), the notion that a close relationship exists between literary fiction and the social sciences can be traced to the very beginnings of sociology (see, e.g., Coser 1963). The modern novel and sociology were born at the same time and remained inseparable for many years (Lepenies 1988). Furthermore, according to Coser, fiction offers social evidence and testimony, together with a commentary on events and morals, making it a better source of sociological insights than the random comments of untrained informants. Recourse to literature cannot replace systematically collected field material but can complement and enhance it.

Indeed, novelist and literary theoretician Milan Kundera has claimed that the novel described the unconscious before Freud did, analyzed class struggle before Marx did, and practiced phenomenology even before the concept had been invented (Kundera 1988). Neither is the event of scholars reaching for fiction a passing trend. In the aftermath of the 2007–2010 financial crisis, Melville's novella of some 150 years ago, *Bartleby the Scrivener. A Story of Wall Street* (1853/2004), was brought to the attention of intellectuals commenting on the crisis. As crime-fiction story writer Val McDermid suggested recently,

> When people lose trust in politicians, they need to find it elsewhere. Maybe, because they trust writers to tell some kind of truth buried in the fictions, we're being listened to in a way we rarely have before.
>
> (2015)

The Fate of Counter-Narratives   197

One could ask why people don't turn to social scientists, but this question would require a very long answer. Here, suffice to say that social scientists cannot "bury truth" in their texts, and when they come out in the open with it, and it has a feeling of a counter-narrative, their stories share the fate of other counter-narratives—the topic of this chapter.

The three novels I have chosen were selected in order to illustrate three different epochs, important for developments within the field of organizing and the field of organization studies. The first is located at the beginning of industrialization; the second in the late 1960s, when it seemed that the world had changed for good; and the third in the late 1980s, when postmodernism was announcing a beginning of a new era.

The Counter-Narrative of Justice

Mysteries of Winterthurn is a trilogy by Joyce Carol Oates, originally published in 1984 and reprinted in 2008. The novels are united by the same place—Winterthurn—and by the same families, but chiefly by the personage of amateur detective Xavier Kilgarvan. In each book, Xavier solves a murder puzzle, but his solutions are, and remain, counter-narratives, if not unknown by the other characters, at least ignored in favor of the official explanation.

The story of greatest relevance in the present context is *The Devil's Half-Acre or the Mystery of the "Cruel Suitor."* Devil's half-acre was the nickname for "rockbound desolation two miles south of Winterthurn City" (157), infamous for the five dead bodies of young women that were found there, the last being the body of Eva Teal, a worker in a nearby textile factory. The law enforcement officers "professed themselves baffled by the heinous crimes; and altogether helpless in preventing further crimes to be committed" (ibid.) A friend of one of the earlier victims was interrogated, resulting in the idea of a "cruel suitor"; she reported that the murdered woman had told her about a mysterious, gallant suitor acquired shortly before her death.

Hopeless as they may have felt, the officers of law did their duty and interrogated "nearly three dozen persons," among whom was "the distraught office manager of the Shaw textile mill, Isaac Rosenwald, a Jewish gentleman of forty-one years of age, who had been called in for questioning as a consequence of an anonymous tip received by the authorities" (168).

The gossip joined Eva Teal—and the earlier victims—with a young local man, Valentine Westergaard. Upon hearing about Eva Teal's murder, he promptly visited the sheriff's office on his own initiative to offer his alibi. At the time of the crime, he was attending a party with his male friends, one of whom was Xavier's brother:

> There could not have been a more painful contrast between young Mr. Westergaard, with his exquisite good manners and his eagerness to cooperate with the investigation, and Mr. Isaac Rosenwald,—who, from the first minute he entered the sheriff's office, escorted by a burly

198 Barbara Czarniawska

deputy, radiated the most disagreeable air: a commingling of alarm, disdain, agitation, and, it might have been, guilt.

(177)

The investigation continued, and its development is told in rich detail, in fantastic imitation of Victorian language, and commented upon by the editor—that is, Joyce Oates. The anti-Semitic prejudices of the officers of the law merely reflect the anti-Semitic prejudices of the rest of the population. Even Rosenwald's unusual caring for and understanding of his workers was interpreted as sinister. The factory owners were pleased to make use of his education and intelligence but did nothing to help him when he found himself in trouble. In general, Oates did not present her readers with the stereotypical image of the textile factory as consisting of bad bosses and good workers. The workers are poor and can be bribed or bought, humane bosses are treated with suspicion, and the anti-Semitism exists across all social classes.

The murders of Devil's half-acre were soon defined as "ritual" killings. A week after the first questioning, Rosenwald was fired from his job, and next day was arrested on suspicion of first-degree murder. The media engaged experts (including university professors) in the history of Jewish ritual murders. All agreed—with the exception of Xavier Kilgarvan.

Having earned some fame as an amateur detective outside Winterthurn, Xavier was allowed to look at the documents of the investigation, marveling at their incompleteness and the resulting arrest. But public opinion had already decided that Rosenwald was guilty of not one, but all five, murders, and sorry as the local sheriff might have been, he understood the need to calm the upset and fearful public. Again, Xavier did not share this feeling, and he began his own investigation. (Oates manages beautifully to convey a mixture of irony at Xavier's rationalistic belief in "principles of detection" and an approval of his courageous quest for the truth.) He questioned the victim's coworkers and the foreman at the mill, receiving confused and contradictory pictures of both Eva Teal and Isaac Rosenwald. Yet the only lead he had was that Teal and some other victims were seen in the company of young Westergaard.

Not even a month after the arrest, "a county grand jury unanimously moved to hand down and indictment of *murder in the first degree* against Isaac Rosenwald" (121)—but not before a Jewish lawyer who came from New York to defend Rosenwald was beaten up at his hotel and hastily withdrew from the case.

Xavier was allowed to see Rosenwald and discovered that the prisoner was luckily unaware of his predicament. Believing that the guilty party would be found sooner or later, he busied himself writing letters to authorities and articles about "rank anti-semitism in America, in the 1890s" (226)—texts that, Xavier was more than certain, never reached their addresses.

The stories that circulated about young Westergaard made Xavier virtually certain that Valentine, as he was appropriately called, killed his sister

The Fate of Counter-Narratives 199

and his maid before murdering the five other young women. Yet only the last murder could be proved—by breaking his alibi or by finding the evidence. But while Xavier, by exerting great effort and risking his life, was working on it, Isaac Rosenwald confessed—not to one, but to all five, murders. At this point, the Second Invisible Empire of the Brethren of Jericho concluded that waiting for the final trial would be a waste of time and public money, and Rosenwald was summarily executed, so that "[*j*]*ustice will be served, and the murderous Jew will not slip away, by one or another knothole in the Law,—the which his New York City attorney would doubtless find*" (260).

Yet Xavier found his proof. He paid for the exhumation and autopsy of the five bodies, inspected Westergaard's quarters during the owner's absence and caused a withdrawal of several testimonies (and, most likely, the sheriff's retirement).

> Elsewhere, he contrived to speak with girls and women,—ranging between the ages of twelve and seventy-three—who toiled, for a modest wage, some twelve or fourteen hours daily (Sundays naturally excepted), in the textile mill owned by Shaws, or in the glove factory owned by the Peregrines, or in the canning factory owned by the Von Goelers, or in the paper pulp mill, owned by his very kinsmen, the De Forrests [. . .] a number of these young persons had, all bravely, volunteered to tell their abashed tales to the police; but had been [. . .] sent unceremoniously away; and had not dared to protest,—not even when Isaac Rosenwald was arrested, and given out to be the killer, and everyone *knew*, ah, absolutely *knew*, that he was innocent.
>
> (278–279)

Oates pinpoints here a typical aspect of public opinion that can sway from a narrative to a counter-narrative, even while erasing the memory of the switch.

Valentine Westergaard was arrested a month after Isaac Rosenwald's hanging, on the strength of the evidence collected by Xavier. The final proof, and the breaking of his alibi, was an unexpected testimony of another of Xavier's brothers, who witnessed and co-perpetrated all five murders.

Does this mean that the counter-narrative won in the end? No, it didn't. Westergaard was explained as having been possessed by the evil spirit at the time of the murders, and therefore not responsible for his actions. Xavier's brother went to prison, possibly awaiting a death by hanging (he committed suicide in his cell), while Valentine Westergaard went abroad, sending an ironic postcard to the detective:

> [I]n such cities as New York, Boston, and Philadelphia, the verdict in Westergaard's favor has been greeted with incredulity, and outright scorn: the *New York Times* condemning it as "so extreme and farcical a miscarriage of Justice, it undermines not only our faith in the jury system, but our faith in human nature itself." [. . .] closer to home [. . .]

200 *Barbara Czarniawska*

sentiments were quite the reverse; and the *Winterthurn Gazette* spoke for the great majority, in hailing the verdict as a "stirring vindication of the American tradition of trial by jury,—nay, a tribute to the American virtues of *common sense*, and *fair play*, and *Christian compassion*."

(340)

A contemporary reader may see in the text allusions to the existing division of the United States into "the Bible Belt" and New England but could also argue that *The Devil's Half-Acre*, characterized even by Oates as a "Gothic novel" (see the afterword to the 2008 edition), frightening as it is, is only a work of fiction. But is it?

In 1913 Leo Frank, a Jewish manager in the National Pencil Company in Atlanta, Georgia, was convicted on weak evidence of a murder of a thirteen-year-old girl who was employed by the company. An angry mob took him out of jail and hanged him (King 2014). Yet the details of Oates's story serve an even better fit with another famous incident, in which, as Charles King deftly put it, "modernity clashed with myth" (King 2014, 3). The body of a young boy was found in a Kiev suburb in the spring of 1911. In July, Beilis, a Jewish man working as a dispatcher at the nearby Zaitsev Brick Factory, was arrested, with no evidence tying him to the crime scene. The prosecution "contended that Beilis was a Jew who worked near the murder site and that Jews were known to use the blood of Christian children as a binding agent in Passover *matzo*" (ibid). Expert witnesses provided testimony regarding Jewish rituals and customs, just as they did in Oates's novel. And like Rosenwald, Beilis was "uniquely unsuited as a stand-in for supposed Jewish fanaticism: he was religiously unobservant and a typical member of the empire's highly assimilated Jewish petite bourgeoisie" (King 2014, 4). This fact probably played a role in writers, politicians and activists from around the world joining protesters during the 29 months that separated the arrest from the trial in 1913. The New England newspapers and other major media covered the trial while the local *Kievlyanin* called for justice for the victim and an end to Jewish crime. Unlike in the Oates's novel, Beilis was acquitted, and no actual perpetrator has ever been found. For once, a counter-narrative won, but as Leo Frank's case suggests, it was an exception rather than a rule.

The American Nightmare

One of the endorsements of Joseph Heller's *Something Happened* (1966/1975) claims that his book served as an undoing of the American dream. Indeed, the novel can be seen as a counter-narrative to the American dream narrative, if not even sadder than that. Whereas Heller's famous *Catch-22* (1961) could be seen as comical, or at least a tragicomic tale, his *Something Happened* is a tragedy, and its humor is very black indeed.

The main protagonist in *Something Happened* is Bob Slocum, a middle manager in a company where he is both a great success and a great failure.

The Fate of Counter-Narratives 201

In the course of the book, he is to be promoted to a yet higher position with yet greater perks, at the expense of a colleague and presumed friend.

Slocum is pleased with himself yet deeply unhappy, as are his family members. Enough to quote the titles of the book chapters: Slocum "gets the willies," his wife "is unhappy," his daughter "is unhappy," his "little boy is having difficulties," "[i]t is not true" that "retarded children" are greatly loved by their parents and although "[t]here is no way of getting away" from such children, even "normal" children can "stop talking" to their parents. At the end, the only consolation is that "[n]obody knows" what Slocum really did. But he does.

Narratives and counter-narratives are typically presented by attributing them to different sources or to the same sources over different periods. The cruelty of Heller's novel, and the cruelty of the predicament of its protagonist and narrator, is that the narrative and the counter-narrative both come from Slocum simultaneously, and neither is given priority. The citation limits do not permit me to quote them all, yet they must be quoted in the author/narrator's formulation to retain their force. They all come from the chapter titled "The Office in which I Work":

> We average three suicides a year; two men, usually on the middle-executive level, kill themselves every twelve months, almost always by gunshow, and one girl, usually unmarried, separated, or divorced, who generally does the job with sleeping pills. Salaries are high, vacations are long.
>
> People in the company like to live well and are unusually susceptible to nervous breakdowns. They have good tastes and enjoy high standards of living. We are well-educated and far above average in abilities and intelligence.
>
> (17)

This is the general situation. Some special jobs have special conditions:

> [T]he salesmen love their work and would not choose any other kind. They are a vigorous, fun-loving bunch when they are not suffering abdominal cramps or brooding miserably about the future; on the other hand, they often turn cranky without warning and complain and bicker a lot. Some sulk, some bully; some bully and then sulk. All of them drink heavily until they get hepatitis or heart attacks or are warned away from heavy drinking for some other reason, and all of them, sooner or later, begin to feel they are picked on and blamed unfairly. [. . .]
>
> The salesmen work hard and earn big salaries, with large personal accounts . . .
>
> (22)

It is the late 1960s, yet much in the description of the company brings to mind the TV series *Mad Men* (2007–2015), not least because of the way women are treated (although the women, when they become bosses, behave

202 Barbara Czarniawska

like men). The similarity is striking because it is a company that depends on sales. Therefore, as Slocum says,

> I am continually astonished by people in the company who do fall victim to their own (our own) propaganda. There are so many now who actually believe that what we do is really important. This happens not only to salesmen, who repeat their various sales pitches aloud so often they acquire the logic and the authority of a mumbo-jumbo creed, but to the shrewd, capable executives in top management, who have access to all data and ought to know better. [. . .] It happens to just about everybody in the company who graduated from a good business school with honors: they are the uniformly the most competent and conscientious people in the company, and also the most gullible and naïve.
>
> (24)

Perhaps those people are unable to tolerate the cognitive dissonance that one would imagine must be experienced by anybody who combines a narrative and a counter-narrative? Otherwise, it can be claimed, in accordance with both Festinger's (1957) original theory and its later variations,[2] that it is exactly the constant state of cognitive dissonance that is making Bob Slocum so deeply unhappy in spite of his successes. The way out would be to articulate the counter-narrative, but he finds it impossible:

> I have this thing about authority, about walking right up to it and looking it squarely in the eye, about speaking right out to it bravely and defiantly, even when I know I am right and safe.
>
> (11)

So the only device that permits Slocum to diminish his unhappiness is a secret counter-narrative device:

> On days when I'm especially melancholy, I begin constructing tables of organization from standpoint of plain malevolence, dividing, subdividing, and classifying people in the company on the basis of envy, hope, fear, ambition, frustration, rivalry, hatred, or disappointment. I call these charts my Happiness Charts. These exercises in malice never fail to boost my spirits—but only for a while.
>
> (29)

The suffering of Bob Slocum is such that the reader hopes that he may be an exception and that the others manage to convince themselves of the truth of their own propaganda and live happily ever after. Yet dialogues with his management colleagues suggest that Slocum is not an exception but a rule. And yet the salaries are high, the vacations are long and the company is an equal opportunity employer.

Scott Adam's cartoons (e.g., Adams 1998) are the best indicator that these problems have not vanished. At least the cartoons are neither as cruel nor as tragic as Heller's book. Do they count as counter-narratives, then? Opinions differ: Solomon (1997) has claimed that although Adams seems to caricature the corporate culture, his satire ultimately supports the aims of top corporate management. Filipczak (1994, 29) has suggested, on the other hand, that "Adams exposes many 'cutting edge' workplace issues to the severe light of day, inviting us to laugh at reengineering, cross-functional teams, business meetings, corporate buzzwords, management fads." In my reading of *Dilbert*, Adams does something similar to what Heller did: showing how narratives and counter-narratives coexist in corporate life (Czarniawska 2014b). *Dilbert* suggests that mainstream narratives create role models that managers cannot live up to, models that alienate people as they try to come to terms with the messy realities of their workplaces.

Although both Heller and Adams target US corporations, the phenomenon is not limited to the United States and not only during present times, when most countries imitate US companies. The contributions to this very volume quote examples from Denmark (Humle and Frandsen; Norlyk—in both cases, field material comes from organizations supported by European Union) and from global organizations (Svane, Gergerich and Boje), where the presence of multicultural narratives confirms that counter-narratives exist in every place where one finds narratives.

Is a Dialogue between Narratives and Counter-Narratives Possible?

Although David Lodge's *Nice Work* (1988) is counted among his campus novels, it is set in two organizations: a university and a company. Accordingly, there are two main characters. Robyn, a temporary lecturer, is a postfeminist, poststructuralist academic specializing in Victorian industrial novels, who lives in a world of symbols and politics (the latter in both the positive sense of the feminist movement and the negative sense of the politics of academia). Forced by academia, she reluctantly visits the world of industry, where she is expected to shadow Managing Director Victor Wilcox. Victor also lives in a two-dimensional world: the world of the political and the practical. Symbols do not exist for Victor. Practical things do not exist for Robyn.

Robyn's counter-narrative is ready practically from the outset, and it consolidates after her visit to the foundry, a truly hellish view that has replaced her image of the industry taken from Victorian novels. She knows in advance that the workers at Victor's company are suffering from a cruel exploitation of their labor and other kinds of repression from the capitalist system, represented by the powerful man: their managing director. Thus, she is ready for a justified act of subversion. Having heard during a meeting that there will be an attempt to get rid of an incompetent worker of Asian origins by sending him to training and therefore proving his incompetence, she reveals it to the worker. The foundry workers walk out. Furious, Victor finds her at her home and forces her to listen to his counter-narrative. He is not powerful; the higher-ups can get rid of him easily (eventually, they do). The factory is in a precarious position, and if it loses its clients, the workers will all be unemployed. The job of a manager, even the managing director, is full of paradoxes that must be solved. The company's production is largely too old-fashioned to survive its competition. Production needs to be automated and rationalized, which may mean redundancies, but if the owners do not update the factory, they will close it down. If they do update, on the other hand, and the update succeeds, there can be new hirings. The same scenario will unfold in the case of a prolonged strike, which can follow the walkout triggered by Robyn.

Faced with this narrative, Robyn reluctantly agrees to meet the foundry workers and tell them she misunderstood the conclusion reached at the meeting: the worker in question is going to be sent for training, and his job is guaranteed. The workers achieve Victor's promise to be given extra paid time for washing themselves after work, and they return to work.

But this is not the only exchange of narratives and counter-narratives. Victor decides that shadowing should go both ways and appears at Robyn's department. Here the text gets truly witty and satirical—after all, campus novels are David Lodge's specialty—but also full of premonition. It so happens that Victor's narrative assumes that universities work like businesses. The counter-narrative, presented in part by Robyn, but in a longer speech by her boss, Professor Swallow, portrays universities as collegial entities, very different from businesses. Again, predicting developments to come (or were they already visible in 1988?), Victor suggests that universities should be managed like businesses, which Robyn counters by saying that businesses ought to be modeled on universities. Lodge seems to think that some mixture of the two would not be amiss.

The swapping of narratives and counter-narratives in *Nice Work* suggests that the two parties have an authentically *dialogical relationship*, in the sense that Mikhail Bakhtin (1981) suggested. It is not a debate (they do not have to convince one another), it is not a Socratic dialogue (in which the teacher prompts the student to come to the correct answer) and it is not a duet (they do not speak in unison). But they both learn from that exchange. Robyn learns what the real foundry looks like and discovers that her job at the university is, as the title suggests, "a nice work" compared to many other possible jobs. Victor learns about the role of poetry and prose in life, about the role of symbols and the use of multiple interpretations. They confront various faces of organizational politics in both their workplaces, and learn more about the relationship between work life and private life. The novel ends on a positive note: Vic loses his job but starts his own company; Robyn gets a job at the university, albeit a temporary one.

Different Fates of Counter-Narratives: Times and Places

Joyce Oates's novel presents the confrontation between narratives and counter-narratives according to a traditional plot: a counter-narrative is formulated with the aim of winning over the official narrative but fails, its correctness and the efforts of its narrator notwithstanding. Although the story concerns events of more than a century ago, this plot has not lost its actuality. Common as it may be, it is probably encountered more often in fiction than in factual literature (more on this point in Gabriel, in this volume), precisely because of the reasons I mentioned at the outset. Were counter-narratives well known, they could be winning. Still, the media constitute a forum in which such meetings can be observed. It needs to be added, though, that the official narratives are not always wrong and that counter-narratives are not always correct. Consider, for instance, the narratives about global warming and the counter-narratives about global warming as a scam, a fraud or a conspiracy.

Late modernity has introduced new possibilities of encounters between narratives and counter-narratives—some dystopian, some hopeful. The idea of a constant coexistence of such narratives in the consciousness of working people—not only in relation to work life but also in relation to life, in general—and the unhappiness it brings, so convincingly depicted in *Something Happens*, is frighteningly realistic. Resolving cognitive dissonance by starting to believe in the propaganda perpetrated by one's organization is certainly a dystopian possibility.

What remains is Lodge's idea of a fruitful exchange of narratives and counter-narratives in a dialogical mode. For the moment, it seems decisively Utopian. Universities are being run as companies, and businesspeople seem none too eager to swap narratives. But things do change, so perhaps a time will come when universities and business can enter an equal dialogue.

Notes

1. Later, he widened the sources of his inspiration to include even quantum physics (Boje 2014).
2. Cognitive dissonance theory if of central importance for Weick's concept of sense-making, see, for example, Weick (1995).

References

Adams, Scott. 1998. *The joy of work*. New York: HarperBusiness.
Bakhtin, Mikhail M. and P. N. Medvedev. 1985 (org. 1928). *The formal method in literary scholarship: A critical introduction to sociological poetics*. Cambridge, MA: Harvard University Press.
Bakhtin, Mikhail M. 1981. "Discourse in the novel." In *The dialogic imagination: Four essays*, 259–422. Austin, Texas: University of Texas Press.
Boje, David M. 1991. "The Storytelling Organization: A Study of Story Performance in an Office-Supply Firm." *Administrative Science Quarterly* 36: 106–126.

206 Barbara Czarniawska

Boje, David M. 2001. *Narrative methods for organizational and communication research*. London: Sage.

Boje, David M. 2014. *Storytelling organizational practices: Managing in the quantum age*. New York: Routledge.

Brown, Richard H. 1977. *A poetic for sociology: Toward a logic of discovery for the human sciences*. New York: Cambridge University Press.

Bruner, Jerome. 1986. *Actual minds, possible worlds*. Cambridge, MA: Harvard University Press.

Coser, Lewis A. 1963. *Sociology through literature*. Englewood Cliffs, NJ: Prentice-Hall.

Czarniawska, Barbara. 1997. *Narrating organizations: Dramas of institutional identity*. Chicago: University of Chicago Press.

Czarniawska, Barbara. 2002. *A tale of three cities, or the glocalization of city management*. Oxford, UK: Oxford University Press.

Czarniawska, Barbara. 2004. *Narratives in social science research*. London: Sage.

Czarniawska, Barbara. 2014a *Social science research from field to desk*. London: Sage.

Czarniawska, Barbara. 2014b. "Hard is soft, precise is fuzzy, concrete is abstract, or, where does the economic information belong?" In *Accounting, management control and institutional development*, edited by Anatoli Bourmistrov and Olov Olson, 217–223. Oslo: Cappelen Damm.

Festinger, Leon. 1957. *A theory of cognitive dissonance*. Stanford, CA: Stanford University Press.

Filipczak, Bob. 1994. "An Interview with Scott Adams." *Training* 31 (7): 29–33.

Fisher, Walter R. 1984. "Narration as a Human Communication Paradigm: The Case of Public Moral Argument." *Communication Monographs* 51: 1–22.

Gabriel, Yiannis. 1991. "On Organizational Stories and Myths: Why It Is Easier to Slay a Dragon Than to Kill a Myth." *International Sociology* 6 (4): 427–442.

Gabriel, Yiannis. 2000. *Storytelling in organizations*. Oxford, UK: Oxford University Press.

Heller, Joseph. 1961. *Catch-22*. New York: Simon and Schuster.

Heller, Joseph. 1966[1975]. *Something happened*. New York: Ballantine Books.

King, Charles. 2014, September. "Kiev, 1913. A Dead Boy, a Dramatic Trial and the Minute Detail in Which Modernity Clashed with the Myth." *Times Literary Supplement*, 19: 3–4.

Kundera, M. 1988. *The art of the novel*. London: Faber and Faber.

Lepenies, Wolf. 1988. *Between literature and science: The rise of sociology*. Cambridge, UK: Cambridge University Press.

Lodge, David. 1988. *Nice work*. London: Penguin.

Martin, Joanne. 1982. "Stories and scripts in organizational settings." In *Cognitive social psychology*, edited by Albert J. Hastorf and Alice M. Isen, 225–305. New York: Elsevier and North Holland.

McCloskey, D. N. 1990. *If you're so smart. The narrative of economic expertise*. Chicago, IL: The University of Chicago Press.

McDermid, Val. 2015. "Why Crime Fiction Is Leftwing and Thrillers Are Rightwing." http://www.theguardian.com/books/booksblog/2015/apr/01/why-crime-fiction-is-leftwing-and-thrillers-are-rightwing [April 4, 2015].

Oates, Joyce Carol. 2008[1984]. *Mysteries of winterthurn*. Princeton, NJ: Ontario Review Press.

The Fate of Counter-Narratives 207

Polkinghorne, Donald. 1987. *Narrative knowing and the human sciences*. Albany, NY: State University of New York Press.

Richardson, Laurel. 1990. "Narrative and Sociology." *Journal of Contemporary Ethnography* 19 (1): 116–135.

Solomon, Norman. 1997. *The trouble with Dilbert: How corporate culture gets the last laugh*. Monroe, ME: Common Courage Press.

Weick, Kark E. 1995. *Sensemaking in organizations*. Thousand Oaks, CA: Sage.

White, Hayden. 1973. *Metahistory: The historical imagination in nineteenth century Europe*. Baltimore, MR: The John Hopkins University Press.

10 Narrative Ecologies and the Role of Counter-Narratives

The Case of Nostalgic Stories and Conspiracy Theories

Yiannis Gabriel[1]

In spite of wide-ranging disagreements about the scale, nature and character of narratives, scholars are in general agreement that counter-narratives emerge *in opposition* to other narratives, sometimes referred to as master narratives. Thus, the literature on counter-narratives has started to identify different ways in which they can subvert, qualify or confront master narratives. Master narratives, for their part, seek to neutralize, discredit or silence counter-narratives, representing as they do the interests of those in power. By contrast, counter-narratives are generally seen as attempts of the powerless, marginalized or disempowered to make their voices heard, to place their stories on record and to challenge the uncontested hegemony of master narratives.

The dynamic of narrative and counter-narrative has become a common and compelling trope. It can be observed in many spheres of social activity, including politics, religion, business and art. It can also be observed in academic discourses where new theories are cast as counter-narratives challenging the hegemony or mainstream theories and concepts. In this chapter, I want to question and qualify this trope. I argue that master narratives do not exist as narratives until and unless they encounter counter-claims and counter-narratives in one form or another. Like Hegel's master–slave dialectic, without a counter-narrative a narrative can hardly be recognized as a master narrative. Master narratives need counter-narratives in order to recognize themselves as narratives, and counter-narratives need master narratives in order to be recognized as counter-narratives. This chapter demonstrates how narratives and counter-narratives co-create each other by examining two particular narrative types, nostalgic stories and conspiracy theories.

Acknowledging many ongoing, unresolved and potentially unresolvable debates on the definition of narratives, this chapter approaches narratives as particular types of *text*, involving temporal chains of interrelated events or actions, undertaken by sentient characters with motives, judgments and emotions. In this way, I adhere to the tradition that approaches narratives as plotted texts with characters (even if these are nonhuman), beginnings, middles and ends (Czarniawska 1998; Gabriel 2004). Narratives are not mere concepts, words, signs, objects, images and 'facts,' although all of these can

Narrative Ecologies and the Role of Counter-Narratives 209

be approached as texts and can spark, sustain or challenge a wide variety of narratives as defined here. In this chapter, I also make another assumption, one that I have sought to demonstrate elsewhere (Gabriel 2000), namely, that narratives (and counter-narratives) *travel*. In this sense, narratives are not constrained by formal organizational boundaries. Instead, they can and often do cross such boundaries, moving from one organization to another, from one discourse to another, and from one narrative space to another. They can emerge at the widest cultural level of societies and even civilizations, they can merge, cross-fertilize and interweave themselves with other narratives that subsist in organizational or group levels and can ferment or animate still other narratives that emerge at the individual level, as subjects strive to come to terms with different circumstances and adversities and create their own life stories. Narratives from one narrative space can and do colonize other narrative spaces; they grow, they shrink and they eventually die.

The view adopted in this chapter is that narratives and counter-narratives *around* organizations cannot be separated from narratives those *in* organizations and those *outside of* organizations. While organizations themselves frequently feature terrains where particular types of narratives and counter-narratives battle it out, the narrative dynamics themselves readily and regularly cross boundaries of organization, group and nation. Thus, the narrative dynamics that pitch modernization against tradition, the individual against the impersonal forces of the machine, expertise against formal authority, egalitarianism against meritocracy, logic against irrationality, compassion against ruthless efficiency and so forth, these may be observed regularly in different group, organizational and social contexts. I, thus, propose that the co-creation of narratives and counter-narratives can be conceptualized as occurring in spaces that are not circumscribed by organizational boundaries, but in spaces that I term *narrative ecologies*, where different narratives, along with their plot lines, their characters and their affective and symbolic resonances, take form, encounter, combine, qualify or contest each other.

Counter-Narratives and Master Narratives

One of the important recent developments in narrative studies has been the realization that a master narrative is not subverted through direct confrontation, inversion or denial, one for example in which the triumphant hero is turned into an absurd fool or one in which a passive victim is turned into a plucky survivor (for a definitive summary statement, see Bamberg 2004). Nor is it always the case that in a counter-narrative the weaker party is recast as the stronger one and vice versa, as demonstrated by Humle and Frandsen, in this volume. Instead counter-narratives emerge out of various counter-claims, claims, in other words, that invoke a master narrative, drawing it, so to speak, into consciousness in order to rebut it or challenge it.

210   Yiannis Gabriel

Counter-claims do not necessarily crystallize into counter-narratives unless they manage to establish a narrative coherence of their own. In doing so, they deploy a formidable range of tropes involving irony, intertextuality, inversion, reframing, double entendres, killer facts and many other techniques to lend them credibility and plausibility. A counter-narrative, therefore, does several things simultaneously: it articulates and posits a particular narrative as a master narrative, it demonstrates some of the flaws and contradictions of this narrative and it proposes an alternative narrative line with a new plot and metamorphosed characters that ostensibly redefine a particular phenomenon and offer a superior explanation for it. In so doing, and this is crucial, the counter-narrative unveils certain political interests and positions served by the master narrative and offers itself as a political intervention that undermines or subverts these interests and positions.

Consider an example that provides an almost paradigmatic account of this process proposed by Wairimũ Njambi, who claims to offer "a counter narrative on 'female genital mutilation' " (2007, 689). This counter-narrative may be viewed as part of academic discourse, it will become readily apparent that it is also a social, a political and even a personal counter-narrative. Njambi argues that far from representing a means of oppression and domination of women and a human rights violation as stipulated by the World Health Organization, traditional female genital practices among Gĩkũyũ women in Kenya were a core feature of an initiation rite (*irua ria atumia*), which represented a means of empowerment. Bans on female genital practices initiated by colonial administrators were part of "a persistent colonial legacy that is embedded well within the feminist discourse of eradication: one that presumes a non-reciprocal right of a 'civilized' west to intervene in the (presumably backward) cultural practices of its Others" (Njambi 2007, 693). While claiming to liberate African women from the oppressive grip of African men, colonial bans were an attempt to curb a rite which "promoted an ethic of boldness and courage that provided a socio-historical platform for women to engage in militant anti-colonial activity in ways that were perceived as coequal of men" (Njambi 2007, 691). Hence, claims Njambi, "*irua ria atumia* can be read as a truly feminist practice aimed at women's equality, promoting a bravery that contemporary feminists should embrace, rather than disparage" (692).

In Njambi's counter-narrative, a set of practices that allegedly deprived women of sexual desire and subordinated them to male power, on the contrary emancipated them from monogamous bondage, bolstered their independent sexual identities and enabled them to play a vital part in the Mau Mau rebellion, the great African liberation movement against colonial rule. In this way, Njambi's counter-narrative challenges not only the master narrative of colonialism (enlightened Westerners ridding primitives of superstition, backwardness and barbarism) but also the feminist master narrative that views 'genital mutilation' as perpetuating women's subordination to men. This latter narrative, once constructed as a counter-narrative to the

Narrative Ecologies and the Role of Counter-Narratives   211

hegemony of traditional genital practices, is now recast as part of the colonial master narrative, nestling with the larger narrative of colonization.

Importantly, at no point in Njambi's counter-narrative is there any reference to the mechanism whereby a ritual involving the removal of parts of a woman's sexual organs at the age of 16 is linked with the effects it is meant to produce. Instead, Njambi constructs her counter-narrative through a variety of arguments which include, first, the revelation that colonial administrators frequently acted at the behest of missionaries and other religious agents who were scandalized by polyandry and permissiveness of traditional Gĩkũyũ society; second, by revealing that these administrators did not seek to impose similar bans to male genital practices; and, third, that far from sexually oppressing Gĩkũyũ women, genital mutilation, now recast as *irua ria atumia*, emboldened them and enabled them to fight colonial rule on equal terms as their male counterparts. In this way, Njambi repositions what was previously a counter-narrative (the feminist narrative against genital mutilation) as a master narrative, demonstrating that counter-narratives can and often do turn into master narratives, once they have started to spawn counter-narratives of their own.

Njambi's counter-narrative demonstrates something else. It is often claimed that history is written by winners—hence that large historical narratives reflect the values, interpretations and above all the interests of the winners. In a famous essay written toward the end of World War II, George Orwell (1944) argued that the history of the war, as well as its meaning, would depend on who eventually won it: "In no case do you get one answer which is universally accepted because it is true: in each case you get a number of totally incompatible answers, one of which is finally adopted as the result of a physical struggle. History is written by the winners." He concluded by expressing some hope that "the liberal habit of mind, which thinks of truth as something outside yourself, something to be discovered, and not as something you can make up as you go along, will survive. But I still don't envy the future historian's job." Njambi's counter-narrative suggests that it is not the winners who invariably write history. Winners usually have better things to do with their victories than writing and rewriting them. Once the celebrations are over and the monuments have been erected, it is the losers (at least the surviving ones or their advocates) who get down to writing history, or, more often, to telling their stories. It is they who seek through these stories to vindicate their own sufferings and celebrate their own endurance in adversity; it is the losers' claim to be proffering counter-narratives that establishes the sovereignty of the master narratives. It is by constructing such narratives that losers cease to be losers, just as the Mau Mau rebels, men and women can no longer be viewed as losers. They become survivors, fighters, rebels, martyrs or, at worst, victims of brutal and illegitimate violence, whose silence has been broken.

Counter-narratives emerge gradually and unevenly. Initially some isolated voices, often those of survivors and their relatives, advocates, journalists,

212 Yiannis Gabriel

academics (like Njambi) and historians, begin to make claims or proffer what in my own work I call "protostories" (Gabriel 2000) or what Boje (2001) refers to as "antenarratives." These are emotionally and symbolically charged narrative fragments that contain the seed or the potential of a story. In the right circumstances, they may gather momentum, detail, cohesion and credibility, coagulating into fully blown counter-narratives. The emergence of such counter-narratives depends crucially on drawing in neutrals and gaining credibility, always in juxtaposition to master narratives. Counter-narratives are thus frequently romanticized as brave attempts by the poor, the weak and the exploited to rise up against their oppressors and claim a moral superiority over them. It is true then that counter-narratives challenge established regimes of power. It is also true that most audiences and neutrals will celebrate the victories of brave little Davids standing up to giant Goliaths or the heroic defeats of Spartacus in the hands of the brutal Roman legions. Yet, it seems to me that advocates for Goliath and even for the Roman legions are capable of creating counter-narratives seeking, for example, to show how badly they have been misunderstood throughout history, how their pain has gone unrecognized or how their brutality was dictated by superior expediencies or served superior ends. The view that history is often written by losers does not contradict the well-rehearsed argument that those in power, notably governments, corporations and other organizations devote extensive resources and efforts in silencing or discrediting counterclaims and stopping them from crystalizing into counter-narratives (e.g., Boje, Luhmann and Baack 1998; Linde 2009). On the contrary, what is argued here is that attempts to discredit and silence counterclaims become themselves significant counter-narrative plotlines, adding fuel to them, in precisely the manner that will be discussed presently in relation to conspiracy theories which thrive on the back of the cover-up, the whitewash and, above all, the silencing of voice. What I am arguing here is that master narratives, too, can claim to be marginalized, ignored or even silenced by the shrill voices of protestors, troublemakers and those in perennial search of conspiracy and victimhood.

Two types of narrative that demonstrate the co-creation of narrative and counter-narrative are nostalgic stories and conspiracy theories. These types of narrative become quite prominent in certain social circumstances, especially when a society, an organization or a group undergoes periods of intense uncertainty, confusion or crisis when many narratives lines compete for ascendancy with no overall narrative hegemony. Such has been the situation in Greece over the past six years, in the face of unprecedented economic crisis, social stress and high levels of anxiety, where many different voices compete to be heard and many outrageous narratives assume a kind of plausibility. In such situations, nostalgic narratives emerge as a sort of consolation for current troubles, making up for these troubles by extolling the greatness of the past. Nostalgic narratives exist in sentimental varieties, but it is increasingly their aggressive, xenophobic, exclusionary versions that

Narrative Ecologies and the Role of Counter-Narratives 213

predominate. Conspiracy theories, for their part, seek to make sense and account for distressing experiences in the present by discovering various scapegoats and conspiracies on which to pin blame. Nostalgic narratives and conspiracy theories can at times combine and reinforce each other. What I wish to examine is how these narratives become features of certain narrative ecologies by setting themselves up as counter-narratives and drawing energy and sustenance from the master narratives which they set out to combat.

Nostalgic narratives have been explored previously in organizational contexts (Brown and Humphreys 2002; Gabriel 1993; Strangleman 1999, 2007; Ybema 2004). Less developed has been the study of organizational conspiracy theories (Brown and Jones 1998; van Iterson and Clegg 2008)—yet there is no reason to doubt that both of these narratives are not uncommon in many organizations. If the two sections that follow draw their inspiration predominantly from the political sphere, it is because it is in this sphere that nostalgia in its xenophobic and aggressive forms that I want to highlight, and conspiracy theories have been most extensively studied. Consistent with the perspective adopted in this chapter, to the extent that these two types of narrative stand in opposition to hegemonic narratives, they can be reproduced at the political, the social, the organizational and even the personal level.

Nostalgic Narratives as Counter-Narratives

Nostalgic narratives are easy to identify, as they are driven by the unmistakable emotion of nostalgia and invariably revolve around the 'golden age' of a nation, an organization, a group or an individual. This is a time in the past, constructed variously as heroic, romantic, happy, free, communal or even as harsh and difficult but always in such a way as to outshine the present which appears lackluster, impoverished and lacking. The nostalgic past is quite distinct from the historical past. It is a mythoplastic past, a past of fantasy and myth, a past that does not require support from historical research or factual verification. In fact, the nostalgic past positively eschews any encounter with the past of historians that may question or undermine it. As a yearning for the past, nostalgia can be experienced as pleasurable or unpleasurable, but most authors are in agreement that it reflects the discontents of today rather than the glories of the past (Daniels 1985; DaSilva and Faught 1982; Davis 1979; Gabriel 1993; Ivanova 2000; Murphy 2009; Werman 1977).

In general, nostalgia can be viewed as the flip side of the ideology of progress (Lasch 1991). When faith in a better future wanes people are liable to experience nostalgia which can then define the prevalent mood of a whole period. Thus, Boym (2001) argues that for Russia, the twentieth century started with utopia and ended with nostalgia. Nostalgia can thus drive social movements, like Fascism, that harp after a return to not only a golden age but also artistic movements like romanticism (Löwy and Sayre 2001; Thiele 1997) that rise as counter-narratives to the values of the modernity. In our days, nostalgia sustains entire empires of consumerist society, such as the heritage and tourist industries and a large part of the entertainment, film, music and the arts sectors. In the hands of advertisers, nostalgic narratives have become a tried and tested means of promoting anything from authentic wholemeal bread to real ale (e.g., Unger, McConocha and Faier 1991).

Nostalgic narratives are quite common in organizations, especially among older employees. Their leading characters may include different aspects of an organization's past—its departed leaders, its old buildings, its family-like atmosphere, its authentic products or its memorable characters. Such narratives tend to have a sentimental quality and serve a consolatory and ego-supporting purpose. Having been a member of an organization's golden age reinforces individuals' self-esteem (Brown and Humphreys 2002, 2006; Gabriel 1993; Strangleman 1999). A 'has-been' becomes a 'somebody' through a narrative that casts him or her as part of the golden past. Inasmuch as they provide a bedrock of loving memories, a life worth having lived and a source of meaning, this sentimental or even mawkish and always bittersweet nostalgia helps people to endure their current malaise.

Nostalgic narratives have distinctly *counter*-narrative qualities. By constructing an idealized past, nostalgic narratives emphasize the discontinuity that separates the past from the present and offer a critical commentary of those the precise qualities of the present that make it inferior to the past. Thus, the caring, family-like atmosphere of the past highlights the dog-eat-dog ethos of the present; the authenticity of the past highlights the phony artificiality of the present; the solidarity of the past highlights the isolation and loneliness of the present (Gabriel 1993). Brown and Humphreys (2002) demonstrated how nostalgic narratives in a postmerger Turkish university opposed the dominant narratives of bureaucracy and Islam and "challenged the university élite's assumptions of unity and integration" (154). Similarly, O'Leary's (2003) study of an Irish newspaper demonstrated how nostalgic narratives celebrating the company's past as a time of camaraderie, honesty, heavy-drinking and serious investigative reporting opposed modernizing narratives of efficiency, careerism, deceitfulness and injustice. By emphasizing the caring, authentic and meaningful qualities of the past, these narratives cast today's organization as a profit-hungry monster. O'Leary's argument also offers a contrast between nostalgic narratives and a different type of counter-narrative—cynical narratives. These, too, cast the organization as a monster, but instead of seeking to sustain identities by incorporating them into an idealized past, they do so through a disidentification and distancing from the organization of today. Denigration of the present, insinuated indirectly in nostalgic narratives, becomes the focal point of cynical ones, which never miss an opportunity to besmirch the organization for its injustice, its deceitfulness, its inconsistency and its brutality. Both nostalgic and cynical narratives can then be seen as part of the organization's narrative ecology, casting themselves as counter-narratives to a neoliberal master narrative of competitiveness, profitability, rationality and efficiency.

Narrative Ecologies and the Role of Counter-Narratives 215

In recent times, a different type of nostalgic narrative, distinct from the sentimental or elegiac variety described earlier, has attracted scholarly attention, not so much at the level of organizations as at the level of nations and regions. Following the fall of communism in Russia and the former East Germany, there were widespread reports about the rise of "nostalgia for real socialism" (Velikonja 2009), a retrospective utopia of the socialist past as a time of order, solidarity, justice and stability. This nostalgia frequently assumed a strident aggressive quality, often aligned with a yearning for a 'strong leader,' capable of restoring order and bringing back the glories of the past (Boym 2001; Marsh 2007). Ivanova (2000, 63) explicitly contrasts *cultural nostalgia* associated with a "desire to bring order to the chaos that developed as a result of the abrupt historical change in the structure of life" and *aggressive nostalgia* maintained by a "persistent desire to remain in the past, to forcibly bring that past back." The narratives of aggressive nostalgia have in recent decades become a trademark of nationalist, right-wing organizations, parties and movements, assuming slightly different shapes and nuances but always extolling a mythologized national past free from the dominant afflictions of the present, economic, political, demographic, ideological or technological. This abrasive and aggressive nostalgia easily assumes xenophobic and chauvinistic overtones. It does not recall a past through rose-tinted glasses but rather seeks to resurrect the mythological past, by force if necessary.

Aggressive nostalgic narratives have been important in various liberation and anticolonial movements, which resurrect national heroes and martyrs from a nation's distant past to inspire new generations of heroes and martyrs. In the twentieth century, both fascist and Nazi movements spawned their aggressive nostalgic narratives, which, at least in the case of the Nazis, fed an exterminationist ideology seeking to rid the country of parasites and traitors (see, e.g., Friedländer 1997). Unlike sentimental nostalgia which fixates on a past that was lived and remembered fondly and tenderly, aggressive nostalgia resurrects a past ostensibly lodged far deeper in the unconscious memory of the folk, a past of racial and cultural purity, populated by heroes and other archetypal characters, like those who populate Richard Wagner's music dramas.

Aggressive nostalgia glorifies those qualities in the mythological past that are experienced as sorely missing from the present—order against chaos, strength against impotence, solidarity against individualism, authenticity against bullshit, purity against bastardization. In Greece today, for example, aggressive nostalgia seeks to re-create the country's heroic past, a past unadulterated by foreigners, economic crises, troikas and memorandums, European creditors and usurers, immigrants and all the other hideous afflictions of the present. While its chief spokespeople are neo-fascists, the appeal of this aggressive nostalgia is far wider, and not only in Greece. Aggressive nostalgia can certainly be found in the United Kingdom, whether in the populist press's diatribes about the chaos wrought to the country by

216 Yiannis Gabriel

immigrants, shirkers and other parasites or United Kingdom Independence Party's (UKIP) wider appeal among the conservative strata of the old working class or the 'countryside' people—they are all after a return to a past that was authentic, sometimes heroic but always free of all those toxic influences of modernity, including intellectuals and foreigners, shirkers and parasites.

In the United States, aggressive nostalgia drives what Murphy (2009) describes as the jeremiads of the Christian Right, narratives that constantly draw attention to the current decline of the nation when compared to the greatness and the promise of the past. What gives these jeremiads their aggressive quality is a persistent attribution of blame to an idea or a practice held responsible for the decline and fall—for example, the 'sexual revolution,' the legalization of abortion, the 'explosion' of the welfare state, feminism—and a strident call for repentance and return to the old values and practices. Thus, the American jeremiad is a counter-narrative consisting of idealization of the past and lamentation for its abandonment in opposition to the presumed master narratives of modernity, multiculturalism, free-thinking, liberalism and permissiveness. The jeremiad, for its part, spawns counter-narratives of its own. Thus, historian Stephanie Coontz (1992, 9) has challenged the nostalgic narrative of 'the traditional family,' supposedly ruined by abortion, sexual freedom and the massive entry of women into the workforce, arguing the traditional family is "an ahistorical amalgam of structures, values, and behaviors that never coexisted in the same time and place." In fact, she points out at evidence suggesting that today's American family may be closer to 'traditional family' than the postwar family. In this manner, Murphy suggests that narratives and counter-narratives are "partial, moralized tales [that] duel with each other in the political sphere . . . by attempting to offer a more compelling story and by appealing to their audiences' sense of concern for the future" (Murphy 2009, 129).

Aggressive nostalgic counter-narratives seem tailor-made for nationalist and xenophobic ideologies. Their presence in organizations has not been systematically examined, in contrast to sentimental nostalgic ones, but, as we argued earlier, organizational boundaries do not represent major obstacles to narratives. Clearly, right-wing, nationalist organizations and political parties, like Greece's New Dawn, are suffused by such narratives; in addition, however, many other organizations may import such narratives from the wider society or may breed them themselves—for example, military organizations may spawn aggressive nostalgic narratives of a past before women were admitted in fighting units. More generally, I would expect to find such narratives in organizations that have recently opened up their ranks to previously excluded groups and constituencies or to organizations that, post merger, experience dislocation and trauma.

In summary then, the narratives of aggressive nostalgia, like those of sentimental nostalgia, form part of a narrative ecology in which an idealized past of purity, authenticity, community, self-reliance and heroism confronts the hegemonic narratives of late modernity—multiculturalism, diversity,

Narrative Ecologies and the Role of Counter-Narratives 217

cultural and sexual equality, intellectualism, urban sophistication and so forth. Unlike their sentimental counterparts, instead of offering solace for the discontents of today, the chief aim of aggressive nostalgic narratives is to accentuate or exacerbate these discontents, by persistently maligning the present from the perspective of a mythical past. Sentimental nostalgic narratives are narratives of loss; aggressive nostalgic narratives are narratives of betrayal and fall. It is not surprising, therefore, that these narratives often merge or cross-fertilize with another type of narrative that focuses on betrayal and fall. Conspiracy theories are a type of narrative that inhabits very much the same narrative ecology as nostalgic narratives and, like nostalgic narratives, they relish their status as counter-narratives, relying on master narratives for their vitality and sustenance.

Conspiracy Theories

Conspiracy theories are narratives, *par excellence*. They are 'stories' that, at their simplest, challenge and dismiss received explanations or official accounts of events by proffering alternative plotlines. Seemingly unorthodox, effective conspiracy theories combine iconoclasm with plausibility, fancy with factuality, absurdity with logic. The range of conspiracy theories is formidable—they include the 'denial' of particular events, like the Americans landing on the moon, the Nazi holocaust or climate change; the reinterpretation of an accident as the result of a conspiracy, like the death of Princess Diana or the reattribution of an event or a catastrophe to a different agent from the accepted one, like attributing the attacks of 9/11 to the Mossad or the Central Intelligence Agency or the assassination of John F. Kennedy to various nefarious agents. A particularly important type of conspiracy theory is the sort that attributes designs for global domination to particular groups of people, like the Free Masons, the Illuminati, the Jesuits or the Jews. Thus, the notorious forgery "The Protocols of the Elders of Zion," partly responsible for the wave of anti-Semitism that swept Europe in the twentieth century and a contributor to the Nazi genocide, alleged that Jewish leaders conspired to take over the entire world. The Nazi Party published numerous editions of the protocols and used it as a means of mass propaganda, long after it had been exposed as a fraud.

As with nostalgia, conspiracy theory can define entire historical periods, notably those characterized by purges and witch hunts, like Stalin's Moscow show trials in the late 1930s and Senator Joseph McCarthy's anticommunist crusade in the early 1950s. In such instances, conspiracy theories, far from being counter-narratives established themselves as hegemonic narratives dominating the narrative ecologies of their time. More often, however, conspiracy theories emerge as counter-narratives seeking to puncture or debunk official accounts and explanations and seeking to account for failure or adversity by appealing to various invisible and dark forces. Unlike nostalgic narratives, conspiracy theories address the past but have no yearning for its

218 *Yiannis Gabriel*

return. Also unlike nostalgic narratives, conspiracy theories are not averse to historical research and to factual verification. Quite the contrary—many of them would appear to be obsessed with factual minutiae which are invoked in establishing the holes, discontinuities and contradictions of official narratives in order to mount a frontal assault on them. Thus, deniers of the American lunar landings scrutinize minutely NASA photographs to demonstrate their lack of authenticity and establish that they were all products of studio photography.[2]

Conspiracy theories have attracted a considerable amount of scholarly attention. The rise of the Internet and social media has provided both conspiracies and conspiracy theories with fertile new grounds on which to hatch. In general, there is widespread recognition that there is a great public appetite for conspiracies or at least for exposing and unmasking them. In the groundbreaking essay "The Paranoid Style in American Politics," written at the height of the Cold War, Richard Hofstadter (1964) argued that conspiracy theories have exercised a fascination on Americans since the revolution, something that he links to an endemic paranoia, fed by mistrust, anxiety, anger and suspiciousness. The paranoid style, he argued, is a powerful force in politics and amounts to a fundamental vision of history, not as progress but as a Manichean struggle between good and evil. This battle to the death emerges as a counter-narrative to the narratives of political pluralism, compromise and institutionalized conflict resolution.

> The paranoid spokesman sees the fate of conspiracy in apocalyptic terms—he traffics in the birth and death of whole worlds, whole systems of human values. He is always manning the barricades of civilization. He constantly lives at a turning point. Like religious millennialists he expresses the anxiety of those who are living through the last days.
>
> He wills, indeed he manufactures, the mechanism of history, or tries to deflect the normal course of history in an evil way. He makes crises, starts runs on banks, causes depressions, manufactures disasters, and then enjoys and profits from the misery he has produced. The paranoid's interpretation of history is distinctly personal: decisive events are not taken as part of the stream of history, but as the consequences of someone's will. Very often the enemy is held to possess some especially effective source of power: he controls the press; he has unlimited funds; he has a new secret for influencing the mind (brainwashing); he has a special technique for seduction (the Catholic confessional).
>
> (Hofstadter 1964, 85)

Hofstadter did not deny the existence of actual conspiracies, nor did he dismiss a priori the paranoid style as hostile to factual evidence, claiming that "style has more to do with the way in which ideas are believed and advocated than with the truth or falsity of their content. I am interested here in getting at our political psychology through our political rhetoric" (77). While

Narrative Ecologies and the Role of Counter-Narratives 219

acknowledging the pejorative qualities of the term *paranoid* and suggesting that the term has a "greater affinity for bad causes than good," Hofstadter envisaged the paranoid style as being capable of serving good purposes as well as bad, and supporting truth as well as lies. A more trenchant critic of conspiracy theories, Karl Popper (1945) argued in *The Open Society and its Enemies* that such "theories" are not merely unscientific but a threat to democratic institutions and a feature of totalitarian thinking. Popper claimed that conspiracy theories and paranoid scenarios feed totalitarianism and are direct threats to democracy.

The twin ideas that conspiracy theories are not liable to scientific validation by evidence to facts (they will incorporate *any* fact as a feature of a conspiracy and a cover-up) and that they harm democratic public life have set the terms for most of the scholarly debates on conspiracy theorists. These have divided commentators in two opposed camps, *implacable critics* and *equivocal defenders* of conspiracy theories. Implacable critics sustain a rationalist critique of their content and a public interest critique of their implications. Such theories, they argue, are irrational, unscientific and damaging (see, e.g., Aaronovitch 2010; Clarke 2002; Keeley 1999). They are peddled by nutters, fantasists or indeed conspirators themselves who stand to gain financially, politically or symbolically. In recent times, however, a more equivocal argument (a counter-narrative?) on conspiracy theories has also started to take shape. In a world full of real conspiracies, secrecy and concentration of power, a suspicious state of mind may be quite justified. In such a world, systematic doubt and skepticism, far from being signs of mental disorders, may be sensible responses to various visible and invisible attempts at deception and manipulation (Basham 2001). Aren't scientists themselves doubtful and skeptical when facing orthodoxy?

Equivocal defenders of conspiracy theories have argued that, far from being unscientific, these theories share many features of science—attention to detail, a questioning attitude, an unwillingness to be fobbed off by ad hoc explanations and a belief in everything having a cause. Thus, Raikka (2009) rejects both the epistemological and the public trust objections to conspiracy theories, noting that science (like conspiracy theory) often suffers from limited falsifiability and offering strong arguments to the effect that conspiracy theories are both liable to correction and to eventual decline and dismissal. Similarly, Pigden (1995, 3) directly turns Popper's argument against itself by suggesting that "the belief that it is superstitious to posit conspiracies is itself a superstition." In a similar vein, Locke (2009) views conspiracy theories as features of a rationalized discourse, informed by "the same logic that produces the sciences of general social analysis" (582). An interesting twist to these defenses of conspiracy theories is offered by Dean (2002), who argues that the surfeit of information available in the age of the Internet and social media, far from bolstering democratic accountability, blurs the lines between fact and story, producing "suspicious subjects ever clicking for more information, ever drawn to uncover the secret and

220 Yiannis Gabriel

find out for themselves" (16). The proliferation of conspiracy theories on the internet is the result of this suspicious attitude bred by the increasing instability of facts, a symptom rather than the cause of the erosion of trust in reality and rational discourse.

In contrast to the views of implacable critics of conspiracy theories, equivocal defenders tend to dismiss absolute separations between fact and story but also between theory and story—scientific theories share many qualities with narratives and cannot be differentiated sharply from them. They both offer explanations and may compete in the same narrative spaces or narrative ecologies (just as Darwinism and creationism do). The narrative qualities of conspiracy theories, the qualities that make them more or less effective as explanations and that enhance their plausibility and appeal, have been less widely discussed than have their epistemological or political status. In this regard, Brown and Jones's (1998) contribution seems very important. Based on research of a failed IT project in a UK hospital, they argue that when confronted with failure, people resort to two different types of narratives, one that casts the failure as inevitable and one that sees it as the result of a conspiracy. Both of these narratives seek to exonerate the subjects of responsibility for the failure but do so in different ways. The narrative of inevitability does not seek to attribute blame but approaches failure as the result of a concatenation of unpredictable and accidental factors. The conspiracy narrative, on the other hand, attributes the failure to the actions of actors, saboteurs and agents who stand to lose from the success of the project. Conspiracy theories deserve to be far more widely studied in organizations, in some of which they form part of the daily gossip. Indeed, in some organizations where paranoia and accompanying anxieties reach high levels (Diamond, Allcorn and Stein 2004; Kets de Vries and Miller 1984; Lawrence 1995), it may be that conspiracy theories become the hegemonic genre of narrative, attracting instant credibility and spawning counter-narratives of their own.

Like nostalgic narratives, conspiracy theories inhabit a narrative ecology in which they generally emerge as counter-narratives in opposition to the ecology's master narratives. They problematize what seems to be incontestable 'fact' ("The Americans landed on the moon in 1969"; "Al Qaida organized the 9/11 attacks") by turning facts into stories born of particular interests that deserve to be debunked. Like nostalgic narratives, conspiracy theories draw their energy and their power from their opposition to master narratives—without the master narrative, they would be pointless. But the master narratives themselves and their rationalist advocates, like Popper, Dawkins and Aaronovitch, need the counter-narratives in order to cast themselves as standing for the forces of reason and order and against superstition, hocus-pocus, prejudice and irrationality. Narrative ecologies then can be viewed as spaces where, by analogy to natural ecologies, different elements and populations of narrative emerge, interact, compete, adapt, develop and die.

In Conclusion—Toward a Typology of Narrative Ecologies

Nostalgic narratives and conspiracy theories are but two types of narrative that by casting themselves as counter-narratives help create and elevate other narratives to the status of master narratives as part of the narrative ecologies they inhabit. Nostalgic narratives and conspiracy theories can and frequently do combine; thus, nostalgic jeremiads noted earlier easily merge with conspiracy theorizing about the forces of darkness that have brought about the fall. They may also borrow or blend with other narrative genres including the tragic and the epic. In all their vicissitudes, narratives and counter-narratives depend on each other for sustenance and virility, like different populations of species inhabiting the same ecosystem. In this way, narratives and counter-narratives are not constrained by formal organizational boundaries. They resemble a certain extent animals and plants inhabiting an ecosystem that are not constrained or limited by formal national borders and frontiers.

By analogy to animals, plants and inanimate resources which interact, compete and support each other in a natural environment, different narrative forms interact, compete and support each other in different narrative ecologies. Just as different natural ecologies spawn different forms of life, it can be argued that different narrative ecologies spawn different types of narrative which interact, compete, adapt, develop and die. In this way we could single out certain types of narrative ecologies:

- Narrative temperate regions, where many different narratives grow together, displaying considerable diversity, versatility and tolerance for each other. This would be the case in organizations that are culturally and functionally diverse, complex and pluralistic.
- Narrative deserts—organizations, groups and societies where few narratives emerge, for example, because they are in acute trauma or because of taboos against narrativization. This is the case in organizations in a state of miasma, which I have described in my own work (Gabriel 2012).
- Narrative monocultures—organizations, groups and societies dominated by a few hegemonic narratives which are only challenged occasionally and tentatively by oppositional voices, protostories and antenarrative that rarely crystallize into proper counter-narratives. This is the case of totalitarian organizations where a very strong culture permits little room for opposition (Lawrence 1995; Sievers 1999)
- Narrative mountains where only lichen-like narratives grow, anemic narratives, devoid of passion and energy. This would be the case of loosely structured networks that only meet occasionally or mainly online, focusing mostly on doing business together rather than constituting any kind of community.
- Narrative marshlands where heavy and wet narratives prosper, tending to sink deep into the morass. This would be the case in what are described

222 Yiannis Gabriel

as 'communities of practice,' most notably those coming together online for the purpose of addressing particularly pressing health, social or political problems and issues.

- Narrative jungles where many plants grow and compete for light, including those analyzed in this chapter, conspiracy theories and nostalgic narratives. This would be the case in organizations during periods of extreme change and stress when uncertainty and anxiety lend credibility to the most fanciful scenarios and plotlines.
- Narrative allotments and gardens, where people grow their private narratives, carefully protecting them from weedlike counterclaims and counter-narratives. This would be the case in relatively small, informal organizations that place much emphasis on happy and harmonious relations between people, where individual's stories and experiences are treated with great interest and consideration.

It will be noticed that some of these narrative ecologies permit a greater degree of 'management' of narratives and counter-narratives than others. Thus, narrative monocultures suggest a near complete control of an organization's or a society's narrative by a ruling elite, as do narrative allotments or gardens in which the individual gardener or grower carefully eliminates weeds and parasites. A narrative jungle or even a temperate region, on the other hand, suggests an absence of any central plan or design, allowing life to emerge, grow, develop and die in unplanned and relatively disorderly manners. Such ecologies would, therefore, be elements of what I have described as the *unmanaged organization*, an organizational space that develops independently of managerial designs and proves difficult to police or patrol, a space dominated by fantasies and desires rather than reason and control (Gabriel 1995).

In this chapter, I have suggested that narratives and counter-narratives can be thought of as co-constructing elements of narrative ecologies and proposed that different types of narrative ecology can be viewed as fostering different configurations of narrative patterns. To be sure, the concept of a narrative ecology is a *descriptive* device, one that does not account for the ways that narratives and counter-narratives interact as dynamic elements of wider sociopolitical realities and help define some of these realities. As a descriptive device, however, it promises to take us beyond simplistic dualities of master narratives and counter-narratives engaged in an endless game of shadow boxing, reflecting the interests of their respective constituencies.

Notes

1. I am grateful to Stephanie Schreven, whose sharp insights and observations provided a constant stimulus for the arguments presented here.
2. Conspiracy theories, like nostalgic narratives, engage with the past, but, like nostalgic narratives, they may spawn future-oriented narratives, such as prophesies, scenarios, utopias and dystopias. Images of a future freed from the afflictions of

Narrative Ecologies and the Role of Counter-Narratives 223

the present or, conversely, plagued by terrible calamities, can animate different visions which can develop into fully blown narratives or counter-narratives. Thus, the Enlightenment narrative of eternal progress may be contested by Huxley's dystopia of *Brave New World*, or the Marxist vision of a socialist Eden may be challenged by an Orwellian nightmare of *Animal Farm*.

References

Aaronovitch, D. 2010. *Voodoo histories: The role of the conspiracy theory in shaping modern history* (1st American ed.). New York: Riverhead Books.

Bamberg, M. G. W. 2004. "Considering counter- narratives." In *Considering counter-narratives: Narrating, resisting, making sense*, edited by M. G. W. Bamberg and M. Andrews, 351–371. Amsterdam: J. Benjamins.

Basham, L. 2001. "Living with the Conspiracy." *Philosophical Forum* 32 (3): 265–280.

Boje, D. M. 2001. *Narrative methods for organizational and communication research*. London: Sage.

Boje, D. M., J. T. Luhmann, and D. E. Baack. 1998. "Hegemonic Stories and Encounters between Storytelling Organizations." *Journal of Management Inquiry* 38 (4): 997–1035.

Boym, S. 2001. *The future of nostalgia*. New York: Basic Books.

Brown, A. D., and M. Humphreys. 2002. "Nostalgia and Narrativization of Identity: A Turkish Case Study." *British Journal of Management* 13: 141–159.

Brown, A. D., and M. Humphreys. 2006. "Organizational Identity and Place: A Discursive Exploration of Hegemony and Resistance." *Journal of Management Studies* 43 (2): 231–257.

Brown, A. D., and M. R. Jones. 1998. "Doomed to Failure: Narratives of Inevitability and Conspiracy in a Failed Is Project." *Organization Studies* 19 (1): 73–88.

Clarke, S. 2002. "Conspiracy Theories and Conspiracy Theorizing." *Philosophy of the Social Sciences* 32 (2): 131–150.

Coontz, S. 1992. *The way we never were: American families and the nostalgia trap*. New York: Basic Books.

Czarniawska, B. 1998. *A narrative approach in organizational studies*. London: Sage.

Daniels, E. 1985. "Nostalgia and Hidden Meaning." *American Imago* 42 (3): 371–382.

DaSilva, F. B., and J. Faught. 1982. "Nostalgia: A Sphere and Process of Contemporary Ideology." *Qualitative Sociology* 5 (1): 47–61.

Davis, F. 1979. *Yearning for yesterday: A sociology of nostalgia*. London: Macmillan.

Dean, J. 2002. *Publicity's secret: How technoculture capitalizes on democracy*. Ithaca: Cornell University Press.

Diamond, M., S. Allcorn, and H. Stein. 2004. "The Surface of Organizational Boundaries: A View from Psychoanalytic Object Relations Theory." *Human Relations* 57 (1): 31–53.

Friedländer, S. 1997. *Nazi Germany and the Jews: The years of persecution 1933–1939* (1st ed.). New York: HarperCollins.

Gabriel, Y. 1993. "Organizational nostalgia: Reflections on the golden age." In *Emotion in organizations*, edited by S. Fineman, 118–141. London: Sage.

Gabriel, Y. 1995. "The Unmanaged Organization: Stories, Fantasies and Subjectivity." *Organization Studies* 16 (3): 477–501.

Gabriel, Y. 2000. *Storytelling in organizations: Facts, fictions, fantasies*. Oxford: Oxford University Press.

224 Yiannis Gabriel

Gabriel, Y. 2004. "Narratives, stories, texts." In *The Sage handbook of organizational discourse*, edited by D. Grant, C. Hardy, C. Oswick and L. L. Putnam, 61–79. London: Sage.

Gabriel, Y. 2012. "Organizations in a State of Darkness: Towards a Theory of Organizational Miasma." *Organization Studies* 33 (9): 1137–1152.

Hofstadter, R. 1964, November. "The Paranoid Style in American Politics." *Harper's Magazine*, November, 77–86.

Ivanova, N. I. 2000. "The Nostalgic Present: Retrospectives on the (Post-) Soviet TV Screen." *Russian Studies in Literature* 36 (2): 55–72.

Keeley, B. L. 1999. "Of Conspiracy Theories." *Journal of Philosophy* 96 (3): 109–126.

Kets de Vries, M. F. R. and D. Miller. 1984. *The neurotic organization*. San Francisco: Jossey-Bass.

Lasch, C. 1991. *The true and only heaven: Progress and its critics*. New York: Norton.

Lawrence, W. G. 1995, October. "The Seductiveness of Totalitarian States of Mind." *Journal of Health Care Chaplaincy* 7: 11–22.

Linde, C. 2009. *Working the past: Narrative and institutional memory*. Oxford: Oxford University Press.

Locke, S. 2009. "Conspiracy Culture, Blame Culture, and Rationalisation." *Sociological Review* 57 (4): 567–585.

Löwy, M. and R. Sayre. 2001. *Romanticism against the tide of modernity*. Durham, NC: Duke University Press.

Marsh, R. J. 2007. *Literature, history and identity in post-Soviet Russia, 1991–2006*. Oxford: Peter Lang.

Murphy, A. R. 2009. "Longing, Nostalgia, and Golden Age Politics: The American Jeremiad and the Power of the Past." *Perspectives on Politics* 7 (1): 125–141.

Njambi, W. N. 2007. "Irua Ria Atumia and Anti-Colonial Struggles among the Gĩkũyũ of Kenya: A Counter-Narrative on 'Female Genital Mutulation'." *Critical Sociology* 33 (4): 689–708.

O'Leary, M. 2003. "From Paternalism to Cynicism: Narratives of a Newspaper Company." *Human Relations* 56 (6): 685–704.

Orwell, G. 1944. "As I please (or 'History is written by the winners')." In *Tribune*, 4 February 1944, London.

Pigden, C. 1995. "Popper Revisited, or What Is Wrong with Conspiracy Theories." *Philosophy of the Social Sciences* 25 (1): 3–34.

Popper, K. R. 1945. *The open society and its enemies*. London: Routledge.

Raikka, J. 2009. "On Political Conspiracy Theories." *Journal of Political Philosophy* 17 (2): 185–201.

Sievers, B. 1999. "Psychotic Organization as a Metaphoric Frame for the Socioanalysis of Organizational and Interorganizational Dynamics." *Administration and Society* 31 (5): 588–615.

Strangleman, T. 1999. "The Nostalgia of Organisations and the Organisation of Nostalgia: Past and Present in the Contemporary Railway Industry." *Sociology: The Journal of the British Sociological Association* 33 (4): 725–746.

Strangleman, T. 2007. "The Nostalgia for Permanence at Work? The End of Work and Its Commentators." *Sociological Review* 55 (1): 81–103.

Thiele, L. P. 1997. "Postmodernity and the Routinization of Novelty: Heidegger on Boredom and Technology." *Polity* 29 (4): 489–517.

Unger, L. S., D. M. McConocha, and J. A. Faier. 1991. "The Use of Nostalgia in Television Advertising: A Content Analysis." *Journalism Quarterly* 68 (3): 345–353.

Narrative Ecologies and the Role of Counter-Narratives 225

van Iterson, A., and S. R. Clegg. 2008. "The Politics of Gossip and Denial in Interorganizational Relations." *Human Relations* 61 (8): 1117–1137.

Velikonja, M. 2009. "Lost in Transition Nostalgia for Socialism in Post-Socialist Countries." *East European Politics and Societies* 23 (4): 535–551.

Werman, D. 1977. "Normal and Pathological Nostalgia." *Journal of American Psychoanalytic Association* 25: 313–320.

Ybema, S. 2004. "Managerial Postalgia: Projecting a Golden Future." *Journal of Mangerial Psychology* 19 (8): 825–841.

Index

actantial model 56, 111–12, 115–17, 120, 122–3
agencement 21–3, 31–4, 38–9
aggressive nostalgia 213–17
antenarratives 9, 91, 92, 108, 109, 123, 125, 129–33, 136–41, 143, 145–8, 150–3, 212, 221
authenticity 9, 73–4, 76–7, 79, 138–9, 161, 214–16, 218
authoritative text 3, 8, 19–24, 27, 29–39, 177–9, 181–3, 185, 187; authoritative text and master narrative 91–2, 176–8, 179–81, 184, 186; authoritative text and power 178; authoritative text and discursive struggles 178; counter-narratives as authoritative text 22–4, 179

being-in-the-world 137, 138, 147, 151
branching fractal 133, 135, 147
branding 65, 67, 70, 72, 74, 173, 177–87; see also corporate branding and national branding
bureaucracy 150, 173, 178–87, 214

causality 45–6, 51–2, 59, 174
CCO see Communication as Constitutive of Organization
coauthorship and ventriloquism 88–9, 98
cognitive dissonance 125, 202
cohesion 51–3, 59, 66–7
Communication as Constitutive of Organization (CCO) 3, 8, 19–20, 23, 39, 46–7, 56, 85, 86, 88, 99, 173, 178–9, 182
conspiracy theories 10, 208, 212–13, 217–23; internet and conspiracy theories 218
consumer counter-narratives 64–5

corporate branding 65, 70, 180, 184, 186; see also branding
corporate social responsibility (CSR) 9, 55, 60–1, 71, 83–6, 90–9, 178
counter-narratives 2–10, 17–19, 22–4, 31, 34, 38–40, 43–5, 51, 53, 55–61, 64–5, 67–71, 73, 77–80, 83–4, 86–90, 94–6, 98–100, 103, 105–6, 108–9, 112, 114–17, 119–27, 129–30, 132–3, 135, 139–41, 143, 145–9, 151–2, 155–7, 159, 161, 163–8, 171, 173–7, 179, 181, 183, 185–7, 195–7, 199, 201, 203–5, 208–17, 219–23; counter-narratives as authoritative text 22–4, 179 (see also authoritative text); counter-narratives and conceptualizing of 2–3; counter-narratives and crisis 43–5, 55–61 (see also crisis); counter-narratives and crisis management 53–6 (see also crisis); counter-narratives and communicative constitution of organization 3–5, 22–4, 43–5 (see also Communicative Constitution of Organization; constructionism); counter-narratives and history 211–12; counter-narratives and interdisciplinary insights 5–6; counter-narratives in and around organization 6–7; counter-narratives and methodology 6–8; counter-narratives and organizational identity 68–9, 77–80 (see also organizational identity); counter-narratives and power 208, 211–12; counter-narratives and recontextualization 56–8; strategies of counter-narrativizing 73–7; critique of counter-narrative

228 *Index*

framework 174–6; fate of counter-narratives 195–205; strategies of counter-narrativizing 73–7
crisis 43–5, 47, 49, 51, 53–5, 57–62, 68, 112, 173, 180, 196, 212, 215, 218; analysis of organizational crisis 43–63; crisis management and mitigation of crisis 53–6; narrative approach to crisis communication 45–6; organizational crisis 8, 43–63, 68; social media crisis 54–5
CSR *see* corporate social responsibility
cynicism 9, 64, 65, 67, 68, 79, 214

discourse 3, 10, 37, 45, 49–51, 57, 69–70, 95, 106, 133, 155–7, 159, 161–6, 173, 175, 178, 182, 209–10, 219–20

ecologies 208–9, 211, 213, 215, 217, 219–23

fascism and counter-narratives 213
fate of counter-narraties 195–205
fiction 1, 6, 10, 45, 111–12, 195–6, 200
fractal 129, 132–54; fractal change management in cross-cultural change 129–54; antenarrative fractal theory and methodology 132–40; fractals in merger 130–1, 140–3, 145, 146, 147; fractals and storytelling definition 129
framing 10, 23, 156–7, 161–5

genre 45, 182, 220; speech genre 45
grand narratives 88, 129, 132, 137, 176, 178

history and counter-narratives 211–12

ideology 68, 213, 215–16
identity 1–4, 6–10, 22, 53, 64–9, 72, 74, 77, 79–82, 84, 92, 103, 105–9, 111–17, 119, 121–8, 131, 142–3, 145, 155–7, 159–68, 173, 176, 181, 183–5, 187, 210, 214; organizational identity 6–7, 9, 64–6, 68–9, 72, 77, 79, 84, 105–28; professional identity 114, 155, 157, 159–68, 173, 183–5, 187
intertextuality 3, 8, 48, 49–50, 52, 53, 66, 69, 70, 77, 88–9, 210; intertextual analysis 69–70, 180;

intertextual counter-relations 52; *see also* transtextuality
irony 9, 73, 77, 79, 198, 210

legitimacy 7, 9, 22, 30, 52, 56, 73–7, 79, 83–6, 95, 99, 109, 112, 178–9, 187
little wow moments (LWM) 136, 141
LWM *see* little wow moments

master narratives 2, 10, 22, 38, 52–3, 55, 58–9, 86–8, 91–4, 99, 156, 167–8, 171–80, 187, 196, 208–10, 211–13, 216–17, 220–2; master narratives and authoritative texts 91–2, 176–8, 179–81, 184, 186; master narratives and stakeholder stories 87–8; struggling master narratives 173–4
metaphors 10, 70, 156, 159–61, 163–5

narrative turn 195
narratives 2–10, 15, 17–19, 22–4, 31–2, 34, 38–41, 43–7, 49, 51–3, 55–71, 73, 77–80, 83–4, 86–90, 94–100, 103, 105–17, 119–30, 132, 133, 138–43, 145–52, 155–7, 159, 161, 163–7, 171–81, 183–7, 195–7, 199, 201, 203–25; narrative cohesion 51–3, 59; narrative definition 3, 45, 110, 208; narrative ecologies 209, 220–2; narrative performativity 178; narrative space 209; *see also* antenarratives; counter-narratives; grand narratives; master narratives; storytelling storywork
nascent organizational narrative 18, 23, 25, 39
nation branding 173, 176–86; *see also* branding
nazi ideology and conspiracy theories 217
nostalgia *see* aggressive nostalgia

organizational analysis 8, 10, 171–4, 176, 178–9, 180–6
organizational crisis 8, 43–63, 68; analysis of organizational crisis 43–63; crisis management and mitigation of crisis 53–6; narrative approach to crisis communication 45–6; *see also* crisis
organizational identity 6–7, 9, 64–6, 68–9, 72, 77, 79, 84, 105–28;

counter-narratives and organizational identity 68–9, 77–80; everyday storytelling practices 106–7 (*see also* storytelling); organizational identity flux 65–8, 77–9; organizational identity negotiations 105–28; organizational outsiders and insiders 105–6; organizational identity and story work 108 (*see also story work*)
organizational unfolding 17–42
organizing 2–5, 8, 17–23, 30, 38–42, 56, 129, 133–6, 139, 144–5, 173, 178–9, 182

paranoia 218–20
performativity 172, 177–9, 181, 187
phenomenology 158, 196
plot 1–2, 22, 45–6, 53, 58, 66, 79, 110, 111, 132, 156, 180–1, 195, 209–10, 212, 217, 222; definition of plot 45–6
polyphony 3–5, 78, 105–8, 125–6, 145, 166
power 2–5, 7, 10, 18, 22, 52–3, 57–60, 67, 78, 84, 86, 88, 91, 93–6, 99, 107, 110, 112, 124, 149–50, 155–8, 164–5, 169–72, 174–80, 182, 186–7, 208, 210, 212, 218–20; power and counter-narratives 208, 211–12; power struggles 10, 99, 171–2, 174, 177–80, 182, 187
professions 10, 155, 157–61, 163–8, 186
professional identity 114, 155, 157, 159–68, 173, 183–5, 187
protostories 212, 221

quantum storytelling 9, 129, 132, 138, 140–1, 151–3

recontextualization 51–9
reinterpretations of plot line 58–9
rhizome 129, 133, 135–7, 143, 145

sense-giving 83, 87, 88, 90, 91, 99
sense-making 45, 83, 87–8, 90, 99, 106–7, 112, 120, 129–30, 135, 138, 141, 144, 150, 175–6, 179; retrospective sense-making 129, 130, 139, 144
social media 5–6, 9, 54–5, 60–2, 64–5, 67, 69, 71, 73–5, 77–81, 218–19; social media crisis 54–5; social media platforms 6, 54, 60
sociomateriality 141
spacetimemattering 132, 141, 151–3
stakeholder 4, 6, 9, 15, 48–9, 53, 55, 60–1, 65, 83–91, 98–102, 122, 124, 126; stakeholder communication 15, 84; stakeholders' stories 9, 83–102
start-up accelerators 24, 39
stereotype 132, 148, 161–3
storytelling 2–9, 105–9, 111–13, 115, 120–33, 136–8, 140–2, 146, 151–3; storytelling definition 129, 137; storytelling and organizational identity 106–7
story work 105–9, 111–13, 115–20, 122–6

temporality 45, 141
transtextuality 47–8, 50, 52, 53, 56–7, 59; *see also* intertextuality

Us–Them cross-cultural identity 131, 142–4, 146

ventriloquism 3, 9, 78, 84, 86, 88–9, 90, 93–8, 99–100; analysis of ventriloguism 93–8; ventriloquism and coauthorship 88–9
villain challenge 55, 56, 59–60

xenophobic counter-narratives 215–17

Printed in the United States
By Bookmasters